BELIEVE AND ACHIEVE

William Clement Stone (1902 – 2002) was a businessman, philanthropist and author. Mr. Stone developed the philosophy of Positive Mental Attitude (PMA), which he viewed as the cornerstone of his success. He believed in the power of optimism and that even in adversity lay seeds of success. He was highly successful and eventually started the Combined Insurance Company of America with a modest initial investment of $100. Combined Insurance grew into a multimillion dollar enterprise that became Aon Corporation in the 1980s. He is the author of several self-help books including *Success Through a Positive Mental Attitude* (co-authored with Napoleon Hill), *The Success System That Never Fails*, and *The Other Side of the Mind* (co-authored with Norma Lee Browning).

BELIEVE AND ACHIEVE

W. Clement Stone's 17 Principles of Success

Napoleon Hill Foundation

HarperCollins *Publishers* India

First published in 1991 by The Napoleon Hill Foundation. Revised edition published in 2002 by The Napoleon Hill Foundation

First published in India in 2017 by
HarperCollins *Publishers* India

HarperCollins Publishers India, Cyber City, Building 10-A, Gurugram, Haryana-122002, India
www.harpercollins.co.in

P-ISBN: 978-93-5264-583-1
E-ISBN: 978-93-5264-584-8

2 4 6 8 10 9 7 5 3 1

Printed and bound at
MicroPrints India, New Delhi

HarperCollins Publishers, Macken House, 39/40 Mayor Street Upper, Dublin 1, D01 C9W8, Ireland

Contents

Contents

Preface

To Succeed You Must Be Willing to Pay the Price

Every normal person has a brain and nervous system and is, therefore, endowed with great mental capacities. Few of them, however, use and develop their natural abilities sufficiently to reach the many goals they could achieve. Most people simply aren't willing to pay the price: the effort of learning the art of motivation with a positive mental attitude (PMA).

You can be different.

You can develop your abilities to their fullest...

If you are motivated to pay the price.

Specifically, you must be willing to make regular investment in *study, thinking, and planning time* followed up by action. Work, in other words. There is no substitute. It will be an effort. You will not have everything you want next week. You will make sacrifices.

Is It Worth It?

When endeavoring to come to any decision concerning your future, you may ask yourself, "Is it worth it?"

By paying the price, you will be able to make discoveries about the human mind that have helped countless thousands transform their lives for the better. Much of what you will come to understand is beyond what is taught in schools or bandied about on the evening news, such as:

- *How to, through your conscious mind, tap the powers of your subconscious as it pertains to instincts, passions, emotions, feelings, moods, attitudes, the formation of desirable habits, and the elimination of the undesirable.*

- *How to influence yourself and others in a desirable direction—for this is the essence of the art of motivation with PMA.*

There will be other rewards, but these two alone should be enough to excite your interest.

Believe and Achieve with the Magic of Motivation

What a thrill it is to know that you possess the greatest machine ever conceived—so awesome that it could only be created by God Himself—a brain, nervous system, and the ineffable human mind! And even more exciting: you can learn to operate and use this machine effectively to deliberately direct your thoughts, control your emotions, and achieve any worthwhile goal that doesn't violate the laws of God or the rights of others.

Motivation is that which induces action or determines choice. A motive is an urge within the individual, such as an instinct, emotion, habit, impulse, desire, or idea, that incites him to action. It is the hope or other force that moves the individual to attempt to produce specific results. When you can motivate yourself and others, the world is no longer a place where something always stands in the way of success.

My greatest discovery was that the secrets to success are so obvious they aren't seen. Once recognized, however, they are easy to teach and easy to learn. They were revealed to me in reading self-help action books, and tested through trial and error and . . . trial and success. I learned:

- *How to recognize, relate, assimilate, and apply principles rather than only learn facts.*
- *How to develop a positive mental attitude and eliminate the negative.*
- *How to motivate oneself and others to desirable action at will, and succeed in achieving worthwhile goals.*
- *How to avoid harmful emotional disturbances, mental illness, and maintain good mental and moral health.*
- *How to acquire wealth even though one earns a small salary.*
- *How to acquire the true riches of life.*

Inspirational self-help action books have inspired and motivated millions of persons through the world, and they can motivate you as well. This book is a wonderful place to begin; don't let it be the place where you end.

Believe and Achieve using the Principles of Success

To get the most out of any book, you must take the time to analyze the ideas you encounter. If you judge them worthy, you must assimilate those ideas into your way of thinking. Just as important, you must then be willing to act in accordance with what you have learned and embraced. This deliberate effort is a significant part of the price of success.

This deliberate effort is also what holds most people back from doing anything significant with their lives. They never get off the dime, so to speak. Armchair quarterbacking is great fun on a Sunday afternoon; it's part of the pleasure of watching a football game. But life is not a football game to be watched. You're not in your living room. You're out on the field and you will never score a down, let alone a goal, if you know what needs to be done but you *don't do it*.

Memorize the self-motivator, "DO IT NOW!" The habit can easily be established by repeating, "DO IT NOW!" several times in the morning, several times in the evening for a week or ten days, to indelibly imprint the suggestion in your subconscious mind. When faced with the need to act, "DO IT NOW!" will flash from your subconscious to your conscious mind and propel you to action.

Also memorize the two following self-motivators that have helped countless thousands of persons motivate themselves to desirable action:

"What the mind of man can conceive and believe, the mind of man can achieve for those who have PMA," and, "AIM HIGH!"

These two key phrases will energize your mind against doubt, which along with procrastination, is one of the greatest enemies of human achievement.

Believe and Achieve with a Positive Mental Attitude

The Positive Mental Attitude approach to success has helped millions around the world take charge of their lives, realize their potential, and reach the loftiest goals they have set for themselves. Many of today's leaders in government, education, business, entertainment, and the arts, and in virtually every other field of endeavor, are living testimonials to the value of the PMA philosophy of success and its seventeen principles of success.

A Positive Mental Attitude is necessary for achieving worthwhile success. Achievement is attained through some combination of PMA and definiteness of purpose with one or more of the other 15 success principles. A few illustrations on how you can develop PMA:

- *Strive to understand and apply the golden rule.*
- *Be considerate and sensitive to the reactions of others.*
- *Be sensitive to your own reactions by controlling your emotional responses to environmental influences.*
- *Be a good-finder—look for the positive elements of any situation or person, no matter how hard it may seem.*
- *The harder you have to look, the more important it will be to find those positive elements.*
- *Believe that any goal that doesn't violate the laws of God or the rights of your fellow men can be achieved.*

Believe and Achieve with Definiteness of Purpose

Definiteness of purpose combined with PMA is the starting point to all worthwhile achievement. Some authors use the term "singleness of purpose" to indicate definiteness of purpose. However expressed, it means that you should have one high, desirable, outstanding goal and keep it ever before you. You can have many other goals that are non-conflicting which help you to reach your major definite goal. It is, in fact, highly advisable to have immediate, intermediate, and distant objectives. When you set a definite major goal, you are apt to recognize that which will help you achieve it.

Only you know what your definite major goal is. Whatever it may be, it must be something you can pursue with passion, with a burning desire that will give you strength when you are weary and the odds are long. Admitting a burning desire requires a kind of courage, for once you recognize what you want most, you will never be satisfied until you know you are on your way to achieving it. Giving up complacency is part of the price of success.

A *burning* desire suggests a compulsive intent, an ardent, intense feeling. An effective way to turn a want, wish, or desire into a *burning desire* is to write your goal down and review it each day to keep it constantly before you. As you develop successful habits and learn through experience, an evolutionary process will take place whereby you will be driven to select higher goals. Aim higher and higher with each achievement.

Believe and Achieve using the Guidelines for Success

1. Decide what hour and where you will engage in daily study, thinking, and planning time regarding yourself, in an environment conducive to concentration. Then, come what may, invest one hour daily for self-improvement.

2. Pray for divine guidance when you begin your self-improvement hour.

3. Know what you want. Write out your objectives, indicating the positive characteristics you wish to acquire rather than the negative you want to eliminate. If you want to eliminate fear, strive for courage. Thus, your self-motivator could be: Be Courageous.

4. Strive to keep a positive mental attitude. Try to achieve your determined objectives each day.

5. Read a chapter in a self-help action book. Also, memorize desirable affirmations, self-commands, or statements that you would like to impress indelibly on your subconscious mind.

6. Inspect your daily activities regarding these guidelines. You will probably fail if you don't check yourself daily to see if you are acquiring the desirable habits and eliminating the undesirable. Determine what progress you are making toward your goals. Play safe. Keep a daily record so that you can evaluate your progress.

Do you want to bring your dreams into reality? You can if you want to by following the principles in this guide. Remember, you have unlimited potential power. Convert it into actual power and USE IT!

Maintain Success When You Believe and Achieve

Have you ever wondered how and why certain persons, corporations, institutions, or organizations become successful or why some that did achieve outstanding success subsequently failed? Did you try to analyze them to gain the knowledge that you could and would try to apply to help yourself or others? Did you study, analyze, and write down, in minute detail, for the purpose of helping yourself and others, HOW and WHY you succeeded or failed? I have! And in doing so, I have made great discoveries that have helped me and countless thousands of persons achieve goals in the realm of the possibility of the improbable.

Do you have high goals? Yes or no? Whether you do or don't, you can now learn how to motivate yourself to set high goals, become successful and . . . stay that way.

I have some exceedingly high goals in many fields of endeavor. But I shall mention only my major one: to change the world and make it a better world for this and future generations. I sincerely believe it will be achieved by applying those ideas, principles, techniques, systems, methods, and formulas that I write about as well as those from what I see, hear, read, think, and experience. As you read these words, try to believe that they were written just for you . . . with the hope that you will respond with PMA and become successful . . . and stay that way.

Please consider "...character is the cornerstone in building and maintaining success...the highest and best achievements are noble manhood and womanhood...the achievement of true integrity and well-rounded character is in itself success...There is something infinitely better than making a living: It is making a noble life…If ever there was a time when America needed the help of a positive mental attitude, it is NOW!"

BECOME SUCCESSFUL ...
AND STAY THAT WAY WHEN YOU BELIEVE AND ACHIEVE!

W. CLEMENT STONE

Introduction

The Napoleon Hill Foundation welcomes you to the Napoleon Hill family of achievers! For more than 70 years, Napoleon Hill's ideas have been helping people like you turn their ordinary lives into remarkable testaments to the power of human accomplishment.

Napoleon Hill was born in 1883 in a one-room cabin on the Pound River in Wise County, Virginia. He began his writing career at age 13 as a "mountain reporter" for small town newspapers and went on to become America's most beloved motivational author. He was the first to publish a philosophy of personal achievement that could be adopted and applied by anyone willing to follow the principles he identified. His landmark books, *The Law of Success* and

Think and Grow Rich have influenced millions of successful people. His work stands as a monument to individual achievement and is the cornerstone of modern motivation.

Apply Time-Tested Principles to Reach Success!

In 1952, W. Clement Stone and Napoleon Hill joined forces and philosophies. Stone added his Positive Mental Attitude (PMA) concept to Hill's principles, resulting in the classic book, *Success Through a Positive Mental Attitude.* The two men spent the next 10 years writing and lecturing about the story of success through PMA. Their formula was to become the foundation for virtually all modern motivational writing.

Now the Napoleon Hill Foundation reports on that ever evolving formula. Under the guidance of W. Clement Stone, we have surveyed today's leaders to discover that the original principles set forth by Hill and Stone are still valid and still being used every day. We reveal how new twists, developed over years of refining and expanding, make those principles even more relevant for today's perceptions, attitudes, and values.

The principles of success are practical, proven and versatile. As we grow and change, the principles expand along with our ability to achieve greater goals and to meet our higher expectations.

Believe and Achieve explains exactly how the personal, intellectual, attitudinal, fraternal, and spiritual principles used by the likes of Andrew Carnegie, Henry Ford, and F. W. Woolworth—as well as modern achievers like Tom Monaghan, Mary Kay Ash, Larry King, and Steve Jobs—

can be applied by you to reach your goals.

Believe and Achieve is not the last word on creating success; that story will continue to evolve as long as the human race endures. Instead, the Napoleon Hill Foundation hopes that it will be nothing more than the first words in the next chapter of your life: the first of many chapters in which success is the theme.

The Foundation was established by Napoleon Hill himself as a non-profit educational institution whose mission is to perpetuate his philosophy of leadership, self-motivation, and individual achievement to make this world a better world for current and future generations by teaching, inspiring, and motivating individuals to help them realize their potential and achieve their highest goals.

To this end, the Napoleon Hill Foundation Library of motivational books and recordings based on Napoleon Hill's philosophy present the most effective ideas available today to help you learn, understand, and comprehend the time-tested principles of success. When you apply them correctly, they will help you reach the most ambitious goals you may set for yourself.

Whatever you believe you want to do with your life, we believe you can accomplish it, and more, by applying the ideas that follow.

The Napoleon Hill Foundation

Foreword

There's a great story about Vince Lombardi and his dedication to the basics. Once, after the Packers played a particularly bad game, Lombardi got on the bus, held up the ball, and said, "Gentlemen, this is a football." From the back of the bus, Max McGee spoke up and said, "Coach, you are going to have to slow down; you're going too fast for us."

Patrick Ryan chuckles, obviously relishing telling the tale, as he segues into a comparison of Lombardi and W. Clement Stone. "He (Stone) is a strict fundamentalist in business principles and in the principles of life. One of his great successes—something that I have always believed in and tried to stay with—is to remember the value of the basics. A trip back to the basics periodically is always important, but it's especially essential when things aren't going so well, to go back to the basics and remember where you came from. He's a great advocate of that, and it has been the cornerstone of his success—something that has allowed his success to endure for so many decades."

Pat Ryan knows something of success himself. The son of a Ford dealer, Ryan pioneered in the sale of credit, life and accident insurance sold through auto dealerships. Since merging his $560 million (assets) Ryan Insurance Group with Stone's Combined International Corp. in 1982, he has built a growing $5.4 billion insurance conglomerate and increased the value of his personal stake in the company to about $240 million.

As President and CEO of Aon, the new name adopted by Combined early in 1987, Ryan has steered the company on a course of rapid growth through cost cutting, diversification, and shrewd acquisitions.

Stone continues to serve as Chairman Emeritus of the Board of Aon, but Ryan runs the company. He's "fabulous" to work with, Ryan says of Stone, describing him as "very supportive, totally predictable (which is good), and very consistent. He is a man with keen insights, therefore a man you can listen to and learn a lot from, yet he is not intrusive. He allows people to do; he doesn't get in the way of people meeting their responsibilities."

The back-to-basics approach to success that Stone advocates was, perhaps, the first really practical guide to achievement ever written. It had its origins in a chance meeting of its two principal proponents—Stone and Napoleon Hill. At a meeting of a suburban Chicago North Shore Kiwanis Club in 1952, the program chairman arranged for the two to sit together at the head table.

Hill, at age 69, was semi-retired, enjoying the fruits of a

lifetime of writing and lecturing; Stone, at 50, was head of Combined, an insurance empire that he built with an investment of $100 and dedication to his Positive-Mental-Attitude (PMA) philosophy.

The two dynamic personalities clicked, and before the luncheon was over, they had struck a deal to collaborate on a series of books and self-help courses. Both were men of action who didn't hesitate to make the commitment, knowing full well the personal sacrifices such a venture would demand.

Hill's life's work had been the development of a series of principles that could be used by anyone in any field to achieve his or her goals, an idea he credits to turn-of-the century industrialist Andrew Carnegie.

In 1908, as a 25-year-old journalist, Hill was assigned by a magazine to write a profile of the steel magnate. During the course of the interview, Carnegie, then in his early 70's, lamented, "It's a shame that each new generation must find the way to success by trial and error when the principles are really clear-cut."

He challenged young Hill to develop a practical philosophy that anyone could use, and by the time Carnegie had finished elaborating on his beliefs, Hill was smitten. It took him exactly 29 seconds to accept the challenge.

Hill assumed Carnegie was offering to underwrite the project and was stunned when the industrialist asked him if he was willing to devote 20 years of his life—while supporting himself—to accomplishing the task.

"It is not my unwillingness to supply the money," Carnegie said, "it is my desire to know if you have in you the natural capacity for willingness to go the extra mile, that is, to render the service before trying to collect for it. Successful people," Carnegie went on, "are those who render more service than they are required to deliver."

The canny Scotsman stuck to his terms. He provided some of the introductions and much of the material, but none of the funding for the work, except some out-of-pocket and travel expenses. Hill kept his end of the bargain as well. He spent almost 20 years interviewing the business and political leaders of his day, cataloging and refining the principles they revealed to him.

Henry Ford, Thomas Edison, Alexander Graham Bell, James J. Hill, Luther Burbank, William Howard Taft, Harvey Firestone, F. W. Woolworth, and William Wrigley, Jr. were but a few of the famous names who freely shared their secrets of success during Hill's marathon years of research. His personal success philosophy of achievement was the first authoritative treatise on the subject, and his books, *Law of Success* and *Think and Grow Rich*, were read by millions around the world.

By the time Hill and Stone met over lunch, Stone had read the books and had found in Hill a kindred spirit whose philosophy paralleled his own. To Hill's original principles, Stone added a Positive Mental Attitude (PMA), which became the fundamental doctrine and driving force of the philosophy.

During the 10 years they worked together, the two men published several books and crisscrossed the globe telling the story of success through PMA. During the 1950's, thousands of people flocked to Chicago hotels to hear them speak. "PMA Science of Success" clubs based on their principles sprang up all over the country. Letters streamed into their offices telling of lives changed and success achieved by following the principles they taught.

But something was missing. They found that audiences responded enthusiastically to their speeches and lectures, but as time passed, spirits were dampened and negative thoughts returned. To fuel the fire and keep the flames of enthusiasm burning brightly, Stone and Hill founded *Success Unlimited* magazine.

Their book, *Success Through A Positive Mental Attitude,* has been translated into many languages and is widely recognized as a classic in the field of motivational literature. It formed the foundation on which many who followed built success models. In fact, virtually all modern motivational books have a germ of Hill's and Stone's philosophy in them.

Nevertheless, the world has changed dramatically in the years since Stone and Napoleon Hill published *Success Through A Positive Mental Attitude*; Stone's *The Success System That Never Fails* also saw the light of day during a different era. In the decades since they were first published, we've put a man on the moon and personal computers in the home. Smoke-stack industries crumbled, services displaced manufacturing, the domestic auto industry lost ground to imports, and the flower power counter culture has gone grey.

Success by any measure is a moving target. It is never completely achieved. "I believe that at each new level of achievement, you have to push yourself or you'll retrench," says Pat Ryan, "so I'm an advocate of reaching one plateau, then springing to another and so on. When you do, your capacity as a person is expanded; success is stretching to meet your goals, then never being satisfied.

"I once said, 'You can't conceive how far up is, except for the limitations of your own mind.' It may not be very good English, but a lot of people—including Mr. Stone—liked and responded to the idea. All I really mean is that once you decide how high it is that you want to go, that's as far as you will go. People sometimes ask me if I ever realized how big my company would become. I tell them that I honestly had no idea, but I knew it would be big from the day I started it back in 1963. I had a goal that it would be a national sales organization. I could have decided that was enough, but I wanted to build to greater heights. I don't want to know how high it is because if you establish the height you want to achieve, that is where you will stop."

The PMA philosophy is not static. It's alive, moving, ever evolving to meet changing needs and situations. Since Stone's early collaboration with Hill, he's refined the principles they developed and added new insights.

"My perception is that Napoleon Hill's and Mr. Stone's basic principles have outlived and endured far beyond the trendy situations we see too often," says Ryan. "It is important for the reader to understand that these principles are not a reflection on a successful man's life, but, in my judgment, are principles that extend into perpetuity. Readers should accept this philosophy as past, present, and very much a part of the future."

This is the essence of a philosophy of success that has withstood the test of time, overlaid with a template formed by the mores of modern life in America.

A Note about W. Clement Stone

I have been privileged to work directly with W. Clement Stone for over 52 years.

When asked to write my most memorable memories of my association with W. Clement Stone for his 100th birthday, I realized I already had done that. In my book *Keys to Positive Thinking*, I dedicated thirty pages to him, examining his life and how it offered a real demonstration of Positive Thinking with words and deeds. He is an inspiring example of the application of "PMA"—a Positive Mental Attitude—with everyone he comes in contact with. His life has been a relentless avocation of sharing his PMA concepts with everyone, to make this a better world for this and future generations.

There is another outstanding quality I admire in W. Clement Stone. It is best described in the following "Definition of a Gentleman" from John Henry Cardinal Newman's *The Idea of a University*. You could easily re-title this "This is W. Clement Stone, The Man."

"Hence it is that it is almost a definition of a gentleman to say he is one who never inflicts pain. This description is both refined and, as far as it goes, accurate. He is mainly occupied in merely removing the obstacles which hinder the free and unembarrassed action of those about him; and he concurs with their movements rather than takes the initiative himself. His benefits may be considered as parallel to what are called comforts or conveniences in arrangements of a personal nature: like an easy chair or a good fire, which do their part in dispelling cold and fatigue, though nature provides both means of rest and animal heat without them.

"The true gentleman, in like manner, carefully avoids whatever may cause a jar or a jolt in the minds of those with whom he is cast...his great concern being to make everyone at their ease and at home. He has his eyes on all his company; he is tender towards the bashful, gentle towards the distant, and merciful towards the absurd...he guards against unseasonable allusions, or topics which may irritate; he is seldom prominent in conversation, and never wearisome. He makes light of favors while he does them, and seems to be receiving when he is conferring.

"He never speaks of himself except when compelled, never defends himself by a mere retort, he has no ears for slander or gossip; is scrupulous in imputing motives to those who interfere with him, and interprets everything for the best. He is never mean or little in his disputes, never takes unfair advantage, never mistakes personalities or sharp sayings for arguments, or insinuates evil which he dare not say out.

"From a long-sighted prudence, he observes the maxim of the ancient sage, that we should ever conduct ourselves towards our enemy as if he were one day to be our friend. He has too much good sense to be affronted at insults, he is too well employed to remember injuries, and too...(affable) to bear malice.

"He is patient, forbearing, and resigned, on philosophical principles; he submits to pain, because it is inevitable, to bereavement, because it is irreparable, and to death, because it is his destiny...He may be right or wrong in his opinion, but he is too clear-headed to be unjust; he is as simple as he is forcible...Nowhere shall we find greater candor, consideration, (or) indulgence: he throws himself into the minds of his opponents, he accounts for their mistakes. He knows the weakness of human reason as well as its strength, its province and its limits...He respects piety and devotion; he even supports institutions as venerable, beautiful, or useful, to which he does not assent; he honors the ministers of religion, and it contents him to decline its mysteries without assailing or denouncing them.

"He is a friend of religious toleration, and that, not only because his philosophy has taught him to look on all forms of faith with an impartial eye, but also from the gentleness and effeminacy of feeling, which is the attendant on civilization...Such are some of the lineaments of the technical character; which the cultivated intellect will form, apart from religious principle."

Respectfully submitted,
Michael J. Ritt, Jr.

Chapter 1

The Seventeen Principles

What the mind of man
can conceive and believe
the mind of man can achieve
with PMA.

The Positive Mental Attitude approach to success has helped millions around the world take charge of their lives, realize their potential, and reach the loftiest goals they have set for themselves. Many of today's leaders in government, education, business, entertainment, and the arts, and in virtually every other field of endeavor are living testimonials to the value of the PMA philosophy and its Seventeen Principles of success.

The principles are practical and proven, they have withstood the test of time, and they are versatile. As we grow and change, the principles expand along with our ability to achieve greater goals and meet our higher expectations. Like anything else, the more we practice the principles of success, the better we can understand and apply them.

It is a continuing process, not something we learn once and have forever. Although we are all born with the potential for both negative and positive thoughts and emotions, the external environment is often unduly negative. In fact, one of the first words we learn is *no*. And the negative influences continue throughout our lives. Seldom do we hear praise when we do something well; it's more or less expected of us. Yet when we err, friends, neighbors, coworkers, and relatives line up at the door to tell us where we went wrong.

To succeed in this environment requires a strong ego, a belief in ourselves and our ability, and confidence that we will ultimately prevail. Maintaining such an attitude requires regular infusions of positive reinforcement to counter the negative influences we encounter daily.

The amount of positive reinforcement we require varies by individual; it is proportional to the negative influences we encounter at home, at work, and in leisure activities. The insurance salesperson, who by the nature of his or her work must face rejection often, may require steady doses of positive thinking. A neurosurgeon whose position and skill commands the respect and acceptance of patients and peers alike might do with a great deal less.

What follows is a brief description of the Seventeen Principles, arranged in our new groupings.

ATTITUDINAL PRINCIPLES

Without question, most of the original principles of success address an individual's attitude. Those we've included in this grouping, however, are driven by attitude more than anything else. These include such things as a Positive Mental Attitude, Definiteness of Purpose, Going the Extra Mile, and Learning from Defeat.

1. A Positive Mental Attitude

This principle is listed first because it is the cornerstone that supports the other 16. It is the process by which you can begin to change your life for the better, for you are the only person on earth who can control your attitude. Others may influence or suggest, but only you can control what your mind accepts or rejects.

A Positive Mental Attitude is the right attitude in a given situation. It is not a Pollyannaish notion that everything will turn out all right if you only look on the bright side. It is, rather, a conscious effort to replace negative, self-defeating thoughts with positive, self-fulfilling thoughts. It is a process that must be practiced during every waking moment until it becomes a habit to greet self-doubt with self-confidence.

Just as your muscles become strong and resilient through exercise and constant use, so does your mind. You know from your own experience that you are at your sharpest and best during periods of intense thought and concentration.

If you suppress the negative influences and replace them with positive thoughts and ideas, you will unleash a powerful force that will allow you to achieve any goal you set for yourself. The secret is control. You must consciously choose to eliminate negative thoughts and replace them with positive ones.

2. Definiteness of Purpose

Napoleon Hill said that Definiteness of Purpose is the starting point of all achievement; you must first know where you are going if you are to ever have any hope of arriving there.

Definiteness of Purpose is more than goal setting. In simplest terms, Definiteness of Purpose is your road map to achieving an overall career objective; goals represent specific steps along the way. Unless you are one of those extremely rare individuals who has such great talent or mental capacity that you are instantly catapulted to the pinnacle of success, you must methodically work your way toward your goal.

Most architects, for example, wouldn't begin their careers designing multimillion-dollar skyscrapers. They would begin with smaller structures or portions of larger buildings until their clients were confident enough in them to risk substantial amounts of capital on their ideas.

Many "overnight successes" have spent years preparing themselves for the opportunity that finally affords them the recognition they deserve.

Having an aim for your life has a synergistic effect on your ability to achieve your goals. By specializing, you become better at what you do, you devote all your resources toward reaching your objective, you become more alert to opportunities, and you can reach decisions more quickly. Every action you take ultimately boils down to the question: Will this help me reach my overall objective or won't it?

Most important, having a definite purpose manifests

itself in a burning desire that will help you focus all your energies on reaching your goals. Your purpose will become your life; it will permeate your mind, both conscious and subconscious.

3. Going the Extra Mile

If you do more than you are paid to do, it is inevitable that you will eventually be paid for more than you do. But that truism is not widely accepted. People seem to naturally divide themselves into two groups: those who cheerfully do their best at their jobs and those who seem to have the attitude, "When they pay me what I'm worth, I'll give them what they pay for."

Ours is a society that demands instant gratification. We want what we want, and we want it now. Most real rewards, however, don't come that way. Usually, you must be willing to do the work, to give more than you are asked, before you begin to collect the interest on your investment.

The principle works for companies as well as individuals. In late 1982, when Johnson & Johnson discovered that poison had been placed in some of its Tylenol capsules, the company didn't hesitate to mount a nationwide recall, despite almost immediate vindication of the company, and convincing evidence that the tampering had taken place only in a few stores in Chicago.

Estimates placed the company's loss resulting from the recall and subsequent lab testing support at more than $100 million. The company refused to distribute the product, however, until its executives were convinced that there was no risk, not even to a single Tylenol user. When the product was back in the stores—in new triplesealed safety packaging—customers repaid the company with unparalleled loyalty. Johnson & Johnson regained market share as customers returned and apparently brought friends.

Then, when it seemed that the company had recovered from the aftermath of the tragedy, it happened again in New York. In response to the cyanide poisoning of a young woman, the company took the new capsules off the market—an action the firm estimated would cost another $100 to $150 million.

Johnson & Johnson Chairman James E. Burke said at a news conference, "We feel the company can no longer guarantee the safety of capsules to a degree consistent with Johnson & Johnson standards of responsibility to its customers.

"While this decision is a financial burden to us, it does not begin to compare to the loss suffered by the family and friends of Diane Elsroth," referring to the young woman who died.

At this writing, the jury is still out on whether customers will accept the replacement "caplets" the company introduced, but that kind of integrity can only pay off in the long run.

History is filled with examples of sports figures, business people, statesmen and soldiers who reaped rewards, both personal and financial, and inspired others by giving more than what was expected of them.

4. Learning from Defeat

One of W. Clement Stone's favorite motivating phrases is: "Every adversity carries with it the seed of an equivalent or greater opportunity for those who have PMA and apply it."

It's true. Think of the people you have known personally who failed at one thing, only to go on to great success at something else. Seldom is defeat permanent.

"Our strength," Ralph Waldo Emerson said, "grows out of our weakness. Not until we are pricked and stung and sorely shot at, awakens the indignation which arms itself with secret forces. A great man is always willing to be little. Whilst he sits on the cushion of advantages he goes to sleep. When he is pushed, tormented, defeated, he has a chance to learn something; he has been put on his wits; on his manhood; he has gained facts; learned his ignorance; been cured of the insanity of conceit; he has got moderation and real skill."

Failure often has the habit of placing one in a position that requires unusual effort. Many a man has wrung victory from defeat, fighting with his back to the wall when he could not retreat.

Caesar had long wished to conquer the British. He quietly sailed his ships to the British Isles, unloaded his troops and supplies, then gave the order to burn the ships. Calling his men together, he said: "Now, it is win or perish. We have no choice."

Of course, they won. Most people do when they make up their minds to do so.

PERSONAL PRINCIPLES

The personal characteristics you possess are almost as important as your attitude. To achieve the level of success you desire, you must develop the traits implicit in the Personal Principles, which include Initiative, Enthusiasm, A Pleasing Personality, Self-Discipline, Budgeting Time and

Money, and Maintaining Sound Physical and Mental Health.

5. Personal Initiative

Author Elbert Hubbard said, "The world bestows its big prizes, both in money and honors, for one thing, and that is initiative. What is initiative? It is doing the right thing without being told."

Initiative often manifests itself in leadership. If you are a person of action who takes responsibility for getting a job done, others will respond to your example. In fact, one of the best ways to develop personal initiative is by teaching it to others. It's like the salesman selling himself before he can successfully sell others.

Initiative is the trait that says "Let's get going; let's do something, even if it's wrong." Henry Johnson, the chairman and CEO of Spiegel, Inc., recalls: "I was always the organizer, the club president, the guy with the bat in his hand who told everyone else, 'let's go.'"[1]

Johnson, who earned wide acclaim for turning Spiegel, the poor stepsister of the catalog industry, into a fairy princess, places a high value on leadership. So high, in fact, that he tells his managers to hire exceptional people even if the company doesn't have an opening at the time.

His advice on initiative and leadership is:

- Make your own opportunities.
- Be serious about doing your job better than it's ever been done before.
- Be willing to stand up and be counted—to make decisions and take risks even in mundane jobs.

Johnson knows whereof he speaks. He is a self-made executive who worked his way up from office boy for

Montgomery Ward & Co. to CEO of Spiegel.

Initiative is not without risk. Years ago, Cadillac observed in an advertisement that when something becomes a standard for the world, it becomes a target for the envious. If your work is mediocre, you will assuredly be left alone, but if you achieve a masterpiece, millions will talk about you. Nevertheless, a true leader will rise above the crowd and will not be dissuaded by the human passions of envy, fear, or greed.

6. Enthusiasm

Enthusiasm is a state of mind that inspires and arouses a person to action. It is contagious and affects not only the enthused, but everyone with whom he or she comes in contact.

Enthusiasm is to a person what gasoline is to the engine of an automobile: the vital moving force. It is the fuel with which great leaders inspire their followers; it is essential in salesmanship; and it is by far the most important factor in public speaking.

If you mix enthusiasm with your work, it will never be difficult or monotonous. It will be fun and exciting. Enthusiasm will so energize your body that you can get along with half your usual amount of sleep and at the same time accomplish twice as much without getting tired.

Some people are naturally enthusiastic; others have to develop enthusiasm. The best starting point for developing enthusiasm is to do something you like, something that helps you achieve your goals. This principle is a good example of the interdependence of all Seventeen Principles. If you have the Definiteness of Purpose, Controlled Attention, a Positive Mental Attitude and the other attributes, it is easy to be enthusiastic.

For enthusiasm to work its magic, however, it must be genuine. The tone and manner in which you speak must reflect the sincerity of your purpose. You can't influence others if you don't believe your own words. When you speak from a heart that is bursting with a message, the fire of your enthusiasm will ignite the hearts of others.

7. A Pleasing Personality

People like to do business with people they like. If competitive factors such as quality, service, price, and delivery are more or less equal, the deciding factor for most of us will be to deal with an individual or organization to whom we can relate. But how do you go about developing a personality that others like?

The first essential is to develop character. It is unlikely that you can have a pleasing personality without the foundation of a sound, positive character. It is almost impossible for you not to telegraph your true character to those with whom you come in contact. That is why when you meet someone for the first time you may have an intuitive feeling about the person; you may instinctively like or dislike him or her without really knowing why.

The person you want to be—your character—is a matter of choice. You decide what kind of person you want to be, and develop good and positive traits by emulating others you admire, by practicing self-discipline to replace bad habits with good ones, and by focusing your mind on positive thoughts. It is a slow and deliberate process.

Honesty and integrity are critical attributes of strong

character. If you do not conduct yourself with integrity in all your dealings with others, you may succeed for a time, but your success will not endure. You need only to read the daily newspapers to see example after example of well-known, highly-respected sports figures, stock-brokers, politicians, and others who have fallen in disgrace because of a fatal character flaw.

It may well be true that success is much more difficult to endure—once you've achieved some measure of it—than failure. A strong foundation built on a solid character is even more essential when others defer to you and you have the means to afford virtually anything you want.

Once you have the solid foundation of good character, there are some specific techniques you can employ to make a good impression. None are new or startling, but all of these attributes combined will result in your being a person that others like to be around. The techniques are:

- Be genuinely interested in others. Find their good qualities and praise them.
- Speak with force and conviction not only in meetings and public gatherings, but in private conversations as well.
- Dress for success according to your age, physical build, and the type of work you do.
- Learn to shake hands in a way that expresses warmth and enthusiasm. (If this seems silly and basic, think back to the last cold-fish handshake you received. What was your impression of that person?)
- Attract others to you by attracting yourself to them. Talk about their interests rather than your own.

- Always remember that your only limitations are those you set up in your own mind.

8. Self-Discipline

We are the product of a million years of evolution. For generations, our species has been refined, animal instincts and baser passions tempered, until finally we represent the finest specimen of animal that has ever lived.

We have the reason, poise, and balance to control ourselves and to do whatever we will.

No other creature has ever been endowed with the self-control you possess. You have the power to use the most highly organized form of energy known to man—that of thought. You have the power to think and to direct your thoughts in any direction you wish.

You also have the power to control your emotions. Emotions are the result of a state of mind that you can control through Self-Discipline. No one can make you jealous, angry, vengeful, or greedy. Others, by their actions, can arouse those emotions, but you alone allow yourself to become the embodiment of those things.

Perhaps the greatest practitioner of Self-Discipline was the Hindu philosopher, Mahatma Gandhi. Few men have held such power or enjoyed such acclaim. He spawned a movement that wrested freedom for the people of India from the British Empire, then one of the greatest military powers on earth, and he did it without ever firing a shot. Gandhi's self-discipline kept his life simple and pure, free of corruption or lust for personal power or riches.

There is great power in Self-Discipline. It is the stuff that keeps you going, even though it's uphill every step of the way, until you reach your objective.

9. Budgeting Time and Money

John Wanamaker, the Philadelphia merchant king, once said, "The man who doesn't have a fixed system for the use of his time and money will never have financial security unless he has a rich relative who leaves him a fortune."

Providers of professional services—doctors, lawyers, accountants, and consultants—are keenly aware that time is the only thing they have to sell. They develop a system of accounting for their time, an hourly rate that covers the cost of doing business and builds in a profit. It's a lesson for us all; time is our greatest asset.

It is the one asset you possess that can be converted into any form of wealth you choose. You can spend it wisely, or you can squander it and spend your entire life without a purpose beyond that of securing food, clothing, and shelter.

The average person's time can be divided into three parts: sleep, work, and recreation. It is the latter portion that is most important as far as your personal achievement is concerned. Your free time provides you with the opportunity for self-improvement and education which, in turn, will allow you to market your work time for a right price. The person who uses all his or her free time solely for personal pleasure and play will never be a great success at anything.

It is vital to allow yourself time for creative thought. W. Clement Stone recommends that at least a half hour daily be devoted solely to creative thinking. The time of the day depends on the individual; some people think more clearly during morning walks, others prefer a quiet time just before going to sleep at night. Experiment with your own rhythms to determine when you do your best thinking, then reserve that time every day for creative thinking without any distractions.

Truly successful people also budget the income and outgo of their money as carefully as they budget their time. A definite amount is set aside for food, clothing, household expenses, for savings and investments, for charity, and for recreation. Naturally, individual circumstances vary, and specific amounts allocated to each will depend on your occupation and earning ability.

Personal savings and investment are frequently the areas that are neglected when other expenses increase, but there is an often overlooked side benefit of saving. In times of emergency, even a modest bank account can give you courage and security; in times of prosperity, it will bolster your self-confidence and reduce anxiety. Worry over money matters can kill your ambition . . . and you.

10. Maintaining Sound Physical and Mental Health

In recent years we have seen increased attention given to holistic medicine—the treatment of the body and mind as one complete unit. Nowhere is the importance of mental attitude in health maintenance more apparent than in the treatment of seriously ill patients. Many cancer treatment centers, for example, now include personal counseling as an essential part of patient care. And the American Cancer Society can provide testimonial after testimonial where the one distinguishing factor between patients who recovered and those who didn't was mental attitude.

You need not be seriously ill to evoke this principle. It might be difficult to document, but no doubt you have known people who simply refuse to be ill—perhaps you've experienced the phenomenon yourself—because they have pressing commitments that they must honor, regardless of the circumstances.

Many of today's leading diseases are lifestyle-related. Heart disease and cancer, two of the most common, are unquestionably related to the substances we ingest into our bodies.

Other success principles such as desire, accurate thinking, and self-discipline can be used perhaps more effectively in health maintenance than in any other area. By eliminating bad habits of over-eating, drinking too much, smoking, or using harmful drugs and replacing them with healthy habits, we can prevent the causes of deadly disease.

What may not be so obvious, however, is the importance of balance in your life. We all need a regular rhythm of love and worship, work and play to maintain high levels of physical and mental energy.

That extra energy can make the difference between winning or being defeated by the competition. The late Sydney J. Harris, syndicated *Chicago Sun-Times* columnist, said that in any large and competitive field, few of us are twice as good or even half again as good as the competition. But, he says, being even five or ten percent better is enough to set us apart from the crowd and elevate us to great success.[2] Your competitive edge might very well hinge on sound health.

A healthy body will help you attain the confidence that,

coupled with a Positive Mental Attitude, will help you achieve your loftiest goals.

FRATERNAL PRINCIPLES

Since the days of early man when hunters banded together because they were more successful as a group than as separate individuals, mankind has struggled with relationships. While we know logically and intellectually that we can better achieve mutual goals if we cooperate with others, our natural reaction is often to "go it alone." That approach may work temporarily, but long-lasting success requires support and assistance from others. As you become more successful, you also become busier. Eventually you reach the point where it is not possible to do it all yourself.

There is also a great deal of satisfaction in helping others grow and develop their potential. Today's successful managers are as much teachers as they are supervisors, and more cheerleaders and coaches than they are authoritarian bosses.

Hence the importance of the Fraternal Principles. These include The Master-Mind Alliance and Teamwork.

11. The Master-Mind Alliance

In contemporary terms, The Master-Mind Alliance might be defined as networking of the highest order. It is the sharing of ideas, information, and contacts in a spirit of perfect harmony to work toward a common purpose.

There's a condition in electronics known as resonance, in which great amounts of power can be generated and sustained by small amounts of electromagnetic force applied at regular intervals. For the condition to exist, however, the power must be applied in perfect harmony with the primary source of power. It's similar to giving a child in a swing a light push at just the right moment to maintain the swing's arc.

The condition of sustained regenerative power also exists when two or more minds developed by a friendly alliance meet to produce a combined power that is far greater than the sum of the individual minds.

The Master Mind is not some sort of parapsychological hocus-pocus. You may have experienced it in a brainstorming exercise when you and others just seemed to click. Ideas built on each other until you finally arrived at the greatest idea of all, the best solution to the problem, or an original new concept. And each mind in the group added to the process.

It's a relationship that should be nurtured and encouraged to develop, but it is not always easy to achieve such harmony. We all have difficulty at times harmonizing our own internal forces; it is far more difficult to harmonize a diverse group of minds even in the most favorable environment.

But it is worth the effort. Choose to associate with people who share common values, goals, and interests, yet who each have a strong individual desire to contribute to the overall effort. Make them members of your Master-Mind Alliance, and you will find there is no problem too difficult to solve, no goal too lofty to achieve.

12. Teamwork

A professional sports team that practices teamwork may win consistently when the players work as a team on the field, whether or not they like each other off the field.

A board of directors may disagree, may even be unfriendly, and still run a successful business.

A husband and wife may be at odds and still raise a family, and to all outward appearances be happy and successful.

All of these alliances will be far more powerful and effective, however, if they are built on a foundation of harmony and cooperation. A simple cooperative effort produces power, but teamwork based on complete harmony of purpose creates superpower.

Teamwork differs from the Master-Mind Alliance in one important respect. Members of a Master-Mind Alliance share a commitment to the same Definite Purpose, while a team may represent the cooperation necessary for each member to realize a goal that may be shared only temporarily. Sports teams are good examples of such cooperative effort; musical groups are another. Individual players may star or solo briefly, but the success of the group will depend on their collective effort, however temporary.

In business today, there is a great deal of interest in strategic partnerships, a sophisticated form of teamwork. Each partner company contributes according to its resources. Large organizations, for example, might provide the capital and worldwide marketing strength while its smaller partner contributes the creativity and the flexibility to adapt to market conditions that are more common in entrepreneurial companies. Some of the better known examples are discussed later in this book.

Any great leader—in business, finance, industry, or politics—understands how to create a motivating objective that will be enthusiastically embraced by every member of the team. Find a motive that people can be persuaded to rally around in an emotional, enthusiastic spirit of cooperation and you have created an unstoppable force.

INTELLECTUAL PRINCIPLES

Researchers are just beginning to explore and explain the workings of the most magnificent of all computers—the human mind. Marvelous advances in the study of brain chemistry, brain wave transmission, and revolutionary new ways to treat brain disorders are reported regularly in the popular press.

This book in no way attempts to examine or explain the intricacies of such complex subjects. Rather, we acknowledge the existence of the principles and concentrate on their application in the development of a well-rounded, successful individual.

The Intellectual Principles include Creative Vision, Controlled Attention, and Accurate Thinking.

13. Creative Vision

Imagination is the workshop of the mind, where old ideas and established facts can be reassembled into new combinations and put to new uses. It might be called the hub of the Seventeen Principles, because every other success principle leads to imagination and makes use of it, just as all telephone lines lead to the exchange office for their source of power.

You will never have a definite purpose in life, you will never have self-confidence, you will never have initiative and leadership unless you first create these qualities in your mind and see yourself owning them.

Two computer whiz kids, Steven Jobs and Steven Wozniak, saw in their imaginations a small, inexpensive, easy-to-operate computer for individual use. Although industry leaders discounted the idea, they persisted and launched Apple Computer, which spawned the personal computer industry that now accounts for many millions of dollars in sales.

The computer giants have since jumped on the bandwagon; almost all offer personal computers, and a whole sub-industry has grown up to satisfy buyers' voracious appetites for software. And the words *user-friendly* have become the marketing catchword of the industry.

If your imagination is the mirror of your soul, then you have the right to stand before that mirror and see yourself as you wish to be. You have the right to see in that mirror the mansion you intend to own, the company you intend to manage, the bank you intend to be president of, the station in life you plan to occupy.

Your imagination belongs to you. The more you use it, the better it will serve you.

14. Controlled Attention

The principle of Controlled Attention could best be defined as the ability, through habit and practice, to keep your mind on one subject until you have thoroughly familiarized yourself with it, and mastered it. It means the ability to focus your attention on a given problem until you have solved it. Controlled Attention is also the ability to think as you wish to think, the ability to manage your thoughts and direct them to a definite end. It is the ability to organize your knowledge into a plan of action that is sound and workable.

You will achieve your goals when you focus your thoughts on your definite, written, realistic plan of action and imagine yourself in the position of having accomplished what you set out to do. Jimmy Carter became President of the United States when he lost his fear of the office and his awe of Gerald Ford. If you watched the televised debates of the 1976 campaign, you saw the transformation take place. At the outset of the first debate, Carter seemed intimidated by the office, by President Ford, and by the crush of the crowd and the TV cameras. But when he began to realize he could handle the situation, when he controlled his attention and directed it to the task at hand, he began to believe he really could become President. And he did.

Nothing was ever created by any human being that was not first created in the imagination, then through a burning desire and controlled attention transformed into reality. When you really concentrate on a goal, and see yourself as you wish to become in one, two, three, five, or ten years—earning the income you desire, owning the new home you want, and being a person of means and influence—you begin to become that person.

If you paint this picture clearly in your imagination, it will soon become the object of a deep desire. Use that desire to control your attention and you can accomplish things you thought were impossible.

You can do it if you believe you can.

15. Accurate Thinking

The human brain has often been compared to a computer, and in many ways it is similar. Both can store and process information, but there is one significant difference in the methods they use. As long as information is put into a computer's memory in a consistent fashion, data can be reorganized, compared, and extracted intact. Our memories, on the other hand, may be clouded by emotions, biases, prejudices, or the simple passage of time.

Yet it is absolutely essential that if we are to make the correct decisions in the wildly varying circumstances that we face in our lives, we must be able to think clearly and accurately. How do we do it?

The best method might be to approach all the "facts" with a healthy skepticism. Ask yourself: Is the expert's opinion supported by adequate research? Is it corroborated by others in the field? Does this person usually exercise sound judgment? Can the facts be substantiated? What other sources of information are available? Does this make sense? Is it consistent with my previous experience, knowledge, and training? Does it make good common sense?

Accurate Thinking is assisted by what W. Clement Stone refers to as the "R2A2 Formula"—to Recognize and Relate, Assimilate and Apply information learned in any field to the problem at hand.

Accurate thinkers learn to trust their own judgment and to be cautious no matter who tries to influence them. They learn to listen to the words and to study the body language, to examine their instinctive reactions that tell them to be careful about getting involved with one person or another, to trust their intuition.

There's an old story about a law school professor who was so rigid in demanding that his students confine themselves to known facts that they decided to trick him. They acquired a white horse and painted one side black. They then assigned one of their group to position the horse so that only the black side faced the road. They summoned the professor and asked him, "What do you see?"

"I see Mr. Thomas holding the halter of a horse, the side of which is facing me is apparently black," the old professor sagely replied.

SPIRITUAL PRINCIPLES

The spiritual principles—Applied Faith and the Cosmic Habit Force—help you harness the power within you to work in harmony with the laws of God and nature. Properly applied, these principles will enrich your business, social, religious, and family life.

16. Applied Faith

Applied Faith, in simplest terms, means action. It is the application of your faith in yourself, your faith in your fellowman, your faith in opportunities that are available, and your faith in God—under any circumstances.

The more worthwhile your goal, the easier it is to follow all the principles of success in achieving it. It is simply impossible not to be enthusiastic and dedicated when your objectives are worthy and desirable.

Inherent in the principle of Applied Faith is the application of the Golden Rule in your daily life. Doing unto others as you would like them to do unto you, if your positions were reversed, is a sound rule of ethical conduct. But there is much more to it.

When you decide to guide yourself according to a code of conduct that is fair and just, you set in motion a power that will run its course for good in the lives of others, and will inevitably return to help you like the proverbial bread cast upon the waters. When you serve another, or perform an act of kindness, your action has a subtle psychological effect on you, even though no one else may know what you did. It brightens some corner of your personality. Eventually, if you perform enough good acts, you will develop such a positive, dynamic character that others of similar bent will be attracted to you, and the kindnesses you extended will be returned to you from totally unforeseen sources.

17. Using the Cosmic Habit Force

We are all ruled by habits; they become a part of our makeup through repetition of our thoughts and acts. We can control our destinies and our way of life only to the extent to which we can control our habits. The reason our habits are so important for success is that after a time they become an unconscious way of doing things or thinking. They are almost instinctive reactions. If we form the habit of doing the right thing without thinking about it, we free our minds of the need to ponder the equities of a course of action and can focus on getting results.

Good habits which lead to success can be learned and acquired; bad habits can be broken and replaced by good ones—at will—by anyone. Man is the only animal that can do this. We alone are not unalterably ruled by instinct. W. Clement Stone is fond of saying that the only way you learn anything is through repetition, repetition, repetition. If you repeat an idea often enough, it becomes yours. If you repeat it aloud, you focus both your visual and auditory senses on learning, and you fix the information in your subconscious mind. Unlike the conscious mind, which functions only during waking hours, your subconscious mind is capable of working for you 24 hours a day. The power and potential are there; all you have to do is tap into the power.

Cosmic Habit Force does not work miracles. It cannot make something out of nothing, and it doesn't tell you which course to follow. But it will help you—even force you—to proceed naturally and logically to convert your thoughts into their physical equivalent by using the natural media that are available to you.

When you begin to reorganize your habits, start with the success habit. Put yourself on the success track by forcing yourself to concentrate on your goals. In time, you will develop the habit of success thinking, and your new habits will lead you unerringly to the object of your desire.

All of your successes and failures are the result of habits you have formed. You can change your life and control your destiny through the application of this principle.

There you have them: Seventeen Principles that have withstood the test of time. They represent the essence of the collective wisdom of some of the most successful people of the past two generations, people who have freely shared their knowledge and allowed us to benefit from their experience. In the chapters that follow, some of today's top achievers describe in detail their own application of the principles of success. Their experiences are yours to take and apply in your own life.

Part 1

Attitudinal Principles

The measure of success you achieve in your lifetime—personal, financial, or otherwise—will be governed more by your attitude than any other single factor. There are no physical, intellectual, or spiritual limitations that cannot be overcome with the right attitude.

W. Clement Stone calls it PMA – Positive Mental Attitude. It's that and much more. It's the passion that manifests itself in mental and physical actions that do what is necessary to get the job done.

It is the inner conviction, the fire in your guts that keeps you going long after everyone else has decided it isn't worth the effort. It is the persistence to follow your plan when everyone you know is telling you that you are making a foolish mistake.

A winner's attitude drives you to give a little better service than the competitor down the street, simply because you are who you are. You wouldn't be content to be as good as everyone else; you need to be better. A winner's attitude is making a few more sales calls after everyone else has gone home, or taking a graduate course on Saturday when your buddies are playing golf.

The "appropriate attitude under the circumstances" is the one that helps—even forces you to set goals for yourself so you can be sure you know where you are going. It is visualizing a goal with such intensity that you lose all track of time when you are working toward achieving it. It is the exhilaration of successfully meeting one challenge, then setting even higher goals next time.

When you've lost a skirmish or even a major battle, the right attitude is the little voice in your head that whispers, "I'll never make that mistake again." It's knowing that the painful lessons learned from temporary setbacks will make you a stronger and better person. It is the assurance that defeat is, after all, only temporary. You'll dust yourself off and charge back into the fray only slightly the worse for wear. Next time, you'll win.

These are the attitudes that carry winners to the top, turn unsuccessful careers around, and give hope to us all. The old-fashioned virtues of maintaining a Positive Mental Attitude, Goal Setting, Going the Extra Mile, and Learning from Defeat do work. In this section, we will review these principles and examine the lives of a few people who made the principles work for them.

Chapter 2

A Positive Mental Attitude

A Positive Mental Attitude, W. Clement Stone says, "is the right attitude in a given environment." It is composed of faith, optimism, hope, integrity, initiative, courage, generosity, tolerance, tact, kindness, and good sense. PMA allows you to achieve your goals, to accumulate wealth, to inspire others, to realize your dreams—however ambitious they may be—as long as you are willing to pay the price.

Of the Seventeen Principles of success they wrote about, Stone and Napoleon Hill concluded that there are two that are the starting points of all worthwhile achievement. The two, A Positive Mental Attitude and Definiteness of Purpose, are essential in order to properly and effectively apply any one or a combination of other success principles.

Stone says, "A Positive Mental Attitude combined with the selection of a specific goal is the starting point to all success. Your world will change whether or not you choose to change it. But you do have the power to choose its direction. You can select your own targets.

"For centuries philosophers have been telling us: 'Know thyself.' What we really should be teaching is not only knowing and understanding yourself, but realizing that you have the potential within you to achieve any goal in life that you desire as long as it doesn't violate the laws of God or the rights of your fellow man.

"What the mind of man can conceive and believe," Stone maintains, "the mind of man can achieve with PMA. We translate into physical reality the thoughts and attitudes we hold in our minds. We translate thoughts of poverty and failure into reality just as quickly as we do thoughts of riches and success. When our attitude toward ourselves is big and our attitude toward others is generous and merciful, we attract big, generous portions of success to ourselves."

Stone says the beginning of applying PMA is understanding and applying the Golden Rule. "Be considerate and sensitive to the reactions of others and your own reactions by controlling your emotional responses to environmental influences," he advises. "Develop the right habits of thought and action. Believe—really believe—you can achieve any goal, and you can.

"With each victory you grow in wisdom, stature and experience," Stone says "You become a bigger, better, more successful person each time you meet a problem, tackle and conquer it with PMA."

Success in any undertaking is easier than failing, although it may not at first appear to be. But if you examine those times in your own life when you experienced temporary failure and defeat, you will find that it took far more time and energy to fail than it would have taken to succeed.

There is no problem that cannot be solved, no obstacle so great that it cannot be overcome if you approach it with confidence, intelligence, persistence, and a Positive Mental Attitude. When you agonize over whether or not you are capable of doing something that is difficult for you, when you substitute self-doubt for self-confidence, not only will you *not* succeed, you will find the experience itself exhausting.

If, on the other hand, you approach the problem or opportunity with the correct attitude under the circumstances, you can direct all your energies toward getting the job done. And get the job done, you will. Because you have a positive attitude, you will succeed. You will no doubt have occasional setbacks. Nothing worthwhile is ever accomplished easily, but if you persist—with PMA—you will prevail.

It's a matter of *expectation*. If you expect to succeed, you will; if you don't, you won't. While this may seem deceptively simple, remember, we are influenced by our environment. We weren't born to think negatively; we were taught to do so.

"There's no such thing as a negative baby," says Dr. Norman Vincent Peale, whose book, *The Power of Positive Thinking*, has sold more than 15 million copies in 45 languages since it was first published in 1952. "When we are born, the world is our oyster. All we have to do is cry and we get anything we want."

As we go through life, however, we are subjected to more and more negative influences from our parents, our peers, our teachers, our brothers and sisters, and countless others.

We are told we can't do this or that, sometimes out of concern, sometimes out of jealousy or competition, sometimes for reasons that make no sense to us at all. The result is that we begin to think negatively about ourselves. This continues until by the time we are 25, 30, 40, or 50, says Dr. Peale, "we have to go through an 'unlearning process' to get rid of negative thoughts."

Perhaps the best known study on the effects of external expectations on our performance was conducted by Harvard University's Robert Rosenthal more than two decades ago. Rosenthal believed that scientists and researchers could unintentionally influence the outcome of their experiments by expecting certain things to happen. The results then became what he called a "self-fulfilling prophecy."[1]

He tested the idea by giving 12 experimenters five rats each, with instructions to teach the rats to run a maze with the aid of visual cues. The rats were identical, but Rosenthal told the experimenters that half the rats had been bred to be "maze-bright" and the other half "maze-dull." At the end of the experiments, the rats whose trainers were told they were brighter actually performed better than the so-called dull rats.

Rosenthal repeated the experiment with a different group of rats and experimenters. The results were the same; somehow the experimenters' expectations were communicated to the rats and they responded accordingly.

To determine whether people responded to expectations in the same way, Rosenthal conducted another study. At the beginning of the school year, he gave an ordinary IQ test to all students in an elementary school, but he told the teachers that the test was designed to help identify "intellectual bloomers."

The school consisted of 18 classrooms, three for each of grade levels one through six. In each grade level, there was one class composed of children of below average ability, one with average ability, and one in which the members of the class were above average.

From the entire school, Rosenthal chose about 20 percent of the children—at random—and told the teachers that these students were the ones the test identified as "intellectual bloomers."

At the end of eight months, Rosenthal gave all the students another IQ test. In the upper grades, there wasn't a lot of difference in performance, but the results in the first two grades were impressive. Rosenthal found that in the first grade, children whose teachers expected them to show gains actually did gain over 15 more IQ points than the control group did. In the second grade, the experimental children gained nearly 10 more IQ points than the control children. Rosenthal found that 47 percent of the children whose teachers expected them to bloom intellectually gained 20 or more IQ points while only 19 percent of the control children gained as much.

The only difference was in the *expectations* the teachers had for the children. We respond to others' influences on us—negative and positive—whether they or we are conscious of it, and apparently we are particularly susceptible to such influences at an early age.

The negative thinking habits we have acquired must be deliberately unlearned. We must form the habit, Stone says, of replacing negative thoughts with positive ones. Every time we find ourselves thinking negatively in any situation, we have to immediately replace those thoughts with positive ones. We have to condition our minds in the same way we condition any other parts of our bodies.

You wouldn't expect, for example, Stone says, to one day get out of bed and say, "Today I am going to become a marathon runner. I know I've never run more than a mile in my life, I'm overweight and out of condition, but I believe I can do it."

What you do is first establish your goal, then start to work toward achieving it. You run a short distance at first, gradually increasing it until you can run the marathon. The same is true with your mind. You don't get up one day and decide to be positive from now on, and that's it. That decision is only the beginning. You work at it every day, consistently, methodically replacing negative thoughts with their positive equivalents until a Positive Mental Attitude becomes such a part of you that one day you are rather surprised to find that you seldom think negatively any longer.

Dr. Peale agrees. "If you are a negative thinker," he says, "you have to do a lot of unlearning of the negative patterns and begin to learn positive thinking. In very few cases can this be done quickly.

"I use the illustration of my farm in Duchess County [New York]. We had a tree up there that was about 200 years old that had begun to develop some problems, so we got a tree man to come down because it was rotten at the center, and a strong wind could cause it to fall and damage the house.

"When the day came, the tree man and his helpers came out to the farm and I watched them as they began their work. I figured they would take out some gigantic saw and just saw the tree off close to the ground and that would be that.

"But they didn't do it that way at all. What they did was climb up to the top and snip off the little branches and work their way down until there was nothing left but the trunk. Then they took that down in sections until they had finally worked their way to the ground.

"That's the way you get rid of negative thinking. You start with the little negative thoughts and eliminate them and keep working on the bigger ones until you finally get to the center or core of your negative thinking. Then you eliminate it, and you are ready to substitute thinking positively."

"I think it is absolutely essential that you have PMA in every aspect of life, and that you start early," says Patrick O'Malley, chairman emeritus of Canteen Company, a $1-billion subsidiary of Transworld Corporation. "I was determined that whatever I got involved with, I was going to be successful and excel at it. Such success only comes with a Positive Mental Attitude that will enable you to commit yourself to whatever challenges you may encounter. I have felt the importance of PMA in everything I've been involved in, whether it be the church, the education of my children, my business, or civic activities. PMA is essential in your life not only as it relates to you but as it relates to those things that you can do to help others as well."

O'Malley, who worked his way up from a truck driver to executive vice president in charge of worldwide sales and bottling operations for the Coca-Cola Company before becoming president of Canteen Corporation, recalls: "I came from a poor family from South Boston where we lived in a third floor walk-up. The only heat we had was a potbellied stove in the kitchen. There were six of us children, and we all had to make a contribution—especially during the Depression—to keep food on the table.

"I started working at age nine shining shoes, and I was using PMA every day, although I didn't know what it was called. I wanted to give the very best service I could give. The end result was that Pasquale Tutello, the owner of the shop, got a nickel for the shoeshine and I was getting a ten-cent tip! Without any equity, I was getting twice as much as the owner himself. That was mainly because I had decided that the best shine anyone could get in South Boston was going to be from Pat O'Malley. It worked. They came back time and time again to have me shine their shoes.

"I went into the newspaper business right across the street from the shoeshine store. I had a newsstand at age 12. I sold papers—we had about eight of them in Boston at the time, and they were all two cents apiece but I sold them two for five cents. People laughed about it, but they paid the five cents. I made a deal with the deli next door to give him my change at the end of the day in exchange for a ham sandwich. I ate half the sandwich and took the rest home for the family.

"I went from that job to delivering groceries driving a horse and wagon. Again, I gave the customers the kind of service I would like for myself, and invariably I got a nice tip. All these things involved having the right attitude, and trying always to have a smile. I believe that no matter what business you're in, whether it's the service business, a technical business, or professional services, if you keep that smile on your face and always have a Positive Mental Attitude, it will carry you a long way."

O'Malley started with the Coca-Cola Company as a truck

driver's helper in 1932, and got a chance to show his ability when the driver was out sick for 10 days. "It was a route sales job, where you sold the product off the truck," he remembers. "I made up my mind that for those 10 days, I was going to sell more than anyone ever did from a truck before. I did. They kept me on as the salesman and moved the fellow I'd filled in for to a different district. Two years later I was promoted to supervisor, then to manager at Stamford, Connecticut, then to a larger district in Oshkosh, Wisconsin, then to Chicago as president of the Coca-Cola Bottling Company of Chicago, and then on to the parent headquarters in Atlanta."

He returned to Chicago a little more than two years later to head Canteen, where he took the company from $195 million in sales to its present position of over $1 billion. Since retiring from Canteen, O'Malley has served in a variety of civic and community leadership positions, tackling them all with the same Positive Mental Attitude that carried him from menial jobs to the top spot at one of the country's largest corporations.

Another person who learned from experience what can be accomplished with a Positive Mental Attitude is Og Mandino, recipient of the first Napoleon Hill Gold Medal Award for literary achievement. From the podium in the Grand Ballroom of the Conrad Hilton Hotel in Chicago, Mandino told the audience assembled to honor award winners what PMA had done for him.

Mandino recalled the time when he was at the lowest point in his life. He had lost his job, his home, his family, and his dream of becoming a writer. In the depths of despair, he saw his shaggy, bearded reflection in the window of a pawnshop in Cleveland that displayed handguns for sale. With his last three crumpled ten-dollar bills, he bought a gun to end the useless life his had become.

"I didn't even have the courage to do that right," Mandino admitted.

From that pit of hopelessness, he began searching for answers, trying to learn "the rules of life I was never taught in school." He scoured the libraries, searching for something—anything—to help him get his life back together.

In a library in Concord, New Hampshire, Mandino found a copy of *Success Through a Positive Mental Attitude* by W. Clement Stone and Napoleon Hill. The knowledge he gained from that book and the encouragement from a girl who believed in him gave him the courage to try again. He applied for a job with Combined Insurance and, applying the success philosophy he learned from self-help books, found the truth for himself: "You really can accomplish anything you want, provided you are willing to pay the price." One success built on another, and he began to attract attention from the home office in Chicago.

When his interest in writing was renewed, Mandino rented a typewriter, took two weeks off, and wrote a sales manual, hoping someone in the company would "recognize the great writing talent they had out in Maine."

Mike Ritt, now head of the Napoleon Hill Foundation, *did* notice and offered Mandino a job as a writer. Mandino went on to become editor of *Success Unlimited*, the magazine founded by Hill and Stone, where he learned firsthand from Stone how to apply the Seventeen Principles of Success.

Mandino didn't lack enthusiasm, but now and then his

inexperience with the production aspects of publishing caused problems. On one occasion, after agonizing at length over a costly mistake he had made, he summoned up the courage to tell Stone what had happened.

"Oh, that's terrific," Stone said, and to Mandino's great relief and amazement dismissed the problem, pointing to the principles of success and how much he had learned from the experience. With his characteristic Positive Mental Attitude, Stone didn't worry over what couldn't be changed. He knew Mandino would never make such a mistake again. Instead he concentrated on showing Mandino how much he had learned from the experience.

As is often the case, necessity gave birth to the idea that Mandino parlayed into the book that garnered the award for literary achievement. When an article for *Success* didn't arrive on schedule, to fill the empty space Mandino wrote a moving story about golf great Ben Hogan's overcoming a handicap that had left him unable to walk.

That story attracted the attention of a publisher who invited Mandino to write a book. The book—which has since become a classic in the field was—*The Greatest Salesman in the World.*

"The cynics say there are no more Horatio Alger stories, but I say the cynics are wrong," Mandino said. "My message is that life is a game. It's spirited and it's holy, but it's a game. And you can't win unless you know the rules.

"The success principles Napoleon Hill and W. Clement Stone shared with the world teach the rules of life that they don't teach in grammar school, junior high, high school, or college: How to achieve success through a Positive Mental Attitude."

The lesson Mandino learned is the same one that has enlightened all great achievers at one time or another. When Henry Ford was asked what had contributed most to his success, he said, "I keep my mind so busy thinking about what I wish to accomplish that there is no room in it for thinking about things I don't want." What he needed most to run his automobile empire, he exclaimed, was "more men who don't know anything about how something can't be done."[2]

According to an account by Napoleon Hill, Thomas Edison, the greatest inventor this country has known, shocked his friends by saying his deafness was his greatest blessing because it saved him from the trouble of having to listen to negative circumstances in which he had no interest, and enabled him to concentrate his aims and purposes in a Positive Mental Attitude.

The great Edison credited his mother with instilling in him the belief that he could make something of himself. According to the author Francis A. Jones, Edison said: "I remember I never used to be able to get along at school. I don't know what it was, but I was always at the foot of the class. I used to feel the teachers never sympathized with me, and that my father thought I was stupid, and at last I almost decided that I must really be a dunce. My mother was always kind, always sympathetic, and she never misunderstood or misjudged me. But I was afraid to tell her all my difficulties at school, for fear she too might lose her confidence in me.

"One day I overheard the teacher tell the inspector that I was 'addled' and it would not be worthwhile keeping me in school any longer. I was so hurt by this last straw that I burst out crying and went home and told my mother about it. Then

I found out what a good thing a good mother was. She came out as my strong defender. Mother love was aroused, mother pride wounded to the quick. She brought me back to the school and angrily told the teacher that I had more brains than he himself, and a lot more talk like that. In fact, she was the most enthusiastic champion a boy ever had, and *I determined right then that I would be worthy of her and show her that her confidence was not misplaced.* My mother was the making of me."[3]

Analyzing that episode, Stone says, "While it was true it was his mother who aroused within him the desire that motivated him to high achievement, Edison was, in fact, the making of himself. Although he attended primary school for a total period of less than three months, he became an educated man and a gifted person, for he was motivated to learn and persevere. Regardless of what you are or what you have been, you have the potential power to be what you want to be."

It was that same Positive Mental Attitude that allowed Stone himself, a poor boy from the South Side of Chicago, to rise to great heights of wealth and success. Fatherless since the age of three, he began peddling newspapers on the street corners around 31st and Cottage Grove when he was six. Competition was fierce, and he was often threatened by bigger, older boys who wanted to protect their territories.

Undaunted, he moved inside, selling his papers from table-to-table in a nearby popular restaurant. Although the owner tossed him out more than once, young Stone kept returning until, finally, the restaurateur gave up. He admired Stone's pluck and persistence, and the two eventually became fast friends.

"As a newsboy, I learned a lot that helped me later as a salesman, sales manager and executive, although I didn't realize it at the time. I know now that I began to learn that if I couldn't solve a problem one way, I could another. Selling out my papers at Hoelle's Restaurant, for example, eventually led me to realize that every disadvantage can be turned into an advantage if one approaches it positively. Everyone experiences problems along the way; you just overcome them—with PMA.

"I also began to learn how to overcome fear through action and persistence, and that I could outsell others by going into places and selling where they were afraid to go. I was also learning to think for myself. I don't think the older newsboys even thought of trying to sell in a restaurant."

By the time Stone was in high school, fortunes had improved sufficiently for his mother to purchase a small insurance agency in Detroit. Although Stone opted to stay in Chicago to finish high school, he spent holidays and vacations with his mother. It was during one of those summer vacations that the then 16-year-old Stone was hooked on the insurance business.

Drawing on the lessons he learned as a newsboy, young Stone went to where the most prospects were. He canvased office buildings, frightened and unsure of himself, until he perfected his technique. By summer's end, he was earning so much money he dropped out of school to work full time. (He later returned to complete his education.)

At age 20, he returned to Chicago to open his agency which became the foundation on which he built his insurance fortune. To maintain a Positive Mental Attitude, he read self-help books. He was inspired, but distressed by the fact that the books told him what to do, but they didn't tell him how. He vowed that one day he would write books to tell others how to succeed, and began to consciously try to discover the principles that bring success or failure. "My obvious goal," he says, "was to employ those principles that bring success and avoid those which bring failure."

Combined International, the company he founded, became a multinational insurance conglomerate (now Aon Corporation) that employs thousands of people, and Stone has shared his success principles with millions through countless lectures to audiences around the world and through several best-selling books. He did it all by following the PMA philosophy of success that he advocates.

Says Dr. Peale, "Clem Stone started very poor, and he made a lot of money. But the money never managed him. He managed it, and he gave most of it away. Money to him was a tool to help others develop self-confidence and to believe, to become positive in their attitudes."

His philosophy has helped millions of others, and it will help you.

Chapter 3

Definiteness of Purpose

From the initial interviews with Andrew Carnegie through his final lectures and writings, Napoleon Hill steadfastly believed that the principal reason some people succeed while others fail is that successful people have a definite purpose for their lives. Failures do not. He spent his life persuading others that they must first know where they are going if they have any hope of ever getting there.

His original ideas have been expanded upon and refined by a host of other writers until there is now a fairly extensive collection of motivational literature on goal setting. But the fundamental principle remains the same.

Hill advocated a four-point formula:

- *First, write down a clear, concise statement of what you want most out of life. This could be reaching a certain salary level, being promoted to the highest position you can imagine, generating a desired sales volume or commission income, acquiring enough venture capital to start your own business, or successfully taking your own company public.*

The only criterion for deciding your chief definite aim is that once you've achieved it, you must feel you deserve to be called a success.

In his book, *Seeds of Greatness: The Ten Best Kept Secrets of Total Success*, author and speaker Denis Waitley suggests writing goals on 3 x 5 index cards that you can carry with you and review several times a day.

"The mind is goal-seeking by design," Waitley says. "Successful individuals have game plans and purposes that are clearly defined and to which they constantly refer. They know where they are going every day, every month, and every year of their lives. They make life happen for themselves and their loved ones."[1]

- *Second, develop an outline of your plan to achieve this major goal. The plan needn't be long; in fact, the opposite is true. The shorter it is, the more likely it is to focus on major issues.*

Contemporary authors take Hill's approach a step further. Waitley suggests writing the goal as if it had already been reached. "Visualize yourself having already reached that goal," he says. "Allow yourself to actually feel the pride of doing well."

Ron Willingham, a sales training consultant, seminar leader, and writer, tells the story (in his book *The Best Seller!*) of Robert Hooten, a new owner of a struggling printing firm. His goal was to buy a Jaguar sports car—on the condition that he would have to be doing at least $40,000 a month in volume and have the cash to pay for it.

Hooten cut out a picture of the exact car he wanted and tacked it to his office wall where he could look at it. And look at it he did. Every day he visualized himself behind the wheel of the Jaguar until, according to Willingham, it became a passion with him.

That single goal kept him going even in the most difficult times, until finally he was able to buy the car. "One day he came into my office," Willingham says, "and pitched a set of car keys on my desk." Outside, parked at the curb was the Jaguar, identical in every detail to the picture he had posted on his office wall a few years earlier.[2]

- *Third, set a definite timetable for achieving your goal. Remember, major goals are seldom reached in giant leaps. Your plan should include the interim steps necessary to reach the top. You may skip a rung or two on the ladder from time to time, but don't expect to jump flatfooted from the bottom rung to the top in one jump.*

Legend has it that in his early days in the auto industry, Lee Iacocca's entire career plan was contained on a small card. It simply listed the promotions and the dates he expected to receive them until he became president of Ford Motor Company.

- *Fourth, memorize your definite chief aim and your plan. Repeat them several times a day—almost like a prayer—ending with an expression of gratitude for having received what your plan calls for.*

Here Hill was advocating a form of autosuggestion, which he said conditions your subconscious to accept as reality the goals you have set in your conscious mind. Repeating your goals aloud reinforces the message.

Denis Waitley, a psychologist by training, labels this approach "self-talk." He says the process speeds up the internalization of your goals. "Your self-image cannot distinguish between reality and something vividly imagined," he writes. "The habit of repeatedly reinforcing your own goals as if they were in the present tense introduces visual, emotional, and verbal suggestions to your creative imagination at the subconscious level. These suggestions, if repeated with frequency in a relaxed environment, will tend to override your previous habit patterns with a new game plan."

Aside from the obvious need to have a plan to give you direction, W. Clement Stone points to several other advantages inherent in having a "big goal" or definite purpose for your life. In addition to getting your subconscious working for you through self-suggestion or autosuggestion, you have a tendency to get on the right track and head in the right direction because you know what you want.

Most important, you get into ACTION! Plans and goals are important—essential, really—but they are wasted without action. You must take the necessary steps to implement your plans.

Also, when you have definiteness of purpose, work becomes fun. You are motivated to pay the price, and to do it cheerfully and willingly. You voluntarily study, think, and plan, building your enthusiasm and intensifying your burning desire to achieve your goals.

Knowing exactly what you want has the effect of alerting you to opportunities that you might otherwise overlook. You will see things in your everyday experiences that will help you reach your objectives, and because you have a definite goal, you are much more likely to recognize and seize these opportunities when they present themselves.

Perhaps the greatest single advantage of having a definite aim is that it helps put the rest of your life in perspective. Few of us have the time, energy, or resources to accomplish all we would like, or to dabble in everything in which we have a passing interest. Your chief goal becomes an instant guide for priority setting. Either the action helps you reach your goal, or it doesn't. It's that simple.

Your definiteness of purpose, if you reinforce it properly, will manifest itself in a burning desire that will allow you to reach whatever goal you have set for yourself.

Curtis L. Carlson, chairman and CEO of the Minneapolis-based Carlson Companies, one of the top 20 private companies in America, has institutionalized goal setting in his organization.

"When I started in business," says Carlson, whose companies include such luminaries as TGI Friday's, Country Kitchen Restaurants, Radisson Hotels, Ask Mr. Foster travel agencies, and E.F. MacDonald sales incentive companies, "I wrote my ultimate goal on a little piece of paper, folded it and carried it with me until I reached it. When I reached that goal—sometimes the paper was frayed and dogeared—I set a new goal and carried it.

"I carried it with me so I would always know it was there. It became part of me. And because it was written, it became crystallized in my mind. It helped clarify my thinking, and made it easier to make decisions. When you have a fixed goal, you can quickly evaluate whether your decisions will be toward your objective or away from it."

When he started the Gold Bond Stamp Company in 1938

with $50 of borrowed capital, his first goal was to earn $100 a week. That little slip of paper was the "white flag" that drove him on.

If at first he didn't succeed at something, he never thought of giving up—he just tried another tack. When Gold Bond had cash-flow problems in 1940, he sold a half-dozen shares to friends (which he quickly bought back), and when food rationing in World War II eliminated the attraction of trading stamps, Carlson rapidly streamlined his organization to preserve his precious capital. It wasn't until the 1950s, when he landed his first supermarket chain account, that Carlson began to realize the prosperity he always thought possible in trading stamps. He replicated his promotion strategy in the food business and expanded into service stations and dry cleaners.

Then, along came the consumerist movement of the 1960s and the demand for lower prices instead of promotions and premiums. Carlson fought to protect his interests, but consumers blamed trading stamps for increasing food prices, and it was clear that their popularity was fading.

Carlson responded by diversification and acquisition. He moved into real estate, hotels, restaurants, catalog showrooms, and manufacturing. He bought businesses where he could apply his promotional savvy—businesses that fit his replication strategy.

"All we have to do," he told his managers, "is keep our eye on the target. Obstacles are those frightening things that you see when you take your eye off the target."

You should never be content, however, with reaching a goal, Carlson says. "I consider a goal a journey rather than a destination."

He proved the importance of Definiteness of Purpose in his own companies. In 1973, Carlson set a goal of $1 billion in sales by 1977 (inclusive). This ambitious objective raised a few eyebrows, since at the time Carlson Companies was posting sales of half that amount; he planned to double sales in a scant 5 years.

He made believers of the doubters when he reached his goal one year ahead of schedule. Never content to rest on his laurels, the ebullient Carlson immediately announced that his company would double sales again by the end of 1982.

Despite a recession that lingered longer than anyone had predicted, Carlson once again pulled it off. "We didn't know for sure if we had reached our goal until January 10, 1983," Carlson said, but when the numbers were all added up, the company recorded sales of $2,150,000 for the year 1982.

"Our goal now is to double sales every five years. That's a 15 percent annual compounded increase," he says. Carlson passed the $3 1/2-billion mark in 1986, and if he meets his 15 percent growth projections, he should surpass $4 billion in sales in 1987. In 1986, Forbes magazine estimated Carlson's personal net worth at $550 million.

Carlson is a proponent of a 5-year plan because he believes that is the best time frame to allow the necessary flexibility to temporarily deviate from the plan to take advantage of new opportunities as they arise, without having to compromise your overall goal. His advice for goal setting includes:

- Set a definite timetable for reaching your goal.
- Be persistent. Never give in to adversity and the usual difficulties that get in the way of reaching your

objectives.

- Tell everyone about your goal. If you keep it to yourself, it is too easy to give up (Carlson posted his sales goals in the lobby of the building).
- Make your goal realistic. Break it down in subsets so you can see how you will actually reach your overall goal. For the coming year, the action plan should be spelled out by months.

Carlson recently applied his goal-setting philosophy—and his considerable persuasive skills—to the challenge of raising $300 million for the University of Minnesota, where 50 years ago he worked his way through college driving a soda pop truck and selling advertising on fraternity and sorority bulletin boards. He never doubted that he would succeed and, true to form, raised 85 percent of the funds in just 2 years. There is no doubt, with another year to go, the $300 million will be oversubscribed, Carlson says. This will be the largest amount ever privately raised, he says, in that amount of time.

Carlson doesn't carry a little piece of paper with his goal written on it any longer; it's become "second nature" for him. After you become more proficient at goal setting, he says, you learn to keep moving toward your goal, and you remember what has to get done to get you there.

"I heard a story the other day," he says, "that illustrates the value of goal setting. Thirty years ago, a professor at Yale asked members of the graduating class if they had written down the goal they wanted to achieve once they entered the real world. Only three raised their hands. When the living members of the class were contacted 30 years later, the three who had set definite goals for their lives had accumulated as much wealth as the rest of the class combined."

That, Carlson says, is the power of goal setting.

Tom Monaghan, who like Carlson climbed from poverty to great heights of success (both were Horatio Alger Award recipients), emphasizes goal setting—Definiteness of Purpose—as essential. "Writing is the key to my system of goal setting," says Monaghan, founder of Domino's Pizza and owner of the Detroit Tigers baseball team. "I carry a yellow legal pad with me everywhere I go. All my thoughts, my plans, my dreams, my analyses of problems—everything that comes into my mind, sometimes even a shopping list—are written down in my current pad. When that one is full, I start another; I sometimes have several pads going at once for different kinds of thoughts. Over the last 20 years I have accumulated dozens of packing boxes full of these pads. But the funny thing is that I never look at them again once I'm finished writing. The reason is that it's the process of writing that's important to me. It's the thinking that goes into the writing, not the words that wind up on the paper, that makes the difference."

In his autobiography, *Pizza Tiger*, Monaghan says, "I set long-range goals, annual goals, monthly, weekly, and daily goals. The long-range goals are dream sheets. But the other lists are specific and action-oriented. My goal list for 1980, for example, began with this entry: '500 units.' To me that meant we would have a total of 500 stores by the end of the year. This was a high goal at that point in our development, but it was attainable. The important thing about this goal, though, is that it was *specific*, it wasn't just 'let's increase the number of units this year.' It was *500 or bust*! If a goal is specific, it is easy to communicate it to others. This is important because when you are dealing with a corporate goal you have to *sell* it to the people who can help you achieve it: They have to understand exactly what the goal is, they must believe it can be done, and they must be convinced that it can be done by *them*."[3]

Monaghan also emphasizes that, in addition to being specific, goals should have time limits. His style is to set goals that he plans to achieve *this* year, not "sometime in the near future." His yellow legal pads include business goals, physical goals, and personal items. He discovered the importance of "going public" with goals in 1952 when he quit smoking. "I told everybody I knew, 'This is it. I have smoked my last cigarette.' That gave me the strength to follow through. If you believe you're going to do something, and tell everybody else you're going to do it, their belief will be a backstop for yours."

Allen H. Neuharth, chairman and president of Gannett Company, Inc., one of the country's largest newspaper chains, had long believed his company needed a flagship property to make it stand out from the competition. The organization owned many profitable and respectable local newspapers, regularly won awards for excellence, and was profitable enough to keep directors and shareholders happy and content.

But Neuharth wanted more. He envisioned a national newspaper, an idea that had enjoyed success in other countries, but not in the U. S. The *Christian Science Monitor,* a nationally circulated 5-day-a-week paper, was acclaimed for a time, but never won mass appeal, and in recent years has struggled to stay afloat. Dow Jones's *The National Observer*, a crisply edited weekly launched in 1962, died an unceremonious death in 1977.

Neuharth believed he could succeed where others had failed, and in late 1979 began intensive research on the idea. His firm tested the concept on 40,000 households around the country.

When *USA Today* hit the streets, it created a sensation. The news organization itself became news as critics sniffed, dubbing the colorful publication "McNews" alluding to the paper's "fast food" approach and its penchant for short, upbeat features.

Neuharth took a big risk in the pursuit of his goal, but it was just one of many in his career. When he was a beginning reporter with the Associated Press in Sioux Falls, South Dakota, he started a weekly tabloid, *SoDak Sports*, which failed. He lost $50,000 for his investors—mostly friends and family.

From that shaky beginning, Neuharth joined the Knight Organization (now Knight-Ridder) as a reporter for the *Miami Herald*, quickly climbing the ranks until six years later he was named assistant executive editor of the *Detroit Free Press*. Gannett recruited him to manage its Rochester, New York papers, and in 1966 sent him to manage the company's operations in Florida. He told his friends, "I'll either come back to Rochester as copyboy or president."

In Florida, he launched a newspaper he named *Today* to serve readers in an affluent area in the east-central part of the state. The publication's success helped him make good on his promise to his friend, and in 1970 he was named president and chief operating officer. Three years later he assumed the title of president and CEO, and in 1979 was elected chairman of the company.

Although there are still plenty of doomsayers and nay-sayers, *USA Today* seems to have found a rapidly growing audience. Today, the publication boasts a readership of 5,541,000. It reported its first monthly profit in May 1987—over $1.1 million. The newspaper's distinctive coin boxes dot the landscape, and it's difficult to check into a first-class hotel or board a airplane these days without being offered a copy of *USA Today*.

Neuharth, Monaghan, Carlson, and many others are living examples of another great benefit of Definiteness of Purpose: When you have the burning desire to achieve your goal, you have the persistence, the determination to stick to the job until it is finished.

"Often," says the Royal Bank of Canada in one of the inspirational letters the firm publishes, "success may depend on knowing how long it takes to succeed." The letter adds:

"If you read the biographies of great men and women, you will find that their accomplishments came not so much from their brilliance as from their energy and persistence. Gregor Mendel, the Austrian monk who discovered the principles of heredity, failed his teacher's examinations three times, but carried on regardless with his experiments in breeding plants.

"He crossbred 21,000 plants over ten years, making detailed statistical analyses of his observations until he was finally able to unlock the secrets of genetics. Mendel was one of those who had to be content with the spiritual satisfaction of having done something lasting; his work was largely ignored in the scientific community until well after his death."[4]

Calvin Coolidge, 30th President of the United States,

said: "Nothing in the world can take the place of persistence. Talent will not; nothing is more common than unsuccessful people with talent. Genius will not; unheralded genius is almost a proverb. Education will not; the world is full of educated derelicts. Persistence and determination alone are supreme."

Definiteness of Purpose gives you the strength to persevere until you reach your goal, regardless of the odds, regardless of the obstacles that must be overcome, and regardless of the temporary setbacks you will inevitably suffer along the road to success.

Chapter 4

Going the Extra Mile

Steve Mecsery is the proprietor of Cos Cob TV, a curious blend of television sales, service, and video rentals. The crowded display aisles bulge with TV sets that range from expensive console models to tiny portables that plug into a car's cigarette lighter. In one corner is a rack of rental videotapes. The back room repair shop is strewn with the carcasses of TV sets in various stages of disrepair.

The store reflects Mecsery's market area. Cos Cob is an affluent section of Greenwich, Connecticut, where some of New York's wealthiest move to escape the crush of Manhattan. Equidistant in the other direction are the low-income housing developments of Stamford. Mecsery's customers are some of the country's wealthiest and some of the poorest. He sells expensive new models to the affluent, repairs their trade-ins and sells them used to the not-so-fortunate, and rents videos to them all.

Mecsery treats both groups the same—with warm hospitality, friendly service, and quality products, including rebuilt models which he personally guarantees for 90 days. He recalls one customer who lived in one of the low income housing units in Stamford. The used set she bought failed just two days after the 90-day warranty had run out. He would have been perfectly justified in sympathizing with the customer and no more; after all, the warranty had expired.

But Mecsery doesn't do business that way. He took the set back without question and gave the customer another rebuilt set. Over the course of the next few days, four new customers from the same housing development came in to buy used sets. Mecsery's customer had told all her friends about the honest guy at Cos Cob TV who goes the extra mile in serving his customers.

"Word-of-mouth advertising is far more effective than print ads in my business," Mecsery says. "The way you treat one customer can pass on to any number of his or her friends and neighbors—good or not so good. Just do what you think is right for all your customers, and by that I mean fair and honest and going that extra step, too. Before you know it, word will get around that your business is a place where people want to come and trade. It really works—and it makes life a lot nicer!"

"That," says W. Clement Stone, "is the way the principle works." He defines Going the Extra Mile as simply "performing more or better service than you are paid to do." It is precisely that attitude which keeps your customers coming back and bringing friends; it is what keeps your boss and coworkers counting on you; it is what will ensure promotion after promotion in your career.

"To get more out of life," Stone says, "you must first give more. The essence of the principle in *The Magnificent Obsession* by Lloyd C. Douglas, a book that was a great influence in my life, is that when you do good solely for the sake of doing good for others, without expecting recognition or any reward, your efforts will come back ten thousand-fold—including experiencing the true riches of life. You can't stop them; I know, from years of experience. *Walk the extra mile* is a biblical concept applied by great achievers in their personal, family, and business lives."

A company that has a reputation for Going the Extra Mile in quality and service will earn customer loyalty that can only be envied by competitors who don't follow such practices. The principle works in every line of business, but if employees are to sustain an attitude of going the extra mile, it has to come from the top down, says Robert D. Nicholas, a regional manager with The Glidden Company.

"Management has to show by example that the company will do more than what might be expected under the circumstances," Nicholas says. "If one of our customers has to shut down a manufacturing line because of a faulty product we provided, he stands to lose a great deal of money quickly. We make every effort to see that that does not happen."

Nicholas believes it is possible to instill the positive habit of going the extra mile by setting a good management example, and by showing employees the direct link between giving customers the extra effort and their own personal success. Helping others reach this realization not only helps the employee and the company, it provides a great benefit to the manager as well. "There is no greater reward," Nicholas says, "than the pride that comes from knowing that as a manager you helped turn a marginal employee—or a failure—into an achiever."

In addition to management by example, another good way to institutionalize an attitude of going the extra mile is to have a published code of ethics that everyone in the company is expected to follow. So says E. Morgan Massey, president of A.T. Massey Coal Company, Inc., a billion-dollar mining and exporting operation headquartered in Richmond, Virginia.

Massey requires all employees to sign a detailed code of ethics at the time they join the company; this ensures that there is never a question in anyone's mind about what is acceptable behavior and what is not. The code covers such things as illegal contributions to politicians and labor organizations, bribes, or any other activities aimed at obtaining special privileges or favored treatment of the company.

The code also prohibits virtually any activity involving secret funds, hidden assets, improper payments or gifts (giving or receiving), as well as disclosing inside information for personal gain, and conflicts of interest.

"Abuses in our industry were very prevalent when I went into the business," Massey says. "We have been a leader in changing that. I believe it is necessary to have an impeccable code of ethics, almost to the point of exaggeration. Anything else is self-defeating; I've seen people ruin brilliant careers just to make a few dollars on their expense accounts."

Johnson & Johnson takes the code of ethics idea even further, explaining the company's philosophy in a few paragraphs. It was that written policy, says J & J spokesman

Robert Andrews, that simplified the decision about what the company's response should be during the Tylenol crisis discussed in Chapter 1.

The credo was written more than 40 years ago by the son of one of the company's founders. "It is a timeless document," says J & J Chairman and CEO James E. Burke, "ideal in its goals but pragmatically effective when its principles are put into practice. Its author, General Robert Wood Johnson, evidenced remarkable vision in the mid-1940s to foresee the critical need for our corporation to embrace its responsibilities in the many communities worldwide, where we live and work."

The credo, which has been updated periodically to keep pace with the times, is reprinted here. The principles, Andrews says, are listed in order of importance:

OUR CREDO

We believe our first responsibility is to the doctors, nurses, patients, and to mothers and all others who use our products and services. In meeting their needs everything we do must be of high quality. We must constantly strive to reduce our costs in order to maintain reasonable prices. Customers' orders must be serviced promptly and accurately. Our suppliers and distributors must have an opportunity to make a profit.

We are responsible to our employees, the men and women who work with us throughout the world. Everyone must be considered as an individual. We must respect their dignity and recognize their merit. They must have a sense of security in their jobs. Compensation must be fair and adequate, and working conditions clean, orderly and safe. Employees must feel free to make suggestions and complaints. There must be equal opportunity for employment, development and advancement for those qualified. We must provide competent management, and their actions must be just and ethical.

We are responsible to the communities in which we live and work and to the world community, as well. We must be good citizens—support good works and charities and bear our fair share of taxes. We must encourage civic improvements and better health and education. We must maintain in good order the property we are privileged to use, protecting the environment and natural resources.

Our final responsibility is to our stockholders. Business must make a sound profit. We must experiment with new ideas. Research must be carried on, innovative programs developed and mistakes paid for. New equipment must be purchased, new facilities provided and new products launched. Reserves must be credited to provide for adverse times. When we operate according to these principles, the stockholders should realize a fair return.

* * *

Another company which prides itself on going the extra mile to serve customers is American Express. In a *Fortune* magazine special section on quality, President Louis V. Gerstner says, "Superior service to our global customer is neither a simple slogan to be recited nor an ancient tradition to be venerated. It is our daily mandate, which we must execute flawlessly under often unpredictable circumstances."[1]

The company, according to *Fortune,* is on the leading

edge of using technology to provide equality, highly personalized service. “Last year [1985], over 22 million of American Express Card members purchased $55 billion worth of products and services in over 150 countries. To handle that volume, American Express now operates 16 major information processing centers, 10 worldwide data and time-sharing networks, 90 mainframe computer systems, 400 minicomputer systems, and 30,000 individual workstations.”

“Technology is only part of our fabric, not the whole cloth,” says Chairman and CEO James D. Robinson III. “We have a two-part pledge to customers: first, to promise only what we can deliver; second, to deliver what we promise. And we deliver our services one transaction at a time. It is our well-trained employees who make this technology work—who ultimately deliver what we promise.”

The company recognizes employees who deliver superior service through an incentive program it calls “Great Performers.”

American Express goes the extra mile with customers in more dramatic ways. Its people were on hand to help passengers of the hijacked TWA Flight 847 when they were released by their captors in Lebanon. They were also there to help passengers of the *Achille Lauro* and to assist travelers and local residents following the Mexico City earthquake.

Going the Extra Mile may take the form of little things that mean a lot. A few weeks after dealership customers drive home in a new Lincoln Mark VII, they receive a package from T.J. Wagner, Vice President and General Manager of Ford’s Lincoln-Mercury Division. In it is a letter from

Wagner—on his personal stationery—outlining the benefits of owning a new Lincoln and promising the full support of your dealer. The package includes a report on the benefits of the "Lincoln Quality Commitment," a toll-free number to call with questions, and a specially designed key and key ring which may be registered with the company for easy replacement should you ever lose your keys.

Compared to the over $25,000 price tag for the car, the key doesn't cost much. You could buy one from the dealer for about $15, but it wouldn't have the same effect as receiving one in the mail from a company vice president. It's a little unexpected extra which makes customers feel that in a small way the company really does appreciate their business.

Auto dealers have borne the brunt of a lot of public criticism over the years (Would you buy a used car from this man?); no doubt criticisms were sometimes justified, but just as surely auto dealers have been falsely accused in other instances. After years of bickering between customers and manufacturers and dealers, as well as occasional courtroom battles, the Better Business Bureau established what it calls its "Autoline" program to settle such disputes. Nineteen manufacturers, ranging from Jeep to General Motors to Rolls Royce, participate in the program.

It works well. Diane Skelton, of the National Council for the BBB, says that of 199,066 cases handled in 1985, almost 90 percent were differences of opinion that were settled in mediation and didn't require binding arbitration.

One dealer who doesn't have many of those kinds of problems is Jack Rowe, owner of Precision Toyota in Tucson, Arizona.

"If one of our customers goes to the BBB with a complaint, the people at the BBB, because of our reputation, always ask first: 'Have you talked to Jack Rowe about this?' The minute that occurs, no matter what the situation, I take whatever time is necessary and do what has to be done.

"I have never had a dissatisfied customer that I couldn't handle. It's all attitude. If you want to do it, you can. As a result of this effort, in 31 years in business we have no negative record in the County Attorney's office, we have nothing from the State Attorney General's office, and I'll wager we have the smallest file on record at the BBB in Arizona.

"But it's worth it. We don't have any attorney's fees because we've never been to court. Our philosophy is that if you go to court, even if you win, you lose. That customer will hate you forever and will tell everyone he or she knows.

"It makes no sense to spend $25,000 on advertising to avoid spending $250 on goodwill. Easily two-thirds of our business comes from repeat customers or because of our reputation. We like that, and we plan to keep it that way.

"We have a policy in our store that the customer is never wrong. There really isn't any magic to it; we just put ourselves in the customer's shoes. Customers today are paying a lot of money for reliable transportation, and that's what they expect—even in a used car. That's what we give them."

Going the Extra Mile is really a simple concept. It's nothing more, as Rowe says, than putting yourself in the customer's shoes. Why, then, do we resist giving that little extra that will pay such big dividends? Perhaps it's ego-driven—we inherently believe that if we do more than we are required to do, we are somehow making ourselves subservient to others.

Perhaps it is an outgrowth of peer pressure. As children we learn that if we do more than our parents expect, our siblings may accuse us of currying favor at their expense.

If we do more than teachers assign, other students accuse us of "sucking up" or being "teacher's pet."

The result is that many people form the habit early of doing no more than what is required. With the passage of time, those negative behavior patterns are so firmly ingrained that they are extremely difficult to change. We react as we have always reacted without even thinking.

The tragedy is that the only people we shortchange are ourselves. We damage relationships with others, we deprive ourselves of learning something new, and we cheat ourselves out of the satisfaction that comes from knowing that we did what was right—and more.

Thomas Corson says he learned the most important business attributes as a newsboy and by doing odd jobs, long before he began his career in the business world. "People appreciate service and a friendly attitude," he says. "Customers like dependability and service with a smile, whether you are a paperboy or the chief executive of a Fortune 500 company."

In 1964, Corson got an opportunity to test his theory when he and two brothers started Coachmen Industries. Inc., in Middlebury, Indiana. They began in a 5,000-square-foot building with little more than "a dream of providing America with quality travel trailers and a recreational lifestyle." The first year, with three employees, Coachmen Industries produced 12 travel trailers, one truck camper, and 80 truck caps. Gross sales were $23,653.

In 1985, Coachmen reported sales of over $350 million. The company has experienced the ups and downs of the RV industry, but has been able to survive and prosper, Corson believes, because "our philosophy from day one was to practice the Golden Rule with all our publics." In good times and bad, he says, the company has made every effort to be forthright with employees, shareholders, and customers. "I don't know any other way to do business except to put myself in other people's shoes, evaluate the situation, and treat them accordingly.

"I try to set an example for my employees by looking for an opportunity in every situation I am exposed to, then proceeding to do it. There are never enough hours in the day to do all that needs to be done. A person who only does what is assigned to him may get by with 40 hours a week, but if you look at the most successful businessmen over the years, you will find that they put in 60 to 80-hour weeks. That's what it takes.

"I like to think that the more energy I expend, the more it benefits my customers, whether it is improved products or improved direction of the people servicing our customers. Every part of a work relationship is affected by an additional commitment to serve. Our credo that I have preached for many years is simply that business goes where it is invited and stays where it is cared for. You and I go to do our business where we are invited, and if they convince us by service and attention that we are well cared for, we will continue to do business there. If they don't, we look elsewhere."

A company that has permeated its organization with the philosophy of Going the Extra Mile with customers is Quill Corporation, a Lincolnshire, Illinois, office products dealer.

The company sells strictly through mail order and telephone sales, serving over a half-million customers nationwide.

Says customer relations manager Gerald Barber, "Quill's owners, Jack, Harvey and Arnold Miller, have an absolute passion for customer service. They back it up with commitment, encouragement, and resources. They have also provided a solid role model to which all members of the organization look for guidance. Quill's commitment is so great that we publish our basic beliefs on how we should conduct business in every semiannual issue of our catalog. Around here, this has become known as 'The Quill Customers' Bill of Rights.'

"A few years ago, when we started attaching a preauthorized return form (the customer does not need to call or come in to receive approval to return goods) as part of the packing slip with every order, many of our competitors thought we were asking for trouble."

It didn't work that way, of course. "For one thing," Barber says, "it reinforced the fact that we are serious about our guarantees. Our customers understand exactly when, where and how to return goods, and they appreciate how easy it is to return them. It also gives Quill more detailed information regarding customer returns such as customer account, name, order number, and the like, since all this is printed on the form. In addition, it has greatly reduced our customer service labor expense since we do not have to handle as many up-front authorization requests. Best of all, our returns did not increase as a result of using this form."

Quill uses a wide array of incentives and internal controls to ensure consistent, quality service. Internal auditors place anonymous orders and report back to management on performance; customer relations supervisors monitor sales agents' calls and help with problem areas; and a quality assurance team investigates products with high return rates.

There is a lot of employee involvement. Quill maintains 12 quality circles which meet weekly to solve work-related problems. The groups have improved efficiency in several departments with the full support and cooperation of the employees involved. Quill also has an active in-house training department and a generous tuition reimbursement policy. "Employees are encouraged and reimbursed for taking job related courses at universities or attending professional seminars," Barber says.

The goal is promotion within. Many supervisors and managers worked their way up from inside the organization, Barber says, adding: "The 'We Care' customer service culture is nurtured and spread throughout the organization. Quill believes in helping employees become the best they are capable of being. In turn, the company expects employees to help it become the best it is capable of being. Both must be aware of, and strive for, the achievement of the same goals."

In the highly competitive world of office products where differentiation from competitors is often difficult to achieve, Quill has gained recognition by going the extra mile with customers. Billing itself as "The nation's leading independent office products dealer," the company, in 1985, completed an "aggressive" expansion program that added 100,000 square feet to its existing space for a total of 442,000 square feet. It presently has 875 employees, a number that Barber says may double in the next few years as a result of increasing business. However large Quill's workforce may become,

Barber says, "each and every new employee will be imbued with the Quill 'we care' culture."

Napoleon Hill studied people for much of his life, trying to quantify the reasons why some individuals achieve great heights of success while others with just as much ability and education have lackluster careers. "It seems significant," he said, "that every person whom I observed applying the principle of Going the Extra Mile had a better position at a better salary than those who simply did enough to 'get by.'"

Hill says "Observance of this principle brings not only financial reward but also the reward of happiness and satisfaction that comes only to those who give such service. If you receive no pay except your salary, you are underpaid, regardless of how large that salary may be. No amount of money could possibly take the place of the happiness and joy and pride that belong to the person who makes an 'impossible' sale, builds a better bridge, or wins a difficult case.

"When you deliver the best service you possibly can, striving each time to surpass all your previous efforts, you exercise and strengthen those forces of mind which are available for your use. If you follow this principle, and let going the extra mile become a habit with you—by always doing more than you are paid to do—before you realize what happened, you will find that the world is willingly paying you for more than you do."[2]

As Elbert Green Hubbard noted years ago, "Folks who never do any more than they get paid for, never get paid for any more than they do."

Chapter 5

Learning from Defeat

When talk-show host Larry King comes on the air, millions of Americans hear his velvety voice on his syndicated radio program or watch him interview the world's elite six nights a week on his Cable News Network TV show.

What they may not know is that just a few years ago the calm, self-assured King they see and hear was dead broke, deeply in debt, and fighting the emotional scars of two failed marriages. To make matters worse, Miami financier Louis Wolfson filed a criminal charge (that was later dropped) against the radio personality, alleging that King had defrauded him of $5,000—money that King was supposed to forward to a third party.

King was fired from his job, and for the next three years survived by living off the generosity of his friends. He told *Success!* magazine, "What helped bring me back was listening to interviews on the radio and watching them on television and saying to myself, 'I'm better than that.' Finally, I realized that the only reason I was no longer on the air was because I messed up. Nobody did it to me. I did it to me. I said to myself, 'Somehow I'm going to get back.'" [1]

He gave up his high-living, free-spending ways and got a job as a public relations manager for a Louisiana racetrack. Soon he became the voice of the Shreveport Steamers of the World Football League, and within a year he was rehired by the Miami radio station that had fired him.

Not long afterward he signed a contract with the Mutual Broadcasting System to host the first all-night national radio show. He turned his finances over to his agent, who pays the bills and gives King an allowance.

The adversity he endured gave King the wisdom to overcome his problems and the determination to make a comeback.

It is remarkable but true that the turning point for many people has been marked by some form of defeat or failure, usually on the same scale as their ultimate success. Viewing defeat as merely a test of your inner strength allows you to accept it for what it is—temporary. As W. Clement Stone says, "Defeat is never the same as failure unless and until it has been accepted as such.

"Do not use the word *failure* carelessly. If you have the real seed of success within you, a little adversity and temporary defeat will only serve to nurture that seed and cause it to burst forth so it can blossom. Success, and all the responsibility that goes with it, always gravitates to the person who will not accept temporary defeat as permanent failure."

One of America's greatest citizens, a man loved and

revered throughout the world, was born in a log cabin in Hardin County, Kentucky. He had none of the advantages we take for granted today, and most of what he knew he learned himself, reading books by candlelight.

He tried his hand at business but went broke. When he sold his interest in the business, the buyer defaulted on the loan. He scrimped for the next 15 years to pay off the partnership's debts. He tried practicing law but attracted few clients. His military career was equally undistinguished; he saw little action, and his principal contribution seemed to be saving an old Indian who was about to be hanged as a spy because his papers weren't in order. It seemed that everything he touched ended in failure.

As if his career failures weren't enough, the woman he loved died. But it was precisely the adversity he endured that reached deeply into the soul of Abraham Lincoln and awakened the great American emancipator.

Sometimes it takes great courage, faith, and imagination to strip away the husks of adversity to reveal the seed of benefit, but it is always there. If you allow it to germinate, if you properly nurture and care for it, that tiny seed will eventually burst forth into the full flower of benefit.

Dr. Henry Viscardi, Jr., winner of the 1984 Napoleon Hill Foundation Award for Meritorious Achievement, was born with stumps for legs. "I spent the first seven years of my life in a hospital ward in Harlem," he says. "I was released from that hospital at age seven to get along the best I could, living in a cold-water flat on New York's west side, where growing up was a matter of survival.

"When I was 12, we moved to a semi-rural area on Long Island where I went to a little wooden school; I got around on a little cart like Porgy in the musical *Porgy and Bess*. When I saw the opera recently, I could relate to Porgy when, at the end, he sings, 'I'm Off to the Promised Land,' to find Bess who has gone to the big city. Most of the audience doesn't believe he will ever find her, but I do because I found my destiny in the world."

Viscardi was 27 years old before he got his first prosthetic legs. "Until then," he says, "in my manhood I stood only three feet, eight inches tall. I know all there is to know about pity and pain and ridicule. Then one day, there I was standing tall and straight, able to look down on my mother's head, to look into the clock on the mantel, to see the tops of cars on the road, to hang onto the strap on the subway, to stand up to a telephone that I could never reach before. A whole new life began and another one ended for me.

"As a child, I wondered, 'Why me? Why was I chosen to go through this?' My mother, a simple woman, an immigrant from Italy, answered in her simple wisdom: 'When the Lord and his council held a meeting to decide where the next crippled child would be born, they decided that the Viscardis would be a good family for a crippled boy.' That's a pretty good substance to hold onto for life as you face adversity!

"The most important thing, I think, is that I never thought of myself as different, even though I knew I was. I always considered myself as being the same as anyone else, and given the opportunity to become a learned man I could succeed in life. I really didn't count it as a handicap, it was just something that made me desire all the more to be successful. I realized very quickly that you have to start early in the game with a positive mental attitude and be willing to work very hard to be successful."

No one would have blamed young Viscardi if he had given up; in fact, most people didn't really expect much of him. But he had much higher standards for himself. During World War II he served as a field officer in the Red Cross, spending much of his enlistment at Walter Reed Hospital, working with the seriously wounded: "I saw thousands of maimed, horribly disfigured young men coming back, first from accidents at training camp, then from the invasions in North Africa, then from the succeeding engagements that brought us into Western Europe.

"It was a terribly sobering experience with those men to try to boost their morale, to tell them that there was a world out there. I came back from the war experiences feeling that I had had enough. I no longer wanted to be identified as a disabled person."

Viscardi turned to the business world to build a career, and was well on the way to a vice presidency in a large textile company, but something kept nagging at him. "I kept meeting men that I had met during the war. They were heroes—there were parades and so forth, but they didn't have the dignity of a productive life. I guess I began to realize that success in the business world didn't really mean that much to me. The challenge of serving these men appealed to me, to help them find a place where they could work and produce, and seek out a dignified life instead of living off the pensions and welfare the government offered them."

In 1947, Viscardi founded an organization to help those disabled veterans, and in the years that followed, went on to establish training centers for the handicapped that now operate in 60 locations around the world. He has been honored by organizations that represent virtually every nation, and he has served as an adviser to every president beginning with Franklin D. Roosevelt. By his own example, Viscardi has inspired millions of handicapped people to overcome their own personal adversity and reach for even higher levels of achievement.

"For me," he says, "success is not monetary. It's the fulfillment of your life, to be able to do even in a small measure those things that you want to do. It's that giving part of life that affects other people. It's being able to face each morning and thank the Lord for giving you the day. It's living life to the fullest by dedicating yourself to the needs of others, by making other people around you happy. In doing that, you're doing something for yourself."

The germ of benefit that always seems to accompany adversity often takes form in unusual ways. The Minnesota Mining and Manufacturing (3M) Company has come as close as any to institutionalizing the process of making lemonade from lemons.

In their book *The 100 Best Companies to Work for in America*, authors Robert Levering, Milton Moskowitz, and Michael Katz write, "Two sayings typify 3M research. One is 'Never kill an idea, just deflect it.' The other, called the Eleventh Commandment, is, 'Thou shalt not kill a new product idea.' The burden is on those who want to stop research, since the company has often found an application for many a seemingly off-the-wall idea."[2]

Take the case of Post-It Notes. If you don't recognize the brand name, Post-It Notes are those little sticky pieces of paper that are as common in most homes and offices today as 3M's Scotch Tape.

Post-It Notes were the result of a botched batch of 3M adhesive and a clever engineer who found an application for a dud product. One Sunday in church, according to a report in *The Washington Times*' *Insight* magazine, Art Fry first thought of an application for an experimental adhesive that hadn't turned out to be as sticky as expected. A member of the church choir, Fry was frustrated because the bookmarks in his hymnal kept slipping out.

"It was then," Fry told *Insight*, "I conceived of a bookmark that would stick to the page but at the same time come off without laminating the paper. The low stick adhesive created by accident seemed perfectly suited for this purpose."[3]

Initially the product had a few marketing glitches, because consumers didn't understand the purpose of Post-It Notes until they started to use them. Once they did, the company says, "they were addicted." Now, the little yellow and pink and blue squares are used for everything from an author's manuscript notes to a scrawled reminder on the refrigerator door to pick up a gallon of milk on the way home.

Another person who knew a good idea when he saw one was Brian Graves. During the last real estate downturn, when most people in the industry were wringing their hands in despair or looking for other lines of work, Graves decided to go into the business. He figured that there must be an opportunity in the larger-than-normal number of houses on the market with absentee owners.

He recalls that when two of his associates who had been home caretakers in a small Washington town told him they would like to expand but weren't sure how to go about it, "a light bulb went on in my head. Here was a niche in the market, a specialized service opportunity. The sum total of all my experiences in the past had prepared me perfectly for this; I knew I could make it work."

What Graves eventually came up with was America's Home Caretakers, a Redmond, Washington, based company that offers an organized, professional house-sitting service for absentee sellers of vacant houses and condominiums. By its third year of operation, the firm was expecting a net income of $100,000.

It's an arrangement in which everyone wins. There is no charge to owners for the service, and the people who occupy the homes pay a monthly fee as low as $150 to $200 a month plus utilities for homes that would normally rent for up to $1,500 a month.

Graves describes his caretakers as "quality people who hope to save a little money and don't mind a little adventure." All applicants are carefully screened—they must be reliable, bondable, and insurable. (The company carries tenant-liability insurance on them.) Graves finds them through referrals from churches, colleges, real estate agents, and other caretakers.

The house-sitters protect the homeowners' investment by keeping the place in tip-top shape, and by minimizing risk of damage from vandalism or undetected frozen or leaky pipes—losses that are not covered by most homeowners' policies if the home has been vacant for more than thirty days. There's an added advantage, Graves says: "I knew from my own experience in the real estate business that occupied houses sell more quickly than vacant ones."

Graves readily admits that the idea of house-sitting is not

a new concept; it's merely an old idea with a new twist. "There's nothing new about a hamburger, either," he says, "but look at what McDonald's did with it."

In an adverse real estate market, Graves found an equivalent opportunity. He quickly points out, however, that recognizing an opportunity is no guarantee of success—you have to take action, take advantage. "You can read all the motivational books you want to maintain a Positive Mental Attitude," he says, "but there comes a time when you have to do something to make it work. You have to roll up your sleeves and get started.

"You can read all that's ever been written about swimming, for example," he says; "but sooner or later you've got to jump in the water if you ever hope to learn to swim."

This is all very good, you may be thinking. *It's fine to read about others who have experienced temporary failure and gone on to achieve great heights of success. Intellectually I agree, but defeat is a very emotional and personal thing. How do I recover when my ego is crushed and my self-esteem is at its lowest ebb? How do I cheerfully stage a comeback when I'm least prepared to deal with it?*

There are no easy answers. Probably the only source of strength is the faith in yourself that comes with experience. We all make little mistakes every day, but we don't let them get us down permanently. We identify problems and we correct them. Learn from those mistakes so that when the big defeats come—and they probably will—you can be confident that you can overcome them.

View every temporary defeat as a stepping-stone to bigger and better things. Every problem you solve, every obstacle you overcome just puts you that much closer to achieving your final goal. If you try to anticipate every problem in advance, if you worry about everything that could go wrong before you even begin, you will never try anything.

Life is a lot like climbing a mountain. If you expect to get from the base to the summit in a few easy steps, you will quickly become discouraged and give up. But, if you are prepared mentally and physically to climb to the top, you will. When you stumble and fall, you will dust yourself off and climb back to the spot where you slipped before and you will pass it. You will keep doing that until you reach the top. Then you will look for newer and higher mountains to climb.

The late Dr. Kenneth McFarland, one of the greatest speakers who ever lived, once likened life to an automobile trip. If you think about the danger of taking a long trip, he said, if you think about meeting all those other cars that are traveling at high rates of speed—just inches from your hubcaps—you will never have the courage to leave home. But you don't go through life that way. You do it a mile at a time and an hour at a time and a day at a time.

That's the same way you should deal with temporary setbacks. Overcome them one at a time, and learn from the experience so you won't make the same mistakes again.

While it may be difficult to recognize the cause of temporary failure while you are still smarting from the wounds, such setbacks are usually the result of one of three things:

- Material loss such as wealth, position, or property;
- Personal loss such as the death of a friend or family member or the end of a relationship; or
- Spiritual loss where the failure comes from within and you quit trying.

We can overcome and learn from any or all of these things. No doubt you have known people who were fired from their jobs only to become immensely successful in another company or by starting their own businesses. Material failures have a way of causing us to reassess our priorities, to decide what's really important to us, to set new goals for ourselves, and to not be distracted by the things that caused us problems before.

Damaged or severed relationships with others, whether they are business partners or spouses, force us to examine our own traits that contributed to the problems and to change our habits in dealings with others. Even in the death of a loved one, many have found a way to redirect their grief by helping others, and in the process have become better people themselves.

A spiritual loss, when we are overcome with discouragement or have lost touch with our religious beliefs, forces us to become more introspective, to find solace within our own souls. In this search you may find an inner strength and peace that you would never have discovered without defeat.

The line between success and failure is so fine that the real cause of failure is often overlooked. It is nothing more than attitude—how you deal with the failures you are dealt or those you cause yourself.

Country music legend Merle Haggard vividly remembers the turning point in his life. He had been in trouble most of his young life until he finally wound up in San Quentin prison.

"I will say that Quentin, unlike some of the prisons I've heard about," he writes in his biography, "gave you a choice. You could either apply for a job, work hard, and build up a good record, or you could lay around in the yard all day. I voted for layin' around in the yard all day. We could make our time count—or just count our time. I did some of both."[4]

His first opportunity for parole came after 18 months, but his lack of motivation did little to attract the attention of the parole board. It surprised no one that his first parole request was denied.

By his own account, Haggard continued to do little to improve his condition. He and a fellow inmate started their "own little business, a gambling operation with a beer concession." That venture landed him in isolation.

"Sometimes it takes one more thing to tip the scales one way or the other. I don't know if it was the execution [of a fellow inmate], the seven days in isolation or the death [of an escapee], or the combination of everything that made a difference.

"Whatever it was, I came off isolation determined to do something positive for Merle Haggard."

Haggard made parole the next time around, and although it wasn't easy, especially right after he was released from prison, he pursued his goal to become a country music star. There are few in the field today who surpass his popularity.

Abe Widra's "cell" was a 9-by-10-foot break in cement blocks at the University of Illinois's Chicago Medical Center that doubled as his office and laboratory. It was in this unlikely setting that the associate professor of medical mycology (the science of fungi) developed Stra-cor, a biodegradable artificial skin that can be used to treat burns and large wounds.

Stra-cor, unlike skin grafts and other types of artificial

skin, acts as a substitute for the epidermis. It is flexible, adherent, and absorbent. It allows air and water to pass through, but stops bacteria. The material is easy to apply and works with the body's natural healing processes, allowing white blood cells to pass through the substance and skin cells to migrate and grow on it.

Stra-cor is made from readily available materials, easily applied, and prevents scarring. It can also be used to slowly release drugs into the body, a trait that Widra believes will have significant implications for implants and bypass surgery.

Widra first toyed with the idea of such a substance over 20 years ago when he was doing basic research on fungi. It was then that he came across a gummy material that he thought might help in the treatment of burns and lesions, but because of other research commitments, he shelved the idea until 1978.

He worked out most of the problems himself with virtually no funding, improvising as he went along. When he needed a way to mold the material into sheets, he bought pie tins at a local supermarket for fifty cents apiece. "They worked fine," he says.

It was four years after he began actively working on Stra-cor that it was first tried on a human patient. Today, the product is under option with a company in Boston. It is being tested by the FDA, but is not yet approved. Widra found new adversities when he applied for a patent, but by concentrating his energies on overcoming the legal hurdles involved in securing a patent on this revolutionary product, he finally achieved his goal.

Widra has also enjoyed some success with another invention he calls "Crudaway," an anti-fungal ointment that clears up skin lesions of virtually any type of fungal infection. It has been tested in medical schools on 50 different individuals with a variety of fungus infections, and "in every case," Widra says, "the problems cleared up, so that's my pension," he chuckles. "When I retire, I'm going to travel around the country selling the product to local dealers. It really is an amazing product."

To deal with the constant trying and failing and trying again that plague a researcher's existence, Widra says, "You have to be stubborn to a fault. You have to search out every possibility thoroughly. If there's one unexplored avenue that you haven't explored, find someone who has. Be flexible; collaborate with someone who has resources other than your own. There's always a network of people out there who can help."

As W. Clement Stone and Napoleon Hill wrote in their "PMA Science of Success" home study course 25 years ago, "All types of defeat will yield readily to friendly, cooperative action. The whole secret of the formula by which you may turn defeat into an asset lies in your ability to maintain a *Positive Mental Attitude* despite your defeat.

"Where and how to make that first step are problems which appear insurmountable to the person who has lately met with failure or defeat, for the wounds of disappointment often cut deeply into the reservoir of faith. So we come to the revelation of the means by which the stumbling blocks of failure may be converted into the stepping-stones of magnificent success. This is the pearl of hope which serves best in the hour of deepest darkness."

PART II

Personal Principles

Ask any achiever the secret of his or her success, and you are likely to get an answer something like this:

"Well, I had the right credentials—education, experience and the like. I worked hard, didn't make too many mistakes, and happened to be in the right place at the right time."

This is true, as far as it goes. The real truth, however, is that in most cases these modest people made their own breaks. They became indispensable to the corporation or to their clients and customers because they developed the right personal attributes. Management, clients, and customers like them, trust them, rely on them, and pay them well for the privilege of doing business with them.

These are the people who take the initiative, who assume

leadership roles, who volunteer for difficult or unpopular assignments because they know someone has to do it. They have the confidence in themselves that they will get the job done right, on time, and on budget. And they usually do.

Others like and admire these successful people. They seem to have a little better understanding of themselves than most; they like others, but work equally well in solitude. They have the enthusiasm to inspire others and the self-discipline to stick to the job until it's finished.

These busy achievers always seem to find a little time for a friend or business associate who needs advice or just someone to talk to about a particularly difficult problem. They dig deep to contribute to a worthy cause, and always seem to have their own financial affairs in order.

Regardless of the number of hours they have worked in the last few days, these people never seem tired. If they've got personal problems, you never know it. Somehow, they always seem mentally and physically fit.

In this section we will examine the personal principles of success: Initiative, Enthusiasm, A Pleasing Personality, Self-Discipline, Budgeting Time and Money, and Maintaining Sound Physical and Mental Health. We will also take a look at the lives of some successful people who are particularly adept at applying these principles.

Chapter 6

Personal Initiative

Stone and Hill defined initiative as "that exceedingly rare quality that prompts—no, impels—a person to do that which ought to be done without being told." It is, they said, the power that starts all action and keeps you going until the job is finished. Personal Initiative is the driving force that transforms your goals and ideas into reality.

Personal Initiative is essential for success in any field, whether it is business, sports, politics, entertainment, or public service. You may have the requisite skills, you may have the necessary education, you may have the greatest ideas in the world, you may even practice all the other principles of success, but unless you alone take the initiative, nothing will happen.

Entire industries have been fathered by entrepreneurs

with the right idea at the right time, the personal initiative to get going, to take a risk, and the determination to stick it out no matter how tough things got. We've seen incredible successes in the face of staggering odds—McDonald's Ray Kroc, Domino's Pizza's Tom Monaghan, Apple Computer's Steven Jobs and Steven Wozniak, and Microsoft's Bill Gates are a few recent examples.

But the phenomenon is not new. Many old-line companies bear the names of founders who revolutionized or started new industries—Ford in automobiles, Edison in electricity, Wrigley in chewing gum, and Marshall Field and Neiman Marcus in retailing. Often, though, the entrepreneurs who changed our lives for the better were ordinary folks with extraordinary ambition and initiative.

Clarence Saunders was such a person. He was a clerk in an old-fashioned "mom and pop" grocery store in Memphis, Tennessee, when he got the idea to have customers select their own groceries from the shelves the same way they helped themselves to food in then-new cafeteria-style restaurants.

When he presented the idea to his boss, he was fired for wasting his time on "foolish ideas." Undeterred, he worked four years to raise enough capital to go into business for himself. His "foolish idea" grew into the Piggly-Wiggly grocery chain, and gave birth to the modern supermarket concept. In the process, of course, it made Saunders a wealthy man.

The idea alone, however, didn't make Saunders successful. Barrooms and locker rooms everywhere are filled with would-be achievers who dream of greatness, but never act on their great ideas. Saunders took the initiative. He got into action, he persuaded others to invest in his idea, and he stuck it out until he succeeded.

Elisha Graves Otis had a great idea for a braking system for an elevator, but the idea alone didn't transform the skylines of America's cities. Visionaries in the mid-nineteenth century knew cities couldn't continue their horizontal growth indefinitely, but few saw the elevator as a possible solution to the problem. Otis had to figure out a way to overcome the complacency of those who were perfectly happy with things the way they were.

Freight hoists were already in use, but most people wouldn't ride them for fear the rope would break, and building heights were pretty much limited to the four or five stories people could conveniently climb.[1]

In 1852, Otis built a freight hoist for the Yonkers Bedstead Manufacturing Company where he was a master mechanic, and added a simple braking device. It was not a very glamorous beginning for an idea that would transform the shape of the cities and change forever the way millions live and work.

Otis saw the opportunities the elevator offered, however, and a year after he developed his braking device, he started his own company to begin manufacturing elevators. To assail public apathy about his invention, Otis seized the initiative. In one of the most flamboyant public relations moves in American business history, he built a tower at the first World's Fair, which opened in New York in 1853. He stood on an elevator platform and had himself hoisted high above the crowd in the Crystal Palace. He ordered the rope cut and, with one swing of a workman's axe, Otis took his place in history.

The brake held, and the thousands who witnessed the spectacle and the millions more who read about it saw that the first safe elevator had arrived. Despite the publicity, however (The New York *Tribune* used the words "sensational" and "daring" to describe Otis's initiative) builders didn't immediately recognize that upper floors could now bring premium prices instead of being wasted or used as storage space. The first passenger elevator wasn't installed until three years later at E.V. Haughwout's five-story china and glass emporium on Broadway in New York. It was another 11 years before passenger elevators were installed in New York office buildings, giving birth to the age of the skyscraper.[2]

Now, Otis Elevator is a part of United Technologies, the Hartford, Connecticut based multinational conglomerate which in 1985 posted after tax income of $636 million on sales of $14.99 billion. Otis is one of the most respected names in the industry, and the company continues to pioneer new ideas.

In an interview published in United Technologies' Annual Report to its shareholders, Otis President Francois Jaulin says:

"Ten years ago the electronics content in the elevator was zero. Today, electronics can account for as much as a third of an elevator's total cost. Electronics are clearly bringing about revolutionary changes in the elevator industry. But we are not pushing electronics for the sake of electronics. They cost less and are more reliable than the electromechanical devices they replace. They save valuable space in the machine room, and they allow the flexibility to adapt to a wide range of differing customer requirements. Otis has moved aggressively to integrate both micro- and power-electronics throughout its product line."

Elisha Graves Otis probably wouldn't have understood what Jaulin was talking about, but no doubt he would have been proud that the products that bear his name continually improve as advanced technology encourages new initiatives in the industry he shaped.

In a field where innovation is central to survival, where a company can leapfrog the competition on the strength of a single idea, Otto Clark recently gave the world a lesson in personal initiative.

When he began negotiating with the Chinese government to help that country build 200,000 copiers that would wholesale for about $250 million, few took Clark seriously. His small Illinois firm didn't even have a working model of its copier.

When the agreement was signed in 1982, Clark Copy International Corporation had only 14 employees and had been in business less than five years. Skeptics who initially doubted that Clark could ever sell the deal to the Chinese then began questioning his ability to deliver.

Clark ignored his critics and concentrated on building a quality product and a management team. According to personnel director Lin Stefurak, Clark's initiative and leadership style attracted other achievers to the company, whose management is now made up of what she calls "non-traditional problem solvers."

Stefurak says that approximately 4,000 Clark Copiers were produced here and shipped to China; by 1984, the company had made good on its promise to make the Chinese self-sufficient. That country is now manufacturing all its own copiers.

The entrepreneurial spirit that Clark nurtures in his company is a definite asset in a field that owes its existence and many of its advances in sales and technology to the initiative and persistence of its early leaders. The dry-copying process was itself a revolutionary advance; it was born out of patent attorney Chester F. Carlson's desire to find a better way to make copies. At the time—during the early 1940s—state-of-the-art technology for copying patent drawings and specifications was the wet, messy, photostatic process.

By 1944, Carlson had developed the process sufficiently to interest The Battelle Memorial Institute in continuing his research; Battelle, in turn, tried to attract a manufacturing company with enough capital to make the process commercially available. Legend has it that the process was offered to dozens of leading companies, including General Electric, Kodak, Harris-Seybold, IBM, RCA, A.B. Dick, and Bell & Howell.

An abstract of an article in a trade journal caught the interest of the Haloid Company, a small manufacturer in Rochester, New York, and eventually an agreement was reached. The combination of Carlson's idea and the management talents of Joseph C. Wilson, Jr., Haloid's president, resulted in one of the great business success stories of this century.

Haloid, of course, went on to become the giant Xerox Corporation, and Carlson's process that was developed in a kitchen laboratory spawned an industry that now produces worldwide sales in the billions.

The initiative and innovation that have characterized the copier field continue to result in advanced generations of faster, better machines in a wide variety of styles and options. Buyers' choices now range from huge high-speed machines that copy, collate, and staple in one operation to laser printers to small inexpensive copiers not much larger than a briefcase.

When you do take the initiative, whether it is to introduce a revolutionary new idea, to find a faster way to perform a mundane task, or to get your group a little more organized, you have changed your life. You are no longer one of the led, you are one of the leaders.

It's been said that no one can really motivate someone else; all you can do is motivate yourself and hope it catches on. While this simplistic statement may overlook the good manager's ability to inspire others to higher levels of achievement, it does underscore the interdependence of personal initiative and leadership. Just as leadership cannot flourish without initiative, neither can initiative accomplish much without the cooperation of others. In most situations, the world is simply too complex and interdependent for anyone to be able to go it alone.

It falls to the leader to show the others the way. When a young officer candidate asked his drill sergeant, "Why is it that the officers always have to lead the men into battle?" the grizzled veteran responded, "Son, did you ever try to push a string?"

One who spent his lifetime showing others the way was the late Strom Thurmond, the senior U.S. senator from South Carolina. He was an educator, attorney, a circuit court judge, a governor, a presidential candidate, over thirty years a U.S. senator, holding several key senatorial committee memberships and chairmanships. His WWII and Reserve service won him 18 medals, decorations, and awards. He landed on D-Day in WWII with the famed 82nd Airborne Division. In his home state, no fewer than seven buildings or facilities are named after him, and there's a life-size statue of him in the town square of his native Edgefield.

His honors and awards covered the walls from floor to cathedral ceiling in his former office across the street from the nation's capitol in Washington, D.C. One wall was for national awards, one was for state awards, one was for education awards and honorary degrees, one was for community service, and another—his president's wall—had photographs of Thurmond with the various presidents he had served with in almost three decades in the Senate, and Franklin D. Roosevelt whom he supported as a Democrat at the 1932 convention.

When he was a freshman senator, Thurmond set out twelve leadership rules for himself:

1. A leader must be honest. Honesty is the heart of character. Unless one is honest, he cannot long remain a leader. Naturally this includes being truthful. People will soon learn whether or not they can rely on what you say.
2. He must have ability. Some people inherit more ability than others, but the average man can train and develop himself to the point where he has ability which can become far above average.
3. He must learn to think, make decisions quickly and accurately; to draw sound conclusions, since good judgment is the core of real ability and success.
4. He must be a hard worker. No matter how honest and

able a man he is, if he is not willing to work, he will not go very far. The fellow who puts in the extra hours when the others are playing around is the one who usually gets ahead.

5. He must be courteous. I don't know of any one quality that brings such large dividends as plain courtesy and kindness. Other than dishonesty, there is no one quality that will hurt a man more than discourtesy.
6. He must be courageous and stand for what is right according to Christian standards, or he is bound to land on the other side with those who have selfish interests to serve.
7. He must love people and want to serve them. He must be willing to make sacrifices to help them.
8. He must be cheerful, optimistic, and inspire confidence in others.
9. He must learn to recognize and use the abilities of other people. One man's time and energy is definitely limited, if he confines his operations to himself and his own abilities.
10. He must learn to organize. The great leaders of this country who have made outstanding records of achievement have been those who had the ability to organize. This requires vision and planning, and execution of plans.
11. He must be aggressive, but not to the point of being offensive. Very few aggressive men of ability and vision are stopped by obstacles and troubles that may appear insurmountable to the less aggressive.
12. He must put his trust in God. No man was ever great and remained great who did not trust in God. And it

> follows that a leader communes with God through daily prayer and reads the Holy Scripture regularly. When matters are under consideration, he will frequently ask himself the question: "What is right? What does God want me to do?" A decision is not too hard to make when one is seriously trying to follow God.

Thurmond attributed his philosophy of life and leadership to his parents. "My mother has had the greatest influence on my life in spiritual and religious matters," he said. "She was a devout Christian, consecrated in every way. My father, Judge J. William Thurmond, has influenced me most in my public life and political ambitions. He taught me law—I passed the bar without ever attending law school and tied for first place with a Harvard graduate —but he also instilled in me the simple truth that anything can be accomplished through honesty, clear thinking and hard work."

During the sixties and seventies, it seemed that many of the basic leadership values Thurmond capsulized fell into disfavor with American managers. It may have been, as some writers have suggested, the result of the country's general disenchantment following Vietnam and Watergate, with the military and political models on which many of our leadership concepts were based. Or it may have been that bottom-line driven managers ever on the lookout for a quick fix became more overseers and administrators than leaders.

Whatever the reason, it seems that today there is a popular resurgence of interest in good, old-fashioned leadership. The nomenclature has changed to fit the times, and approaches have been modified to appeal to a better educated, more sophisticated work force, but the fundamentals are the same. Good leaders set high standards for themselves and inspire others to follow their example.

Author Tom Peters, in his best-selling *A Passion for Excellence*, calls it leading by coaching and teaching.[3] He writes:

"Fine performance comes from people at all levels who pay close attention to their environment, communicate unshakable core values, and patiently develop the skills that will enable them to make sustained contributions to their organizations. *In a word, it recasts the detached, analytical manager as the dedicated, enthusiastic coach.*

"Coaching is face-to-face leadership that pulls together people with diverse backgrounds, talents, experiences and interests, encourages them to step up to responsibility and continued achievement, and treats them as full-scale partners and contributors. Coaching is not about memorizing techniques or devising the perfect game plan. It is about really paying attention to people—really believing them, really caring about them, really involving them. Former New Orleans Saints coach Bum Phillips observed: 'The main thing is getting people to play. When you think it's your system that's winning, you're in for a damn big surprise. It's those players' efforts.'

"To coach is largely to facilitate, which literally means 'to make easy'—not less demanding, less interesting or less intense, but less discouraging, less bound up with excessive controls and complications. A coach/facilitator works tirelessly to free the team from needless restrictions on performance, even when they are self-imposed."

Good coach/leaders are good teachers, Peters says, citing

a survey by The Center for Creative Leadership in Greensboro, North Carolina. When the Center asked successful managers to talk about their best teachers, in most cases they turned out to be former bosses. "The following," Peters writes, "were the most frequently mentioned characteristics of these managers-as-teachers:"

- They counseled. *They gave younger managers constructive advice and feedback. They used younger managers as sounding boards.*
- They excelled. *Whether in finance, production or marketing, these managers were the best in some aspect of their business.*
- They gave exposure. *They made sure that the work and accomplishments of young managers were seen. They opened doors for them.*
- They provided latitude. *They gave young managers the freedom to try, the courage to fail. They involved them in important tasks.*
- They were tough taskmasters. *They challenged; they demanded excellence.*

John Sculley, chairman and CEO of Apple Computer, which celebrated its tenth anniversary in 1987, says that today's leaders will have to "find new role models in terms of how we want to run our businesses. To the more traditional companies and industries," he says, "it means that they have had to rethink the way that they approach business management.

"Most of us in business—and I include myself because the majority of my career has been in a traditional industry that was labor and capital intensive (it has been only in the last few years that I have been in the high technology industry)—have used the old models of the Catholic Church, with its hierarchy of structure and its hierarchy of process, and many levels of organization with clear authority coming from the top down. Another old model was the military organization; even the vocabulary of the military has worked its way into strategic documents; attack plans, and defense programs as we try to outflank the competition.

"These models," Sculley says, "may not be appropriate as we move forward into the information age. At Apple we are experimenting with the kinds of models that are more akin to team sports; the leader is no longer an autocratic ruler who determines from on top what will happen, but the leader becomes a *coach*. The leader becomes responsible for creating an environment in which people can find a quality of life that can be enjoyable.

"Why should working be a tedious experience? At Apple, the average age of our employees is only 29 years. At a lot of companies, 29 years would be the number of years of service. Young people today are looking for more than just good pay or moving up the career ladder. They are looking for quality of life—an environment where they can grow and enjoy what they are doing. They expect their top management to provide this kind of culture for them as much as people from traditional corporations expect to be provided with pensions.

"In fact, at Apple, we do not have a pension program—the only one there who is old enough to worry about pensions is probably me. In its place, we have the largest stock option program for employees of any company in the Fortune 500, because ownership means a lot to young people. They want to buy into having a real role in the company. The reason why young people come to a company like Apple is that they believe it is possible, particularly for people at their age, to do things that have never been done before."

Their leaders, Sculley says, *"have to inspire them with a vision that is exciting enough to follow!"* Sculley knows firsthand the difficulty of making cultural and environmental changes—the move from Pepsi on the East Coast to Apple in Silicon Valley is a lot more than 3,000 miles, he says—and he is keenly aware of the difficulty in leading in an increasingly technological society.

"At a company like Apple," he says, "we have found that we have to be in constant communication. I spend a lot of time wandering around just talking to the engineers, listening to what's going on in their heads, and trying to tell them what we're really trying to do is become more market-driven. Sometimes when I talk to them, I see glassy stares and know I'm not getting through; I'm sure sometimes when they're talking to me, they must get a glassy stare and wonder whether or not they're getting through to me. At least we're talking eyeball to eyeball.

"Perhaps that's one of the big differences between the new corporations and what we've seen in the past. The old ways of talking to the organization were through memorandums or large public address of some sort. Today that just isn't enough. You've got to be out wandering around listening to, talking to, and exchanging ideas with people. If you don't, you can get into deep trouble, particularly in an industry like ours. I include all of high technology in this, where things happen so rapidly that if you miss a beat you can lose your whole company."

Perhaps one of the most interesting observations about leadership comes from Warren Bennis, a professor of management and organization at the University of Southern California. After interviewing and observing some 90 leaders in business, public service, the arts, and sports, Bennis concluded, "Unsuccessful leaders are all alike; every successful leader is successful in his own way."[4]

Bennis told the *Chicago Tribune* he was floored by their diversity. "I was faced with what I call the Anna Karenina syndrome in reverse," Bennis says, referring to Tolstoy's wisdom about families.

The former University of Cincinnati president and consultant to the last four U.S. presidents did, however, find some similarities in the leaders. The one trait common to all is what he and others refer to as "vision."

"I cannot exaggerate this difference," he told the *Tribune*. "It's as if they are drawing people to them, but it's not necessarily the quality we think of as charisma. It's a kind of laser beam intensity they get when they're talking about their vision. When they're talking about something else, they can be as boring as the next person."

Bennis also found that his subjects were able to communicate their ideas to others. Ronald Reagan's skill has earned him the nickname "The Great Communicator," but it's an ability Bennis says Jimmy Carter never mastered. One of Bennis's subjects, Carter's Commerce Secretary Juanita Kreps, told him she did not know what Carter was working for as president. "It was like looking at the wrong side of a tapestry," she told Bennis. "Everything was blurry and indistinct."

"Good leaders are also persistent. Admiral Hyman

Rickover told Bennis that the nuclear submarine would have never been built if he had not kept the idea alive." The effort required, in Rickover's words, "courageous patience" because the idea seemed at first, like so many workable ideas, cockeyed. In the words of Bennis's "favorite management philosopher," Woody Allen, "If you want to be a success in life, just show up 80 percent of the time."

The fourth quality of leadership, Bennis said, "is harder to define but comes down to a healthy self-respect, out of which grows a profitable respect for others. They discovered, usually at an early age what their strengths were and nurtured them.

"Such leaders are often able to bring out the best in others. They see latent talent and encourage it, they listen to their subordinates, and they realize that a person's inability to do one job does not mean he is incompetent at all jobs. An executive at IBM was surprised when he was not fired for a decision that cost the company $10 million. 'Fire you?' his superior said. 'We just spent $10 million educating you.' "

Bennis emphasizes that all his subjects were leaders, not managers. He defined the difference at a seminar sponsored by the National College of Education: "A manager is someone who does things right, but a leader is someone who does the right thing."

Admiral Grace Hopper put it more succinctly. In a recent television interview, the ranking female Navy officer told *60 Minutes's* Morley Safer, "You manage things. You lead people."

The old saying that "the more things change, the more they remain the same," seems to apply aptly to leadership.

Technology may change our world, and our customs may evolve along with our ways of doing business, but leaders who can get results through people will never go out of style. Examine the lives and careers of successful people in any line of work and you will find that when the situation called for action, they took the initiative to act. They did the job without being told.

Chapter 7

Enthusiasm

Most authors of motivational books tell you that you must be enthusiastic if you want to be successful. Few, however, spend more than a paragraph or two on the subject, and almost none of them give any practical advice about how to be enthusiastic. This book is an exception. We will tell you why you need enthusiasm and how to generate it.

What is enthusiasm and how do we catch it? The word itself originated in ancient Greece. Loosely translated, it means "inspired by God." Webster's more modern definition is "strong excitement of feeling on behalf of a cause or subject; ardent zeal or interest; fervor."

About enthusiasm, Emerson said, "Every great and commanding movement in the annals of the world is the triumph of enthusiasm. Nothing great was ever achieved without it."

How do you achieve and maintain such a feeling about the tedious tasks that are part of every job, every profession, every career? How do you convey enthusiasm to others when you don't always feel enthusiastic yourself?

It begins with your own Definiteness of Purpose. Your goals must be so firmly entrenched that they are a part of your psyche, your very soul. Unless you have the courage of your convictions, it is impossible to enthusiastically sell your ideas, your products, or your services to others. The "God within you" is your belief in yourself and what you do.

Former chairman and CEO Lee Iacocca's enthusiasm for Chrysler came across in his television commercials because he believed in his company's products and in what he was saying about them. Although he at first resisted the idea of making commercials when Kenyon & Eckhardt, Chrysler's advertising agency, tagged a few seconds of Iacocca addressing his dealers onto the end of a commercial, they liked what they saw.

The agency finally prevailed, and Iacocca went on to become one of TV's most successful and best-known pitchmen. The commercials became more aggressive until they evolved, according to Iacocca in his autobiography, into the "now-famous line in which I pointed my finger at the camera and said: 'If you can find a better car—buy it.' That one was my own, by the way, which may explain why I could deliver it with such conviction."[1]

There is no limit to what can be accomplished with enthusiasm. W. Clement Stone likes to tell the story of Leo Fox, a man whose boundless enthusiasm seemed to attract others to him the way a magnet attracts iron filings.

"I first met Leo during the Depression when he answered my ad in the newspaper. He was so enthusiastic that I hired him as a salesman on the spot. I didn't find out until later that he was so broke his wife was afraid to leave their room when he was out because the manager would lock her out until some of the back rent was paid. Leo used his first day's commissions to pay back rent, and had to get up early the next morning to sell enough to buy breakfast for his family.

"Leo had been working for me just a few weeks when a salesman from his old organization came up to see me. He had met Leo on the street, and Leo had appeared so happy and prosperous that he wondered if I had another opening. Of course I did.

"In the next couple of months, I hired five additional salesmen from Leo's old organization. They also had met him on the street and asked where he was working and applied, too.

"Leo Fox is a man I hold in high esteem. He had a personal problem that has ruined many men; he was an alcoholic. That's why, he told me, he was 'kicked out of the house' by his father, John Fox, owner and president of the First National Casualty Company headquartered in Fond du Lac, Wisconsin. A year or so after he joined me, Leo told me about the problem and said: 'I'm going to the Keeley Institute in Dwight, Illinois, and I'm going to win this battle with myself.' He did go to Dwight and he did win his battle.

"At a social gathering, or at a convention, if someone asks, 'Will you join me in a drink?' Leo is enthusiastic. 'I'll be glad to,' he says. When the orders are taken, he makes no apologies. He's proud to state, 'Make mine a cup of hot coffee.' He hasn't had an alcoholic beverage since the day he entered the Keeley Institute.

"Leo and his family drove to Fond du Lac to see his

parents before he was to move to Pennsylvania to become my sales manager there. When his father saw what Leo had done to improve himself, he said, 'If you're good enough to be a sales manager for Mr. Stone in Pennsylvania, then you're man enough to become president of First National.'

"Leo accepted the job with his father, and eventually did become president. Later, it was through Leo that I had the opportunity to purchase the First National Casualty Company. Today Leo is a wealthy, successful man. I've told his story often, and it has been an inspiration to thousands."

Stone also recalls a conversation he and Dr. Norman Vincent Peale had about enthusiasm. "'Clem,' Dr. Peale said to me, 'you have more real, genuine enthusiasm than any man I know, and it is of the kind that never takes defeat for an answer. What is the secret of your enthusiasm as it applies to problems—either business or personal?'

"Feeling humbled by his generous compliment, I responded: 'As you know, the emotions are not always immediately subject to reason, but they are always immediately subject to action—mental or physical. Furthermore, repetition of the same thought or physical action develops into a habit which, when repeated frequently, becomes an automatic reflex'" (see Chapter 18).

To be enthusiastic, you must act enthusiastic, Stone says. If you *act* enthusiastic your emotions will follow, and soon enough you will *feel* enthusiastic. He offers the following specific advice from his own experience:

1. Talk loudly! This is particularly helpful if you are emotionally upset or if you have butterflies in your stomach when you stand before an audience.

2. Talk rapidly! Your mind functions more quickly than you do.
3. Emphasize! Stress words that are important to you or your listeners—a word like *you*, for example.
4. Hesitate! Talk rapidly, but hesitate where there would be a period, comma, or other punctuation mark in the written words. When you employ the dramatic effect of silence, the mind of the person who is listening catches up with the thoughts you have expressed. Hesitation after a word you wish to emphasize accentuates the emphasis.
5. Keep a smile in your voice! This eliminates gruffness as you talk loudly and rapidly. You can put a smile in your voice by putting a smile on your face, a smile in your eyes.
6. Modulate! This is important if you are speaking for a long period. Remember, you can modulate both pitch and volume. You can speak loudly and intermittently change to a conversational tone and a lower pitch if you wish.

Stone points out that there is a difference between having enthusiasm and being enthusiastic. "*Enthusiasm*," he says, "is a positive mental attitude—an *internal* impelling force of intense emotion, a power compelling creation or expression. It always implies an objective or cause that is pursued with devotion.

"Being *enthusiastic* is an impelling *external* expression of action. When you act enthusiastically, you accentuate the power of suggestion and autosuggestion. Thus, the salesman or sales manager, public speaker, minister, lawyer, teacher, or executive who acts enthusiastic by speaking in an enthusiastic, sincere manner develops genuine enthusiasm.

"The little difference that makes the big difference is *attitude*—especially where Enthusiasm is concerned."

You've probably seen enthusiasm work its magic in your own acquaintances, your friends and coworkers. When they talk about something in which they believe—really believe—they take on an intensity that is unmatched in anything else they do. They become more animated, their voices become stronger, and they have a vibrancy that is difficult to resist. You begin to find yourself aligning with them emotionally, even though you know intellectually that you disagree.

The fervor that is fueled by an unquenchable fire within is contagious and undefeatable. Hill and Stone compared Enthusiasm to the engine of an automobile; it is, they said, the vital moving force.

If you mix enthusiasm with your work, your work will not seem difficult or monotonous. Enthusiasm will so energize your body that you can get along with half your usual sleep and do twice the amount of your normal work without getting tired. Enthusiasm recharges your body and helps you develop the kind of dynamic personality that attracts others to you. It is simply impossible not to like an enthusiastic person.

Some people are blessed with a natural enthusiasm. The late Mary Kay Ash, founder of Mary Kay Cosmetics, considered herself such a person. She said that she first discovered she could sell on sheer enthusiasm when she was a young housewife and mother.

One day, a woman by the name of Ida Blake came to her door selling the *Child Psychology Bookshelf*, a series of books for children. "If you had a problem with your child," Ash said, "you simply looked up the problem in the back of the book, and there was a story to tie in with it. All the stories included very good morals, and whatever the problem was, there was a story to fit the situation. As a young mother trying to teach her children the difference between right and wrong, I just thought those were the best books I'd ever seen!

"When the saleslady told me what they cost, I almost cried. I just couldn't afford them. Sensing my interest, she let me keep them over the weekend, and I read every page. When she came by to pick them up, I was heartbroken. I told her I was going to save my money, and one day I would buy those books, because they were the best I'd ever seen.

"When she saw how excited I was, she said, 'I'll tell you what, Mary Kay, if you sell 10 sets of books for me, I'll give you a set.' Well, that was just wonderful! I started calling my friends and the parents of my beginner Sunday School students at Tabernacle Baptist Church. I didn't even have any books to show them—I just had my enthusiasm."

In a day and a half, Ash sold the 10 sets, and Ida Blake signed Mary Kay as a saleswoman. Mary Kay went on to make the line of cosmetics that bears her name a household word, and made millions for herself in the process. The company's song says it all: "I've Got That Mary Kay Enthusiasm" (to the tune of a popular old hymn). "It's so much a part of our company that it is sung everywhere," Ash said.

Even if you weren't born with enthusiasm, it's easy to develop, according to Stone and Hill. They recommend that you begin by selling a product or service that you really like.

Although money or circumstances may require you to do something you don't particularly like for a time, nothing and no one can stop you from deciding for yourself what your major goal in life will be. No one can stop you from developing plans to make your goal a reality, nor can anyone stop you from injecting enthusiasm into your plans.

Their simple formula for developing enthusiasm is:

- Associate with others who are enthusiastic and optimistic.
- Work to build financial success. With it comes enthusiasm.
- Master and apply the principles of success in your daily life.
- Take care of your health. It's tough to be enthusiastic when you are physically ill.
- Maintain a Positive Mental Attitude. If you feel positive about what you are doing, others will catch your enthusiasm.
- Help others. Whether it is helping others through the product or service you sell or through your own kindness and benevolence, helping others will help you sustain your enthusiasm.

Dressing for success also will help you maintain your enthusiasm. Many books have been written and many careers have been built on the "dress for success" concept, so we won't deal with that in depth here. We simply wish to point out that you feel better and you are more enthusiastic when you *know* you look good and are appropriately dressed for the situation. Conversely, if you don't think you look prosperous and professional, it's difficult to project enthusiasm.

As you work to build your own enthusiasm, it's also important to remember that it's not so much what you say as *how you say it*. Your tone and manner make a lasting impression on others. Naturally, *what* you say must reflect what you believe or others will see right through you. A phony is easily identified. You must be sincere in your purpose, honest and earnest, if you are to make a long-lasting favorable impression.

You can't afford to express, either through your words or your actions, things you don't believe. If you do, you will soon lose the ability to influence others.

As Napoleon Hill wrote many years ago, "I do not believe I can afford to try to deceive anyone about anything, but I know I cannot afford to try to deceive myself. To do so would destroy the power of my pen and render my words ineffective. It is only when I write with the fire of enthusiasm burning in my heart that my writing impresses others favorably; it is only when I speak from a heart that is bursting with belief in my message that I can move audiences to accept that message."[2]

Grant G. Gard, a veteran salesman, sales trainer, and public speaker with close to 40 years' experience, believes that Enthusiasm is at the bottom of all selling success. In *Championship Selling* he writes:

"You can arouse your enthusiasm and keep it aroused. Far too many salespeople are dependent upon someone—spouse, sales manager, other salespeople—to arouse and supply the enthusiasm needed to sell successfully. Basically, I have found that salespeople can arouse their own enthusiasm by (1) knowing everything there is to know about the product, that it's made the best and is of high quality, and (2) being confident that their product will greatly benefit the buyer. Your first-class product and the many product benefits it provides should set you on fire with enthusiasm. Enthusiasm sells! It sells you, and it sells your product. If you aren't honestly and sincerely excited about your product and the benefits it brings to the user, stop selling immediately! You'll never be very successful as a salesperson. A salesperson without enthusiasm is just an order taker."

Gard goes on to explain that he isn't talking about "shouting, yelling at the top of your voice, or waving your arms frantically and jumping up and down. I'm talking about a genuine, sincere, dedicated belief in the product you sell and a red-hot burning desire to transmit this feeling to your prospect so that he or she can enjoy the benefits. The salesperson who is excited sells. Enthusiasm is the greatest power you have to move you on to greater accomplishment. You must have it before you can give it, but when you've got it, everyone around you also has it."[3]

Oral Roberts and Billy Graham have thrilled audiences all over the world, gathering converts in unbelievable numbers. But take Enthusiasm out of their ministries and they would lose their effectiveness.

Clarence Darrow was undoubtedly one of the greatest lawyers this country has ever produced, and much of his success was due to his great capacity for expressing himself with enthusiasm and arousing enthusiasm in his listeners—courts and juries alike. He was no more knowledgeable about the law than any of the other lawyers of his day.

Someone once said, "There is rejoicing in Heaven and

the gritting of teeth in Hell when God turns loose a man on earth with a capacity for unlimited use of faith and enthusiasm." If you have the courage of your convictions and the habit of thinking positively, Enthusiasm will follow.

You become enthusiastic by acting enthusiastically in your thoughts, your words, and your actions. One of the greatest life insurance salesmen in the world used to send himself a telegram every day so it would be at the breakfast table every morning. It told him how much insurance he was going to sell that day—and he did it. Sometimes he even went far beyond the goal he set for himself.

The telegrams were signed: *Doctor Enthusiasm*.

You may think the idea is a little silly, but that silliness made him one of the top salesmen for one of the largest insurance companies in the country. It worked for him.

We all have to develop our own ways of inspiring enthusiasm in ourselves, but there's no better starting point than believing in yourself, your company, and your product. If you do, and if you act enthusiastic and concentrate on positive thoughts, honest, sincere, contagious enthusiasm will follow—and success will follow enthusiasm. As IBM Chairman Thomas J. Watson, Jr., once observed, "The greatest accomplishments of man have resulted from the transmission of ideas and enthusiasm."

Chapter 8

A Pleasing Personality

People like doing business with people they like. That's a fact. If quality, service, and price are comparable, it is human nature to choose to buy from people we like, to hire people with personalities similar to our own, or to choose to work for pleasant people. Sometimes, even if there are pronounced differences between the products, services, or jobs we are considering, we develop a rationalization to justify buying from one person or accepting one job over another simply because we like the people involved.

Is it possible to make others like you? You bet it is. There is a silly old movie that appears on TV from time to time in which a mother advises her daughter that the secret of a happy marriage is to train her husband the same way she would train a puppy. The mother even goes so far as to give her daughter a handbook on dog training to serve as a guide in the process.

It isn't until the end of the movie that the daughter realizes that while she thought she was training her husband, she was actually training herself. To teach him to be faithful, she had to first prove herself faithful. To receive love, she had to give it.

While the movie is no Academy Award winner, its message is worth noting: To train others to like us, we must first train ourselves to be likable.

It all begins with character. Your personality is what others think you are, it's said, while your character is what you really are. But it's difficult to separate personality from character because each is a reflection of the other.

You may be able to mask your true feelings for a time, but most people can quickly spot a phony. If your motivation to get others to like you is strictly selfish, if you are simply trying to use your personality to take advantage of others, your true character will almost always be revealed eventually.

Likewise if, deep down, you are a positive, pleasant person, others will be genuinely attracted to you. If you can sincerely generate feelings of enthusiasm, happiness, and kindness, people will respond in kind. It is very difficult not to like an enthusiastic, cheerful, considerate person.

The degree to which we exhibit positive personality traits may vary greatly from individual to individual, but we all have them, or at least have the potential to develop them. If we encourage rather than suppress them, we become more proficient at calling up the personality traits—on demand—that will help ensure success in any situation.

In their book *Modern Persuasion Strategies: The Hidden Advantage in Selling*, Donald J. Moine and John H. Herd refer to "pacing," by which they mean revealing your own personality traits that are similar to those exhibited by a person you are trying to influence. Pacing, they say, is "a sophisticated form of matching or mirroring key aspects of another's behavioral preferences."[1]

While they are offering advice in selling—a profession in which a pleasing personality is critical to long-term success—the concept will work in any situation. What Moine and Herd suggest is not a contrived sort of cozying-up that most of us automatically find distasteful, but rather a genuine form of identifying with another, stepping into stride with that person.

Some people do it naturally while others have to work at it, but the net result is the same. "You are pacing," the authors say, "when the prospect gets the feeling that you and he (or she) think alike and look at problems in similar ways. When this happens, the prospect identifies with you and finds it easy and natural to agree with you. You seem like emotional twins. Pacing works, because like attracts like."

Another reason pacing works is because selling, like most other people relationships, is emotional. People don't buy your products, your ideas, or fund your projects on sweet reason alone. They respond emotionally to a well thought out, logical, persuasive, and *emotional* appeal. Regardless of the degree of sophistication of today's prospects, Moine and Herd believe, selling is still more emotional than objective.

In the course of doing research for their book, the authors studied 100 of the country's top sales producers who say they "cannot consciously describe how they perform their own sales magic." After studying them in action, reviewing their tapes, and testing the newfound insights in the field, Moine and Herd realized that these super salespeople so naturally identified with people that prospects instantly liked them, and bought their products and services. Teaching others these pacing techniques resulted in sales increases in some companies of as much as 232 percent in the span of one year.

While it is possible to pace yourself to align the compatible aspects of your personality with another's, this is not to suggest that you should become a chameleon so adept at mimicking others that you lose sight of the real you. W. Clement Stone's style and flair are a part of his personality. Others might prefer a more subdued approach. Whatever makes you unique, use those traits to your advantage.

Emphasize those aspects of your personality that you like in yourself and that others find attractive. Because we are all complex individuals with a full range of positive and negative emotions, it would be totally unrealistic to expect everyone you meet to like every aspect of your personality. But, by directing your thoughts, you can control the kind of person you wish to become; a positive thinker becomes a positive person, someone others like to be around.

When you are dealing with others, look for common ground. Identify the subjects you are both interested in, not just those *you* like or are particularly knowledgeable about. When you are having a conversation with someone else, don't just take turns talking, *listen* to what the other person is saying.

To borrow another technique from the sales field, allow

the other person to talk by asking probing, open-ended questions. Super salesman Hank Trisler says in his book *No Bull Selling*, "A salesman should talk twenty percent of the time and listen eighty percent of the time, and that twenty percent ought to be questions to get the customer talking more. The quickest way to establish rapport is to get the other guy talking about himself. The more you let me talk about myself, the better I like you," he says.

Trisler tells the story of a young woman he once met who so delighted him with her interest in him and his business that by the end of two and a quarter hours together, "I'd determined that this was one of the most intelligent, perceptive, best conversationalists I'd ever met. By the time we were through dinner and a half dozen rusty nails, I was ready to make a lifetime commitment. I was in love."[2]

Trisler's story illustrates the old axiom: when you can't think of anything to say, ask the other fellow about himself. That's sure to keep the conversation going.

How people respond to you is often established in the first few minutes after you meet them. First impressions may be right or wrong but, as the saying goes, you never get a second chance to make a first impression. To underscore the importance of a first impression, sales trainer Lloyd Purves suggests thinking back to the people you have met.

"How many of them that came on like wooden horses do you still have as friends? How many of their names can you recall? Do you remember anything about them except that they irritated or bored you?"

In his book, *Secrets of Personal Command Power*, Purves says that creating a strong first impression begins with the knowledge that people will treat you as you expect to be treated. “This,” he says, “is always true on the first contact. If you step out in a bold confident manner and immediately begin projecting yourself, you will be accorded the respect and attention due any leader.”[3]

Purves recommends that when you are introduced to any group, you begin by shaking hands all around, repeating each name aloud, and leaning slightly toward each person as you are introduced, and as you introduce yourself. When you first meet the group, you can also direct the conversation by asking members of the group about themselves, their interests, their likes and dislikes. This gives you an advantage in establishing yourself later because you will know something about members of the group. The procedure works equally well in one-on-one situations.

Don’t feel obliged to listen to people who have little to say but have a “motor mouth.” They are time wasters. Don’t be trapped by them, Purves advises. Instead, spend your time with people on whom you need to make a strong first impression.

It’s also a good idea to know something about any group you are meeting for the first time. Prepare for a first meeting the same way you would prepare for a job interview. Read any available literature about the organization, and know something about its goals, programs, and reason for existence.

If you are making a sales call on an important prospect, know something about the company so you can tailor your message to his or her situation. Although this might seem very basic, it is surprising how few people do spend any time and effort in advance preparation. Many salespeople use a standard approach to every situation, expecting to learn about the company from the prospect.

One telemarketing salesman we know bombed badly in a major presentation to a group of accounting firm executives because he kept referring to the "company sales force," and how his telemarketing specialists could supplement their efforts. In discussing the presentation after the salesman left, the group realized that each had independently come to the conclusion that the salesman hadn't even taken the time to learn that the firm does not have salespeople. It is a partnership with partners who are responsible for client relations. It would simply take too long to get the telemarketing firm up to speed. The executives weren't tremendously interested in teaching the salesman how to sell his product. Eventually the firm retained another telemarketing company whose sales representative demonstrated that he understood the accounting firm's culture and how his services would complement their efforts. Doing your homework goes a long way toward making a good first impression.

How you dress can also have a significant impact on how others perceive you. There are plenty of good books available on how to dress for success if you are interested in learning more about the subject, but a good rule of thumb is to be sure you are dressed appropriately for the situation. Even if an invitation to some event identifies proper dress for the situation, there is a great deal left unsaid. "Dress casual" may mean jeans and shorts to a group of advertising agency people while the same words mean sports jackets or blazers and trousers at a gathering of attorneys. If you are unsure, ask. Nothing makes you feel more uncomfortable than being over- or under-dressed for the occasion.

The same holds true for work attire. Acceptable dress at

one company may be entirely inappropriate for another. If you want to fit into the culture of any organization, observe how the president dresses and follow his or her lead. If he's an entrepreneur who shuns ties and prefers sneakers to wingtips, however, proceed with caution. He may think it's fine for him to dress that way in the office, but it wouldn't work so well for the sales force to dress the same way when making sales calls on conservative companies, and the vice president of finance wouldn't instill much confidence in bankers if he wore jeans instead of pinstripes to a business lunch. The kind of work you do and the type of people you are likely to come in contact with during the normal course of business should also influence your attire. Again, appropriateness is the key.

Like it or not, voice quality is another factor that greatly influences how people perceive you. To instill confidence, you must project it in your manner, your dress and your voice. If you are soft-spoken to the point of timidity, you may arouse pity, but it will be unlikely that you will inspire respect.

Exercise your voice the same way you do your other muscles. Tape-record your voice so you can hear yourself as others hear you. If your voice quality and inflections or your mannerisms are really a source of problems for you, get a video camera and recorder and videotape yourself in action. Mount the camera on a tripod, turn it on, and tape your presentation. When you review it afterward, be extremely critical of your every move, and work to correct weaknesses until you are satisfied with the results.

This technique works especially well in preparing for a stand-up presentation to a group or a speech where the setting may be more uncomfortable than a meeting with one or two people. The impression you make in such settings will be entirely governed by how you project your personality. Rehearse your presentation before the camera, play back the videotape, and make notes of areas that need improvement. Observe your facial expressions, gestures, and voice quality. There are three rules to a successful presentation, one speech coach noted: rehearse, rehearse, and rehearse. If you know what you are going to say, how you are going to say it, and how the audience sees you, the confidence you feel will be apparent to others.

One of the most powerful personalities this country has ever produced was Lyndon Johnson. Few could resist his formidable persuasive skills on the telephone or in person, yet on television he came across as something of a humorless hick. He never seemed to come to grips with the way television cameras intensify the lack of animation or expression in a speaker. If you are dynamic on videotape, you can be sure you will be dynamic in person. Use this tool and the knowledge it brings to your advantage.

The power of A Pleasing Personality is very apparent in high visibility jobs such as politics, government, or television, but it works equally in virtually any line of work. Ask any member of "The Carlos Corps."

Carlos Karas runs a Texaco station at 9503 Westheimer Road in southwest Houston. On just about any given day, if you hang around the station, you can watch the induction process into the Carlos Corps. One customer comes in with a lawn mower that won't start, obviously irritated about the inconvenience; but he leaves with a broad smile on his face. Karas has quickly repaired the balky mower. "No charge," he says, and says good-bye with his trademark, "Come back and chat sometime." Another "inductee" is a woman whose car engine problem is corrected after a competitor twice tried to repair it and failed.

"It's not going to cost you a dime," Karas tells her when she comes to pick up the car. "Next time you need gas, or have a problem, you come to Carlos." After the woman leaves, Karas says: "She'll never forget that." Karas says of the customer, "Things like that help business. That's how I advertise. She'll come back. I guarantee, she'll be back."

Texaco marketing rep Chuck Campbell, who coined the term *Carlos Corps*, says that what sets Karas apart from others in the service station business are his warmth and friendliness.

When Karas opened his station in 1972, he began by offering "the best service around. I wanted to make them feel as though they were getting something special they couldn't get anywhere else. So that's what I gave them."

"Specifically, what he gave them—and continues to give them—is extraordinary service that borders on pampering," says *Texaco Marketer*. "Windshields of cars on the full-service island are scrubbed by enthusiastic attendants, the oil is always checked, and if there are no cars waiting, a gauge is put on the tires."[4] Karas guarantees that all work will be completed within 24 hours; customers are driven home when they leave their cars, and picked up when the work has been completed.

But Karas's real secret of success is his irresistible personality. He's simply a kind, decent, honest, friendly businessman whose customers like him and keep coming back. His consideration for others paid off recently when he made a loan to one of his customers who was down on his luck. The customer was a driver for a company that operated a small fleet of trucks. "Not only did he pay me back," Karas says, "but he convinced his boss to fuel all his trucks here." The whole company was "Carlos-ized."

You, too, can be Carlos-ized, says W. Clement Stone, if you really want to be. He offers the following tips for developing A Pleasing Personality:

- Begin by taking inventory of your personality traits. Identify as many as you can—good and bad. Ask yourself: Do people generally like me? Why or why not?
- Decide what you and others don't like about yourself and how you plan to change these traits. Use the Cosmic Habit Force and Positive Mental Attitude principles to replace negative characteristics with positive ones.
- Listen in on your own conversations. Are you giving others the opportunity to speak, or are you monopolizing the discussion?
- Be considerate of others. Be genuinely interested in them as people. Use your natural curiosity about others to learn what makes them tick. You will probably find that once you get to know them, you will like them. Best of all, they will like you, too.
- Remember, if you want to make a favorable impression, be attentive. Make the person you're talking to feel that he or she is the most important person in the world.
- Look directly at the person you are speaking to. If you have trouble looking someone in the eye, look at

their forehead. They won't know the difference, and you will give the appearance of rapt attention.

- Nod occasionally even if you don't agree. This encourages the speaker to be more expressive; you can register your views when he or she is finished.
- Don't interrupt. Everyone is entitled to his or her opinion. Listen to the speaker's view before you offer your own.
- Be respectful of the other person's dignity. Don't try to make yourself look good at someone else's expense.
- Don't minimize others' accomplishments and abilities. Give credit where credit is due.
- Don't boast of your own achievements. Deeds always speak louder than words.
- Give others a chance to stand in the spotlight. We all get our turn; be modest when your turn comes.
- Be magnanimous in victory and gracious in defeat.
- Don't use flattery to ingratiate yourself with others.
- Respect others as individuals and expect respect in return.
- Don't try to impress others with your intelligence. Use words to communicate, not to establish your superiority.
- Be discreet about the subjects you choose to discuss. Don't discuss controversial topics such as religion, politics, and race at inappropriate times or places.
- Don't gossip or agree with someone who does. If you don't feel like defending the person who is being maligned, change the subject or walk away. Always assume there are two sides to every story; you are only hearing one of them.

- Don't bore others with tales of your misfortunes, problems, or personal interests.
- Don't let others make you angry. When you lose control because someone else has gotten to you, you have put them in control of your reaction. Don't let that happen.
- Always, always follow the Golden Rule. If you treat others as you would like to be treated, you will never have to worry about whether or not people like you. Your biggest problem will be finding as much time as your friends would like you to spend with them.

Perhaps a note of caution might be in order to end this chapter. A Pleasing Personality may get you some, even all, the things you want—for a time. But in the long pull, there has to be some substance. You can't get by forever simply because people like you.

Your personality may help you get the job, but it's important to know when to stop selling yourself and get down to business. Personality alone isn't enough to cut it. Eventually, you have to produce.

Chapter 9

Self-Discipline

In the philosophy of success promulgated by Napoleon Hill and W. Clement Stone, Self-Discipline might be described as the counter-balance of Enthusiasm. As Hugh Stevenson Tigner once observed, "Enthusiasm always exaggerates the importance of things and over-looks their deficiencies." Self-Discipline is the principle that channels your Enthusiasm in the right direction. Without it, Napoleon Hill said, Enthusiasm resembles the unharnessed lightning of an electrical storm; it may strike anywhere and it can be destructive.

In simplest terms, Self-Discipline is taking control of your mind, your habits, and your emotions. Until you master Self-Discipline, you cannot be a leader of others and you cannot be a great success at anything. As William Hazlitt said, "Those who can command themselves, command others."

Like so many of the other principles of success, Self-Discipline is something that must be practiced constantly. It is never completely learned; it only becomes easier with practice. If you force yourself to make a prescribed number of sales calls every day, rain or shine, whether you feel like it or not; if you force yourself to meet deadlines in your job; if you force yourself to stay with a project until it is finished; if you consciously replace negative habits with positive ones, you are on the way to developing Self-Discipline.

Examine the lives of highly successful people in any business or profession, and you will find that they have the discipline necessary to do what it takes to get the job done. They focus on their goals with an intensity that sweeps aside trivial things so they can concentrate on the situation at hand, and they stick with it until they succeed.

J. Peter Grace, chairman, president, and CEO of W. R. & Grace Co., was close to 70 when he was tapped by President Reagan to head a committee on waste in government, an assignment he accepted with obvious relish. But the voluntary assignment meant that he would have to juggle an already almost impossibly crowded schedule to accommodate the time pressures inherent in trying to bring the massive federal budget under control. Not only did he get his report out on schedule, but he managed to find the time to make two television commercials and barnstorm the country, building grass-roots support for his cause.

At the same time, he was busy redirecting the company. In early 1986 he paid $598 million to the German Flick interests to buy back a 26 percent interest in his company, later sold for $227 million Grace's majority interest in Herman's sporting goods stores, and also generated another $500 billion in cash from selling other retail and restaurant businesses.

At this writing, Grace is also working on a joint venture with a major foreign cocoa manufacturer to strengthen Grace's position in the cocoa business.

In an article about Grace's dramatic reorganization of the company, business columnist Maxwell Newton wrote, "So Grace has paid out $598 million to the Germans, and has mobilized something like $1 billion in cash through the various dramatic moves he has made. At seventy-four, Peter Grace has transformed his company with a vigor and a zest that would be envied by men half his age. Possessed of some unfathomable source of energy, he has fathered nine children who in turn produced sixteen grandchildren. A remarkable life."[1]

Grace's budget-bashing job earned him a lot of publicity—some good, some not so good—but he was already legendary in business circles for his amazing stamina and personal discipline. When asked what success principles he personally practices and admires in others, he responded without hesitation: "Complete dedication. You have to make whatever sacrifices are necessary to get the job done. If you are not disciplined, you can't do that. If you want to have a cocktail or watch TV, you can't do what you need to do. That's not discipline."

Grace doesn't drink alcohol, smoke cigarettes, or watch TV, preferring to devote his energies to the more important things in life. His day usually begins at 6:00 A.M., and he doesn't waste a minute from the time he gets up in the morning until he retires in the evening. He bathes the night before to save commuting time, and during the drive from his home on Long Island to his office in Manhattan, he dictates correspondence for one of his six or seven secretaries to handle. He eats lunch at his desk while reading his mail, and on the way home often dictates more letters and memos or talks on one of his two car telephones. After dinner with his wife, he usually spends another four hours poring over reports and other paperwork before calling it a day.

To review his far-flung operations firsthand, Grace travels constantly in his "flying office," a plane equipped with desks, phones, photocopiers and a full staff. To keep himself on schedule, he wears two watches. The one on his left wrist always keeps Eastern Standard time, the right one is local time wherever he happens to be at the moment.

Grace has elevated Self-Discipline to an art form that most of us can only marvel at.

In his bestseller, *Creating Wealth*, Robert G. Allen writes, "In the locker rooms and lunch halls they will talk about success, and hitting the jackpot, and luck. 'One day my ship will come in.' 'One day I'll strike it rich.' Not a second thought about the years of preparation that go into most successes. The sacrifices. The planning. The coordination. The sleepless nights. The prices paid."[2]

As a young man, Don Miller didn't seem to have the stuff of which success is made. A lackluster student when he was growing up in St. Petersburg, Florida, Miller was kicked out of Florida State University his junior year. Two years later, at 22, he was assistant manager at the Lake Tahoe Sahara Hotel and going nowhere in particular. Then Uncle Sam called, and Miller discovered that where he was going was Vietnam.

That marked the turning point in his life. As a helicopter pilot, he learned discipline and self-reliance, lessons that paid off when he returned to the United States. When the company that promised him a pot of gold vanished in the 1974 recession, he took the loss in stride and hit the road in search of a new rainbow.

With a borrowed $6,000, Miller and his wife Lea Anna opened RainSoft of Denver, a water-conditioning operation. Their office was a card table in their basement. They didn't know anything about prospecting, so they began with the A's in the white pages of the phone book, and started calling. Their first sale was to Karen Abbot, and that was the beginning of a franchise that today posts sales of more than $3 million. The card table long ago gave way to spacious offices, and the husband and wife team has been augmented by a staff of 110. Their two franchises do more business than any of the company's 300 other dealers.

"Nobody goes through high school and college and says, 'Boy, I can't wait to get out and sell water-treatment systems,'" Miller says. Indeed, many would have wrinkled their noses at the idea, but Miller attacked the challenge with the same discipline and enthusiasm that he applied to his life-and-death missions in Vietnam.

That same self-discipline still keeps him in the office 12 to 14 hours a day, and helps him to grow and learn constantly. He learned about goal setting, for example, when he realized that he should follow his own advice to an employee who was floundering because he hadn't established his personal goals. That night, Miller set an immediate goal to increase his unit sales from 20 to 30. The company hit the target right away; Miller then aimed for 50. Then 100. Now it's 250 and up.

Miller's climb from poverty to success is a study in the self-discipline necessary to keep going no matter how tough it may be. Self-discipline is not a success principle that is learned and then saved until it is needed. It is a habit that is developed by constant use so you are prepared to take advantage of it when the right opportunity comes along.

The late Albert E. N. Gray perhaps put it best in an address at the National Association of Life Underwriters annual convention in Philadelphia. He said:

"The common denominator of success—the secret of success of every man who has ever been successful—lies in the fact that he formed the habit of doing things that failures don't like to do.

"It's just as true as it sounds and it's just as simple as it seems. You can hold it up to the light, you can put it to the acid test, and you can kick it around until it's worn out, but when you are all through with it, it will still be the common denominator of success, whether we like it or not.

"The things that failures don't like to do are the very things that you and I and other human beings, including successful men, naturally don't like to do. In other words, we've got to realize right from the start that success is something which is achieved by the minority of men, and is therefore unnatural and not to be achieved by following our natural likes and dislikes nor by being guided by our natural preferences and prejudices."[3]

Jack and Gary Kinder, two brothers who head a hugely successful insurance consulting agency in Dallas, have taken Gray's idea a step further. In a training video for their clients' salespeople, they say, "Any resolution or decision you make is simply a promise to yourself which isn't worth a tinker's damn until you have formed the habit of making and keeping it. And you won't form the habit of making it and keeping it. And you won't unless right at the start you link it with a definite purpose that can be accomplished by keeping it. In other words, any resolution or decision you make today has to be made again tomorrow, and the next day, and the next, and the next, and so on. And it not only has to be made each day, but it has to be kept each day, for if you miss one day in the making or keeping of it, you've got to go back and begin all over again. But if you continue the process of making it each morning and keeping it each day, you will finally wake up some morning a different man in a different world, and you will wonder what has happened to you and the world you used to live in."

That kind of determination and commitment requires an enormous amount of self-discipline and persistence. How do you develop such personal drive? Wally Armbruster believes it comes from having only one competitor—yourself. For most of his career, Armbruster was executive creative director for the St. Louis office of one of the world's largest advertising agencies. During those years, he won several advertising industry creative awards, including being named one of the 100 Outstanding Creative People in America—twice. In his book, *Where Have All the Salesmen Gone?* Armbruster says, "There is only one Ultimate Competitor. I regard him so highly that I wrote a tribute to him—which hangs on my wall to remind me he's there."

In part, the tribute goes like this: *For me, the Ultimate*

Competitor exists within myself. You can only find yours within yourself.

The difference between this competitor and others is that you can never beat him or her. He is always a shade ahead. As you get stronger, so does he; each time you reach a new level of excellence, he shows you a new level you had never seen before. Each time, he challenges you to give more, try harder, reach higher, dig deeper, do better than you've ever done before.

There is no perfect score—not even for him.

The Ultimate Competitor is so demanding that he can sometimes be depressing, or at least a pain in the ass. But he is the only thing that makes The Game worthwhile. He is fantastic fun to compete with.

But if I ever beat him, I will know that I have lost.

Armbruster relates the tale of the time he directed Joe Namath in a videotaped commercial.

"He had the script memorized when we got to the studio in New York. I gave him a few rehearsal readings and some direction—and we did Take 1. Take 2. Take 3. Take 4. Each time I'd suggest a change here or there, and he got a little better. As an actor, Joe was a helluva good quarterback. After seven takes, I decided that was about as good as he'd get—and about all I could ask of him, under the circumstances.

"I said, 'That's a wrap, Joe. Thanks.'

"He said, 'Wally, can I do a few more? I'm not satisfied yet.'

"In the control room, I remarked to his manager that I was impressed with his determination to get it right, especially since I thought Joe Namath was kind of a hot dog—

all talent, but more interested in girls and nightlife than work.

" 'Ha!' the manager said. 'How the hell do you think Joe learned to throw a football that well? Talent only?

"Listen, every day, he threw hundreds of passes at a basket, by himself, until he got it right, to his satisfaction.'"

"It's obvious," Armbruster says, "who Joe Namath's Ultimate Competitor is. And Pete Rose's. And Jonas Salk's. And Mother Theresa's."[4]

George Washington Carver was the greatest agricultural scientist this country has ever produced. He is credited with single-handedly transforming the pattern of agriculture in the South. When he arrived at the Tuskegee Alabama Normal and Industrial School in 1895, much of the land had been depleted by years of growing cotton. Crop rotation to replenish essential minerals was unknown at the time; farmers simply cleared more timberland and let the barren soil erode away. It was an endless cycle. Without vegetation, more and more topsoil washed away.

Carver knew that peanut and sweet-potato plants drew their nourishment from the atmosphere and that they replaced nitrogen and other essential minerals that would make the land fertile again. The problem was that there was no market for them. Peanuts were considered to have little value other than as food for circus animals, and sweet potatoes spoiled too quickly.

Carver set out to change things. He made flour, alcohol, vinegar, and syrup from sweet potatoes; and dyes, stains, cheese, Worcestershire Sauce, and facial cream from peanuts. In all, he made 118 different things from sweet potatoes and found 300 uses for the peanuts.[5]

By the time the United Peanut Associations of America held their convention in Montgomery, Alabama, in 1919, peanuts were second only to cotton as a cash crop. They comprised an $80-million business in the United States, but most of the peanut growers didn't even know it was Carver who had brought them prosperity.

To them he was just an eccentric old colored man who dabbled in agricultural research at Tuskegee Institute. Nevertheless, one of the group insisted that they should learn as much as they could about their product so they could educate the American public. They invited Carver to come to their meeting to talk about his experiments.

When he arrived at the hotel, the bellman wouldn't let him in because he was black. But Carver was accustomed to such indignities. He had come to the South to help his people and promised himself he would bring credit to his race regardless of the personal humiliation he might be forced to endure.

The peanut growers were so impressed with his discoveries that one association member—a congressman—invited him to Washington to address the Congressional Ways and Means Committee. He rode the train all night, sitting upright on a wooden bench in a segregated car designated for blacks, to have the opportunity to present his findings to the committee.

The self-discipline that allowed Carver to ignore the prejudice and work tirelessly toward the achievement of his goals earned him the respect of many of the great men of his day. Thomas Edison sent an assistant to Tuskegee to persuade Carver to come to work in Edison's laboratories at a salary of six figures. Other offers followed. Henry Ford is said to have considered Carver the world's greatest scientist. Nevertheless, the answer was always the same. Carver turned down the offers and sent the checks back. He only wanted to help his people and to show America that a black man could do whatever a white man could.

A museum honoring his work was opened at Tuskegee, 18 schools were named for him; and in Theodore Roosevelt's home in New York City, before a group of 200 dinner guests, the Roosevelt Medal for Distinguished Service in the field of science was presented to a man who as a baby had been traded to Moses Carver for a $300 race-horse.

Napoleon Hill wrote: "Self-Discipline makes it possible to turn on more willpower and keep on going when the road is hard and failure seems just around the corner.

"There are two times in your life when you need highly-refined habits of self-discipline to save you from ruin. One is when you are overtaken by failure or defeat, and the other is when you begin to rise to the higher levels of success.

"Self-Discipline teaches that silence is often appropriate and gives you more advantages than spoken words inspired by anger, hatred, jealousy, greed, intolerance, or fear. It is the means by which you develop and maintain that priceless habit of thinking about the possible effect of your words—before you speak."[6]

Chapter 10

Budgeting Time and Money

The number of books written by experts about virtually every nuance of time and money management would no doubt fill a substantial library. We are not going to attempt to deal in detail with all aspects of these rather complex fields. Rather, we are going to look at this principle as W. Clement Stone does: from the point of view of time and money management as motivator—how they can help you motivate yourself and inspire others.

The plain fact is that both time and money are immensely important factors in determining how you feel about yourself. When you spend your time wisely and budget your money carefully, you feel good about yourself. Conversely, if you fall into a pattern of wasting your time or squandering your money, you begin a downward spiral that manifests itself at worst in a feeling of uselessness and at best in a nagging feeling that you could have done more with your life if you had only been more prudent in the management of your resources.

Like most other success principles, Budgeting Time and Money is a habit that expands exponentially with use. As you become better at budgeting your time, you will accomplish far more because you not only use time more wisely, you use it more efficiently. You find faster, more efficient ways to perform routine tasks, and you become better at establishing priorities. You will find that you can quickly dispatch things that previously seemed boring and time-consuming; you can then get on to the more interesting and challenging tasks. In volunteerism there's an old saying that goes: "If you want to get something done, find a busy person."

Somehow those who already have more than they can do seem to be able to accomplish more than those who have plenty of time to get the job done. They have learned that taking action makes even the most dreaded jobs easier. Once you begin the job, it never seems as difficult as it did when you sat around wondering about how tough you thought it was going to be. W. Clement Stone's motivator "Do it now!" works overtime when it comes to time management. Procrastination leads to self-doubt, needless worry, and more procrastination.

Careful money management is also a great motivator. Increasing your net worth, accumulating wealth for what you can do with it to help others, and for the advantages it can offer you and your family, are worthwhile objectives.

The greatest advantage of budgeting your income and expenses, however, is that it frees your mind to concentrate on achieving your goals. If you know that expenses are covered and you don't have to worry about paying your bills, you can devote all your time and energy to achieving your goals. And achieving them becomes easier. You simply feel better and more successful; you attract others to you because they like dealing with successful people.

There is also a peace of mind that comes with financial security that allows you to set your own agenda for your life. A healthy investment portfolio eliminates many of the "what ifs" associated with money worries. You no longer have to worry about an unexpected expense that could throw your business or family budget into a tailspin, nor do you worry about losing an important client or even your job. You can make career and business decisions based on merit rather than expediency, and you can take a risk on an idea that has great potential if you know you are protected against disaster. A healthy cash reserve is the best career and business insurance policy.

Although budgeting time and money are closely related (As Baron Lytton said, "Time is money"), for purposes of discussion, let's examine the two separately.

The eighteenth century British clergyman Legh Richmond once noted: "There is a time to be born, and a time to die, says Solomon, and it is the momento of a truly wise man, but there is an interval between these two times of infinite importance."

Richmond's tongue-in-cheek understatement underscores the fact that time is ours to do with as we wish, but time squandered can never be recovered. It is gone forever.

For this reason, perhaps, much of what has been written about time is negative. We've come to view time as little more than a relentless taskmaster. Walter John de la Mare portrayed time as "age's rushing, soundless river;" an English proverb says, "Time and tide wait for no man."

A better definition comes from an Italian philosopher who compared time to an "estate." Commenting on that comparison, a newsletter published by the Royal Bank of Canada says, "It's an estate of considerable magnitude." If you consider that the average life span is 71 years, that adds up to 25,915 days or 621,960 hours, according to the bank's calculation. "Given that a large proportion of that must be spent on necessities such as sleeping, eating, and earning a living, we are nonetheless left with a sizeable sum to call our own.

"The parallel with an estate extends only so far, however. If we were to fritter away a financial inheritance, there would always be a possibility of replacing at least some of it. But if we live to 100, each of us has been allotted an absolutely fixed amount of time, and there is no chance of begging, borrowing or stealing any more."[1]

For most of us, the 24 hours we are allotted each day can be divided into three parts:

- Sleep time,
- Work time, and
- Leisure time.

There's not much you can or should do to alter sleep time. Some of us require more sleep than others, and some require less, but the average person generally functions best on six to eight hours a night. (More about this in Chapter 11, "Maintaining Sound Physical and Mental Health.")

With respect to productive work time, there are many variables that influence our effectiveness. Perhaps the most difficult management technique for most of us to learn is delegation. We begin our careers as "doers" responsible for performing a job or completing a project ourselves. As a result, we develop a style of doing things that we believe is correct, and we have trouble accepting the fact that there are many ways to do the same thing. It's natural to believe that we can do the job better than anyone else.

The problem is that as you are promoted to higher levels, you have less and less time to perform actual "work." Your time is taken up in planning, in meetings, in administration, and in providing guidance to your employees. Unless you learn to delegate effectively, your effectiveness will decrease drastically. You will eventually reach the point where it is not possible for you to do—or even check—all your employees' work. You have to hire good people, rely on them to do the job right, and create an atmosphere of mutual trust where they can feel free to come to you with problems—not for an answer, but for a discussion of the alternatives. Your wisdom and experience should be useful to them as a decision-making aid, not for making the decision itself. If you do solve all problems for them, you deprive them of the opportunity to grow and mature as managers.

Naturally, there are questions of policy, large expenditures, and the like that require your approval as a manager, but if you encourage employees to come to you with recommendations rather than questions, you encourage them to think for themselves—and you allocate your own time better as well. If they have thought through the alternatives, you can reach a decision quickly, and not waste your time exploring approaches to problems that they should have developed. One manager we know always responds the same way when people come to him with problems. "I'm not interested in problems," he says, "I'm interested in solutions."

If you are reading this at a time when you are just beginning your career, you may be thinking: *That's all terrific, but I don't have anyone to delegate anything to. I have to do it all myself.* Rarely, however, is that precisely the case. You may not have employees reporting directly to you, but you do interact with peers, with managers, and with other departments whose efforts should complement your own, and vice versa. If you call on them for help in their areas of responsibility, you leverage your time. You free yourself to do more of the things you do best.

If, for example, you are a field salesperson, you *are* the company to your clients and customers, and the company knows it. Accounting, credit and collections, customer relations, advertising, public relations, and other support groups exist to help that customer. Call on these departments for assistance or with ideas that may help with your selling effort. Help from the PR department in placing an article in a trade publication about something new and different your customer is doing with your product or service can be a valuable sales aid. And *that's* a form of delegation. It boils down to expanding your capability by working with and through others.

If your job is so specialized that it is entirely self-contained, get some management and coordination experience by volunteering to serve on committees and task forces in the trade associations and professional societies in your industry. Most such groups are woefully understaffed and would welcome a willing worker. Not only will you get valuable management experience, but you will also increase your visibility. People inside and outside the company will recognize your talent and drive.

Another common problem in time management is the activity trap. If we're constantly busy, we reason, we must be getting a lot done. The obvious flaw in this assumption is that activity doesn't necessarily produce results. Peter A. Turla and Kathleen L. Hawkins, in their book, *Time Management Made Easy*, liken it to the difference between hunting elephants and stomping ants. "An important key to being successful with time management," they say, "is to make elephant hunting your highest priority. This means to go after your big, high payoff goals every day and to minimize the time you spend stomping on ants, those trivial details that take up so much time.

"There will always be ants and elephants in our lives. Unfortunately, many people who are elephant hunters at heart end up stomping on ants. The danger lies in making a career of ant stomping."[2]

At the heart of the authors' approach is, of course, goal setting. You must first identify your elephants before you can hunt them. If you have your definite purpose in life identified, then it becomes a matter of deciding whether or not this activity helps you reach your goal. If it does, it's worth spending your time on; if not, it's time to reevaluate where you are spending your time.

To illustrate the point, Turla and Hawkins invoke the 80/20 rule, which roughly states that 20 percent of your efforts generate 80 percent of your results. The principle cuts across virtually every activity. If you are doing housework, for example, 20 percent of the home accumulates 80 percent of the dirt. Clean the high-traffic areas frequently and let the rest wait longer.

The same holds true in sales. If your situation is like most, 80 percent of your sales come from 20 percent of your customers. Spend your time, Turla and Hawkins advise, in areas that will offer the biggest payoff. You could apply the 80/20 rule to just about every area of business. Twenty percent of your employees are probably doing 80 percent of the work; recognize and reward them accordingly. Not only does this motivate the 20 percent to even higher levels of achievement, it may catch on with the majority that this is the road to success. You get the idea.

The key, of course, is that all time management techniques are planning aids. Whatever system you use, the end result is that you alone determine how you will spend your time. By establishing priorities and setting deadlines, you determine when and how much time you will spend on any given activity.

Control begins with planning. But the problem with most plans is that we formulate them, put them in a drawer, and forget about them until it's time to update them the next year. That, of course, is not the way plans should work.

Time management consultant Alan Lakein likens the difference between a professional planner and an amateur to their counterparts in photography. An amateur photographer takes a few pictures, anxiously awaits the outcome, and is disappointed when only one or two pictures on a roll turn out as expected.

The professional, on the other hand, shoots several rolls, discards the poorly exposed or composed photographs, and ends up with a few that he is happy with. The professional may actually have more bad shots than the amateur, Lakein says, but because he has taken so many he sees some that he is quite pleased with. The professional takes the process a step further, working in the darkroom to bring out the best in the best of the negatives. By altering exposure times and cropping when printing the best of the best, he ends up with a prize-winning photograph.

The same sort of disparity exists between the occasional time planner and the serious time planner. Lakein says, "The occasional time planner gets a fuzzy shot of his goal, and may even miss the mark entirely. He's uncomfortable with the results; they seem hardly worth the effort. He concludes, and rightly so, that he's not a good planner, and gives up.

"On the other hand, the serious time planner will take many and frequent shots of his plans. What begins as a fuzzy, ill-defined jungle of conflicts gradually comes into focus. A wild shot that does not really represent a desired goal gets weeded out. The more important aspects of the plan are refined and elaborated on so that more and more meaning is built into them.

"He checks as the days go by to see how he is following through on his plans. He looks for problems, false assumptions, hang-ups, and difficulties, and makes corrections where he has to. Like (the) professional photographer, he makes some readjustments and becomes better and better at what he does."[3]

A final thought on the importance of allocating your work time comes from W. Clement Stone. He recalls that when he first began selling insurance, he was instructed to "try to sell everyone he called on.

"So I stayed with every prospect," he says. "Sometimes I wore him out, but when I left his place of business, I was worn out too. It seemed to me that in selling a low-cost service, as I was doing, it was imperative that I average more sales per hour of effort.

"I decided *not* to sell everyone I called on, *if the sale would take longer than a time limit I had set for myself.* I would try to make the prospect happy and leave hurriedly, even though I knew that if I stayed with him I could make the sale.

"Wonderful things happened. I increased my average number of sales per day tremendously. What's more, the prospect in several instances thought I was going to argue, but when I left him so pleasantly, he would come next door to where I was selling and say, 'You can't do that to me. Every other insurance man would hang on. You come back and write it.' Instead of being tired out after an attempted sale, I experienced enthusiasm and energy for my presentation to the next prospect.

"The principles I learned are simple. Fatigue is not conducive to doing your best work. Don't reduce your energy so low that you drain your battery. The activity level of the nervous system is raised when the body recharges itself with rest. *Time is one of the most important ingredients in any successful formula for any human activity. Save time. Invest it wisely.*"[4]

Just as you should choose carefully what you spend your time on, you should be equally selective about whom you work for and whom you spend your time with. Choose a company whose corporate culture and style mesh with your own goals and personality. If you like and respect your company and the people you work with, you will be far more successful than if you were to work at a job you disliked or for a company whose business you believed to be irrelevant.

If you are an entrepreneurial type who prefers to run your own operation, choose a business line you value and work with customers and clients you like. Hire employees who share your goals and work style. Choose your associates, business acquaintances, and friends—don't let them choose you. Be "proactive," not reactive!

While it would be impossible to overestimate the importance of managing the work time you spend in pursuit of your goals and objectives, how you spend your leisure time may well have a greater influence on your career and ultimate success than the time you spend on the job.

If you sleep six to eight hours a day and work eight to ten, that still leaves six to ten hours each day for you to do with as you will.

Leisure time is very much like surplus income, that which remains after you have paid all your living expenses. If you invest your disposable income wisely, it will grow and pay dividends; the same is true with disposable time. It will pay a far greater return on your investment than money will—if you invest it wisely.

Napoleon Hill said that Andrew Carnegie attributed every promotion he ever got while he was a salaried worker to the things he did with his time off. In his spare time he did things that he was not paid to do and those were the things that made him the enormous success he became.

While it is important to rest and relax, it is equally important to devote some of your leisure time to self-improvement activities. Watching a football game on TV won't provide nearly the degree of satisfaction or prepare you for success nearly as much as reading a good self-help book, working toward a high-school diploma, a college or graduate degree, or attending a seminar. At a minimum, you should spend an hour or two each day doing the things that will move you up to the next rung on your ladder of success.

Stone recommends that you also dedicate a half hour to an hour each day to creative thinking time. Find a quiet place where you can be alone with your thoughts, use the relaxation techniques outlined elsewhere in this book, and think about your goals, and desires. Get in touch with your inner self. Develop your ability to use the power of your subconscious mind to solve problems, to visualize goals, and to rededicate yourself to success habits. At an age when most men of his wealth and position would be content to relive past days of glory, Stone is often in his study until the wee hours of the morning thinking and planning the future directions of the many business interests and philanthropic organizations he oversees.

You will never be a great success at anything, he believes, unless you are willing to spend some of your "free" time in productive, creative pursuits. It takes more than eight hours a day.

Most successful people also devote a portion of their leisure time to supporting professional societies, trade organizations, and charitable and civic groups. Part of the reason may be a sense of duty—to give back something to the business or profession that has been good to them or to share their knowledge with younger people to help them advance in their careers; part of it is the satisfaction that comes from helping those less fortunate. But the big benefit from such involvement is that it provides variety, a break in the usual routine that is, by its very nature, uplifting and regenerative.

Money may play many varied roles in your personal success formula. Early in our career most of us struggle to make ends meet and provide a few luxuries for ourselves and our families; every promotion is valued more for the additional income it provides than for the status and position it offers. Later, as our basic needs are provided for, we begin to concentrate on investment and accumulation of wealth to provide for our children's education, for our retirement, and to build an estate to pass on to our heirs. Eventually, if we accumulate enough wealth—according to the greatly successful people we interviewed—money becomes mostly a scorecard for measuring success. We reach a point, they say, when money is no longer a motivator unless it is of sufficient amounts to significantly alter our lifestyles.

What the careful budgeting of money does for us, as pointed out earlier, is to provide security and a dispassionate, objective view that allows us to make intelligent career and business decisions.

While the experts may vary on their methods of accumulating wealth, there are some basics that most agree are sound fundamental approaches. The first rule is that money management takes time. Even the most basic activities—such as planning your purchases and living expenses, paying bills, keeping records, and balancing your checkbook—are time-consuming. More involved transactions—purchasing a home or rental property and managing investments are even more complex and time-consuming. Financial consultant Allan Willey estimates that 10 to 20 percent of the time you spend earning your money must be spent managing it, and this applies, he says, to all family earners.[5]

Then, of course, there are taxes. As the saying goes, "The only certainties in life are death and taxes; the principle difference between the two is that death doesn't get worse when Congress is in session."

That statement underscores the fact that tax laws have become so complex, and in recent years have changed so much and so rapidly, that the average person can't possibly be fully informed about the fine points of tax law. Even if you do keep up with newspaper and magazine accounts of changes in law and regulations, even if you buy and study manuals and self-help guides, you won't be privy to IRS private rulings and interpretations. Unless you simply file a standard deduction return (Form 1040A), you probably need a good tax accountant. They are worth their weight in gold, and will usually save you far more in taxes than they charge in fees.

Even if you do file a Form 1040A, you are probably paying too much in taxes, and need a tax accountant to advise you on investment strategies that will allow you to itemize deductions and save more. An aggressive tax adviser looks out for your interest; he or she tries to legally minimize the taxes you are required to pay. After all, when it's you alone against the thousands of people in the IRS, you need all the professional help you can get. There's an added benefit to having a tax adviser; if you are ever audited by the IRS, your tax adviser goes with you to act as your advocate, explain your position, and protect your interest. You should no more act as your own tax adviser than you should act as your own attorney.

And remember, tax savings can be used to fund investments. When you legally cut your taxes, you give yourself a raise.

Like any other aspect of your success formula, if you are to achieve financial independence, you must first set goals for yourself. You should decide how much you can save and invest. You know your financial situation better than anyone else; you alone can decide how much and in what you should invest. Financial advisers agree, however, that unless you work as diligently toward the achievement of your financial goals as you work toward your career goals, you will never accumulate much in the way of wealth.

Nationally known financial adviser and author Venita Van Caspel says in her book, *Money Dynamics for the New Economy*, that after searching for the reasons for financial failure, she has found six.

The first is procrastination, usually brought about by poor spending habits developed early in life. "Don't procrastinate with your financial future," she emphasizes, "Make 'Do It Now' your slogan for the rest of your life."

The second cause of failure, she says, is not establishing a goal. The difference between successful people and others is that they know where they are going. "Each has a goal," she writes. "If anything sidetracks a goal, or if something doesn't work out the way they planned, they just dust themselves off and go right back in the direction of their goal."

Third, people are ignorant about what money must do to accomplish a financial goal. In large measure, Van Caspel blames an educational system that concentrates on teaching vocational skills but falls short when it comes to teaching money management. The message here is: if you don't know how to manage money, you should learn.

Dr. Norman Vincent Peale said, "If you don't manage your money, it will manage you."

Fourth, people fail to learn and apply tax laws. "Learn the rules of the money and tax game," Van Caspel says. "You are playing a serious game of financial survival."

Fifth, make sure you buy the right kind of life insurance.

Sixth, and finally, Van Caspel says people fail to develop financial independence because they fail to develop a winning mentality: "The demarcation line between success and failure is often very narrow. It can be crossed if the desire can be stimulated, if competent guidance is available, and if sufficient encouragement and incentive are provided. There are many vital parts to the psychology of winning, but some of the most important for financial independence are attitude, effort, lack of prejudice, persistence, enthusiasm, the ability to make a decision, and self-discipline."[6]

Half the battle in achieving success it seems, is coming to the realization that there isn't an easy road to the top. Budgeting time and money are difficult and require huge amounts of self-discipline and hard work. But both are necessary. When you consider the alternative, though, that isn't such a high price to pay.

Chapter 11

Maintaining Sound Physical and Mental Health

Years ago, Napoleon Hill pointed out the interdependence of mind and body. You cannot have a healthy body without a healthy mind; neither can you maintain a healthy mental attitude or think accurately if your body is unwell. While his observations went relatively unnoticed at the time except among his own loyal following, the surge of interest in holistic medicine in recent years validates many of Hill's beliefs. The emphasis today on preventive medicine and the continuing attention to both the mental and physical needs of the body would, no doubt, have pleased Hill greatly.

Hill also stressed the importance of a rhythmic life in harmony with our surroundings. "We are born into a world of trees and mountains and moonlit skies, peopled with all forms of living things, and subject to the same natural laws that govern all things, even the smallest grain of wheat," he said. "Understanding this will allow us to swim the river of life and not exhaust our energies fighting against it.[1]

"The waves of the ocean, the flow of changing seasons, and the waxing and waning of the moon show us that there are rhythms to life. There is a rhythm to our own life from birth through childhood and adolescence to full maturity to old age, and finally the rebirth of a new generation.

"Nothing about life is static or unchanging. There seems to be a constant wavelike motion to life that is actually a progression of rhythmical patterns. Review your own life. Do you live a rhythmical life? Are you following work with play, mental effort with physical effort, eating with fasting, seriousness with humor?"

In their book, *Quantum Fitness: Breakthrough to Excellence*, Dr. Irving Dardik and psychologist Denis Waitley point out that true fitness is more than just working out, eating right, or feeling good about yourself. It is a combination of physical, nutritional, and mental wellbeing. They divided the holistic approach to fitness into four building blocks:

- Quantum Force (the power of the mind)
- Quantum Nutrition
- Quantum Exercise
- Quantum Leap (how to command your hidden inner potential)

They also liken the physics of the human body to that of the order of the universe. "Like an invisible atom," they write, "you, too, are a microcosm of the universe, composed of many different systems." By properly ordering your own mental and physical universe, they promise, you can bring your key systems into a "dynamic balance. It is this balance that will allow you to tap the limitless potential of individual energy that you alone possess."[2]

Probably the most important single quality necessary to sound mental health is a Positive Mental Attitude and all that involves. Two of the most destructive forces in the human mind are fear and its close counterpart, anxiety. They kill enthusiasm, destroy faith, blind vision, and destroy harmony and peace of mind—all qualities necessary for a Positive Mental Attitude.

Larry Wilson, chairman of the Minneapolis-based Wilson Learning Corporation which trains 185,000 men and women each year, has an unusual approach to dealing with anxiety. He tells executives to imagine the worst thing that could happen in any given situation, then decide if they could live with the consequences.

The way it works is something like this: Imagine yourself caught in a traffic jam and late for an important business appointment. There's no way out of the traffic and no way to call your client. Your anxiety starts to build and you start thinking, "What happens if I miss this appointment? My client is going to be very upset. If he is that upset, he probably will never see me. If he doesn't see me, I'll never get the order. If I don't get the order, I'm going to be in big trouble with the boss. He might even fire me. If I get fired, I will starve to death."

So, what you are really telling yourself is that if you are late for an appointment, you are going to die. Of course that's ridiculous. You aren't going to die. You can explain the situation, and most likely the client will understand. He's probably been in the same situation himself at one time or another. If he is totally uncooperative, you aren't going to lose your job over one call. You'll go find another prospect. So why worry about something you can't control?

How many people do you know who have a heart attack *before* they can come to that simple realization? Once their lives are really threatened, they realize how foolish they were to worry about every little, insignificant thing. Suddenly they become experts on stress, something they should have done long before the problem led to such serious consequences.

There are two types of stress, according to clinical psychologist William D. Brown, PhD. In his book, *Welcome Stress! It Can Help You Be Your Best,* he writes:

"*Eustress* (from the Greek root *eu* meaning 'good') is one type of stress. Eustress is the conversion of stress within you when you choose the harder right over the easier wrong, when you live up to what you want to be rather than down to what you might become.

"Stress converted to positive energy is stress helping you to be your best. It is what has enabled you to accomplish much in the past, reach those high goals you set for yourself, and contributed to your reputation as a person to be counted upon, even when you didn't feel like coming through. Eustress is stress being converted and used positively and responsibly. This is a desirable outcome of stress.

"The opposite of eustress is *distress* (coming from the Latin root *dis*, meaning 'bad'). Stress converts to distress when you tell the first lie, when you cheat, or when you wrestle with the knowledge of having done something wrong or illegal, even though other people may never know.

"Stress which becomes distress in your life is stress serving you at your worst. This occurs when you fail to be the person you could be or dwell on thoughts which you know will only cause you difficulty later. It's distress when you allow yourself to get down, choosing to be negative. Negative thinking never seems to need substantiating as does the positive, so it is much easier to be pessimistic than optimistic."[3]

Brown also points out that it is just as possible to have too little stress as it is to have too much. If you have no stress in your life, you soon lose your motivation. How dull life would be if you had nothing to do, or if your job provided no challenges, no deadlines, no pressures whatever. The trick is to balance the amount of stress you place on yourself to achieve the rhythm that is so important in your life.

Stress is mostly self-induced. For example, you place unnecessary stress on yourself when you attempt to do more than is humanly possible in the time frame allowed. You also place unnecessary stress on yourself when you have conflicting goals—like the manager who is torn between the need to cut costs by eliminating jobs and the knowledge that he will damage his employees' lives and careers if he fires them.

How do you cope with such situations? By not internalizing the problems. The manager who knows he must lay off people deals with it positively; he attempts to find other opportunities for these people within the organization or at another company. If that is not possible, he treats them with as much compassion and generosity as he can under the circumstances. Once the decision is made, however, he no longer agonizes over it. He goes on with his life, knowing he treated his people fairly and did the best he could.

One of the best ways to turn distress into eustress, Brown says, is by refusing to play the "if only" game. "Saying 'If only' permits us to loll in the luxury of what could have been if only we had invested in IBM in the late fifties, bought a house years ago when prices were much lower, or had seized some other lost opportunity.

"Substituting 'and yet . . .' for 'if only. . .' raises the chances of succeeding with any task, for emphasis is placed on what can be done now as opposed to what might have been. In his profound book, *Reality Therapy*, Dr. William Glasser emphasizes starting from where you are with what you have. Rather than returning to the past, wasting time figuring out how you got where you are, Glasser's therapeutic approach is to confront you where you are now, help you view your options realistically, and then give support in choosing a course in light of these options. Regardless of what has occurred in your life, distress can be turned around, as you pick up and continue from where you are, rather than stagnating over some error or mistake from the past."[4]

Dr. Estelle R. Ramey, a nationally known endocrinologist, has long studied the effects of stress on the life expectancy of humans as well as laboratory rats. What she found in both species is that the ones who have control of their lives live longer. Those whose circumstances are controlled by someone else are far more likely to succumb to a stress-induced death.

In an interview with the *Chicago Tribune*, Ramey said: "Contrary to what everyone believes or would like to believe, top-level, high-paid, successful women and men live longer than anyone else. People at the top are in control of their lives, and people in control live longer.

"It's not hard work that kills. It's not competition. It's not even having to count all that money that kills. What kills is not having control over your life." Ramey believes middle managers are the most likely to have stress problems because they don't have as much control over their lives as top executives do.

"Middle managers are the ones who are killing themselves," Ramey said. "They're the ones who are highly subject to cardiovascular problems. They're the ones who suffer from stress because their lives are neither predictable nor secure."[5]

Ramey found the same characteristics in rats. "When animals know what to expect," she said, "they can handle stress. When it's unpredictable and they have no control, they start to bleed internally and die."

Charles Mayo, who with his brother built the famous Mayo Clinic in Rochester, Minnesota, said, "Worry affects the circulation, the heart, the glands, the whole nervous system. I have never known a man who died from overwork, but many who died from doubt."

But perhaps the best advice regarding worrying about things you can't control comes from author Alice Caldwell Rice. She said, "Ain't no use putting up your umbrella till it rains."

Relaxation and rest are essential to sound health; if worry keeps you from resting or relaxing, it can be doubly damaging. If you have trouble relaxing, remember that the conscious mind is a selecting mechanism. We choose the things we concentrate on. If we concentrate our thoughts and energies on a hobby or diversion, we forget the worries of the day and relax.

Napoleon Hill suggested exploring many and diverse hobbies. Nature, crafts, good reading, music, and other people can help you redirect your interests to something apart from the problems you've been wrestling with. Again, it is a question of balance and rhythm. If your job requires a good deal of physical exertion, your hobbies should be quiet and relaxing. If you work at a desk, you should make sure your hobbies include some physical exercise. Golf, tennis, jogging, or just taking long walks can provide some of the exercise your body needs while you are enjoying an interesting diversion.

Dr. Herbert Benson, associate professor of Medicine at Harvard Medical School and author of the best-seller *The Relaxation Response*, was among the first to introduce to the public the positive effects of meditation. Ten years later he added another dimension: "the faith factor." In *Beyond the Relaxation Response*, he makes a case for how a strong belief in something, whether it is a traditional religious system, faith in oneself, or even in a state achieved while exercising, can measurably alleviate tension and anxiety, lower blood pressure, relieve pain, overcome insomnia, lower cholesterol level, and reduce stress.

Benson, the director of the Division of Behavioral Medicine and the Hypertension Section of Boston's Beth Israel Hospital, is not some sort of mystic who believes that faith can overcome all. He believes faith should be used in concert with sound medical care. But faith can heal and it can be documented scientifically, he says.

His studies have convinced him that faith does make a difference in broadening a person's inner potential.

In *Beyond the Relaxation Response*, Benson describes in detail his studies of Tibetan monks in the Himalayas who are known to perform remarkable feats with their bodies through meditation. He writes, "If you truly believe in your personal philosophy or religious faith—if you are committed, mind and soul, to your world view—you may well be capable of achieving remarkable feats of mind and body that many only speculate about."[6] Benson doesn't advocate belief in any particular system or idea; he says it is the act of believing itself that has healing power.

Benson's approach is to let the body and mind work together—without the aid of drugs to block the actions of the nervous system that cause stress, tension and insomnia. There are no side effects of meditation, he says, except peace and tranquility. His step-by-step approach toward involving your faith in maintaining sound health is:

1. If you feel ill, don't hesitate to go to the doctor.
2. Find a supportive doctor you trust.
3. Go to a doctor who emphasizes the positive.
4. Don't expect a prescription from your visit with a doctor.
5. If drugs or surgery are prescribed, find out why.
6. Use the relaxation response regularly.

To combine the faith factor with the relaxation response, Benson suggests the following techniques:

- Pick a brief phrase or word that reflects your basic

belief system. This can be a religious phrase such as "Hail Mary, full of grace," or "Make a joyful noise unto the Lord." If you have no religious convictions, choose a neutral word like *one*.

- Choose a comfortable position. Sit with your legs crossed or in any other position that is relaxing, but not to the point of falling asleep—unless, of course, you are meditating to overcome insomnia.
- Close your eyes. Don't squint or force it in any way; just let your eyes close naturally.
- Relax your muscles. Start with your feet and gradually work your way up to your neck and shoulders. Roll your head gently, shrug your shoulders, stretch and relax your arms.
- Become aware of your breathing, and start using your faithrooted focus word. Breathe slowly and naturally. Breathe in, and as you exhale repeat silently your focus word or phrase.
- Maintain a passive attitude. As you sit quietly, repeating your focus word or phrase, other thoughts will begin to bombard your mind. Don't fight the distraction. Just say, "Oh, well," and return to your phrase.
- Continue for a set period of time. Benson recommends 10 to 20 minutes. Don't set an alarm or anything else that would startle you, but rather keep a clock in plain sight and sneak a peek occasionally.
- Practice the technique twice daily. The exact time, Benson says, is up to you, but the technique seems to work best on an empty stomach. Most people use the method before breakfast and before dinner.

Another important aspect of maintaining sound health is, of course, nutrition. It's obvious that nutrition will dramatically affect your physical health, but only in recent years has nutritional therapy been used by psychiatrists in treating mental disorders.

According to Dr. Stuart M. Berger, it began with two-time Nobel Prize winner, Dr. Linus Pauling, who explained two important concepts: "First, that a change in behavior and in mental health can result from changing the concentrations of various substances that are normally present in the brain, and second, the idea that substances in our environment can have a profound effect on mental health and behavior."[8]

Dr. Berger points out that nutritional deficiencies can affect every body tissue and organ including the brain. If the body is malnourished long enough, it can lead to an improper metabolism and finally to a state of degenerative disease.

"When the brain's metabolism becomes disordered by nutritional deficiencies, it can change the brain's sensual perceptions, resulting in alternate mood and behavior." he says.

"Heavy consumption of refined carbohydrates (flours and sugars), lack of variety in the diet, prolonged emotional or physical stress, chronic use of alcohol and tobacco, all lead to nutritional deficiencies."

Berger says that any substance that is ingested into the body frequently, including food, can lead to addiction. He cites Dr. Theron Randolph, "the father of our modern understanding of food allergies," who believes that "symptoms that were once diagnosed as psychosomatic are in fact about

70 percent of the time due to a maladaptive reaction to foods, chemicals, and inhalants." According to Dr. Randolph, "If the body is exposed to the same food often enough, it responds by recognizing the substance as 'foreign' and the body's immune system mounts an attack to fight off the invader, which in turn produces uncomfortable (withdrawal) symptoms."

Commenting on a study conducted by Dr. John Crayton of the University of Chicago Medical Center on the effect of food allergies on the brain, Berger says Crayton found that there was "a significant relationship between foods ingested and subsequent behavior." The two foods he used were milk and wheat.

"Another factor in the chemical imbalance of the body that can affect mood and behavior," Berger says, "are the biochemical 'messengers' known as neurotransmitters, and if there is a change in one of them, there is a corresponding change in the way a person thinks and feels."

Again, the experts seem to be saying that in all things, including diet, variety seems to be the desirable approach. Dardik and Waitley recommend plenty of variety in diet. They recommend staying away from large quantities of meats and fats, concentrating instead on fish, poultry, vegetables, fruits, and grains.

In *Quantum Fitness*, they discuss recent research into the effects of body rhythms and the "set-point" theory, both of which seem to significantly influence body weight. The net result, they say, is that researchers have discovered that people function more efficiently on smaller and more frequent meals than the traditional breakfast, lunch, and dinner.

Dardik and Waitley advocate four meals a day, each of

equal calories. They say that such a regimen makes for faster, easier digestion, more stable blood sugar, moderated hunger, and a high and constant energy level resulting from less fat storage.

As far as the set-point theory is concerned, Dardik and Waitley say there has been significant evidence indicating that our bodies arrive at a level of fatness that is psychologically comfortable. Even if we reduce our caloric intake, our body metabolism slows down to keep us at our "fat equilibrium," resulting in little, if any, weight change. The most effective weapon in changing your own set-point, they say, is exercise. And regardless of the set-point theory, we can and should maintain responsibility for selecting foods that optimize health, performance, and longevity.

Peter M. Miller, founder of the Hilton Head Health Institute, agrees with the four-meal approach. In *The Hilton Head Executive Stamina Program* he writes, "Your body needs its fuel in moderate doses throughout the day to keep energy nutrients at their optimum levels in the cells of your body. If you usually just grab a cup of coffee and juice for breakfast and don't eat lunch until 2 P.M., *you are functioning well below your peak stamina level for more than half of the day. Your mind and body cannot function without fuel.* [9]

"By spreading out your food intake over the day," he says, "you also are burning calories more efficiently than you would with any other food plan. My studies of metabolism to help people lose weight have verified this fact over and over again. The reason has to do with a phenomenon called *dietary thermogenesis*. Whenever you eat a meal, your body starts to burn calories at a higher than normal rate. Food actually stimulates your body's natural calorie-burning processes. Of course, if you eat more than your body is able to burn you'll put on weight, but if you eat four moderate-size meals a day, *your metabolism will be triggered to increase its rate of burning for two to four hours after each meal.*"

Miller also advocates a low-protein, low-fat diet that is high in carbohydrates such as vegetables, cereals, pasta, breads, potatoes, and fruit. Like most health experts today, he also recommends plenty of fiber in the diet, such as cereals, whole-grain breads, potatoes, and high-fiber vegetables and fruits such as broccoli, carrots, string beans, oranges, strawberries, and the like.

He emphatically discourages eating anything with refined sugar in it, but for the chocoholics who will never give up sweets permanently, he says that if you restrict your intake of sweets to two small indulgences per week, your system can handle it.

Miller also comes down hard on caffeine, alcohol, and salt. Drink more fluids such as water or noncaffeinated beverages, he advises, and stay away from stimulants.

The books written on nutrition and diet no doubt number in the thousands; every few days a new fad diet seems to be introduced. It would, of course, be impossible to deal thoroughly with the subject here. Suffice it to say that any diet should be planned in conjunction with your doctor, and you should use good common sense in your eating habits. If you would like to learn more about how your diet affects your performance and your mental and physical health, the two books cited here, *Quantum Fitness* and *The Hilton Head Executive Stamina Program*, are two of the best we've run across.

Both books also offer some good advice about exercise. Dardik and Waitley cover everything from traditional jogging and push-ups to exotic stretching and endurance exercises developed by Olympic coaches. Miller's approach is designed for busy executives who spend a lot of time in a sedentary position, and many of his illustrated exercises can be performed in the office.

Whether you follow their suggestions or any number of other programs, the important thing is, you need exercise to round out the balance of your life. Adopt an exercise program that is suitable for your age, size, weight, and lifestyle, and stick with it. Moderate exercise, according to a study whose findings appeared in the *New England Journal of Medicine*, and were cited in *Newsweek* magazine, can add up to two years to your life.

The study, begun in the mid-1960s, included 17,000 Harvard graduates aged 35 to 74. Dr. Ralph S. Paffenbarger, Jr., and his colleagues at the Stanford University School of Medicine asked participants to complete detailed questionnaires about their general health and living habits. A follow-up study conducted in 1978 showed that men who burned at least 2,000 calories a week through exercise "had mortality rates one-quarter to one-third lower than those burning up fewer calories.

"The life-prolonging level of activity cited in the report is the equivalent of five hours of brisk walking, about four hours of jogging, or a shade more than three hours of squash. More exercise meant a better chance at a long life—up to a point. A regimen that burned more than 3,500 calories tended to cause injuries that negated most of the benefits derived from exercise."[10]

The study, which *Newsweek* says was the first to show a favorable effect on mortality from all diseases, showed that even when there was a family history of death at an early age, exercise helped. Even among smokers, exercise reduced deaths by about 30 percent. Exercise is indeed good for you physically, and you feel better about yourself when you are in shape.

No discussion of maintaining sound physical and mental health would be complete without a mention of the detrimental effects of alcohol, tobacco, and narcotics. Every society decides which it will allow and which it will not; every individual has to decide for himself whether or not he will partake of these things.

Alcohol and tobacco are perfectly legal in our society, and many believe that smoking and drinking in moderation are not harmful. Society has become less and less tolerant, however, and is exerting increasing pressure to ban smoking and minimize drinking. The public outcry against illegal drugs has also forced many to examine their consciences about the legal stimulants they ingest into their bodies.

The grass-roots support for eliminating cocaine and other harmful drugs will, hopefully, have a positive effect on public attitudes. It is now socially acceptable to say *no* to the use of any stimulants, and we may see the day when drugs are no longer a problem in this country. Whatever happens in society or in Congress or the White House, these things simply have no place in the life of an achiever. Anything that creates an artificial high is temporary and cannot compare with the natural high that comes from taking care of the greatest gift you have—a healthy mind and body. As the old Arabian proverb says, "He who has health, has hope; he who has hope, has everything."

Part III

Fraternal Principles

You don't have to travel far in the United States to recognize the accuracy of the observation that "Ninety percent of the people in this country live on ten percent of the land mass." Huge numbers of people are packed into relatively tiny urban areas. Drive on any freeway around Los Angeles or along the New Jersey Turnpike from New York to Philadelphia, and it's difficult to tell where one city ends and the next begins. Yet, out in the "great heartland," the miles and miles of open space stretch endlessly.

Such concentration is not really necessary in today's technological society. We are no longer dependent on coastal shipping centers or midwestern transportation hubs to either get the goods to market or the products to consumers. Far-reaching transportation and distribution networks, portable computers, and inexpensive telecommunications service are available to virtually everyone. We could live or work anywhere.

Yet we choose to congregate together. Perhaps it's a holdover from our tribal instincts, but it does underscore our belief that we can accomplish much more working together than any one of us could accomplish separately.

As the old saying goes, "Ain't none of us as smart as all of us." Although there is a great deal to be said for passive introspection and quiet thoughtfulness, there is nothing like the rush that accompanies a successful Master-Mind Alliance. When two or more like-minded people connect in a spirit of perfect harmony to work toward a common purpose, the power generated is nothing short of awesome.

The other fraternal principle—teamwork—has become increasingly important in today's complex, interdependent world. These days, it is not only politics that engenders strange bedfellows; some of the more unlikely alliances of recent years have been in the business arena. Joint ventures, strategic alliances and partnerships are formed regularly in an attempt to leverage the strengths of disparate team members in pursuit of a temporarily shared goal.

Many venture investments and strategic partnerships include the lifetime of the partnership as a part of the contract. Such business arrangements realistically recognize that a team may well be a unit in constant flux, but one that—at least temporarily—is far stronger than the sum of its individual parts.

This section analyzes the principles of the Master Mind Alliance and Teamwork, and illustrates how you can apply those principles in your own life.

Chapter 12

The Master-Mind Alliance

The concept has been around a long time. Napoleon Hill wrote that Andrew Carnegie coined the term *master-mind alliance* to describe his group of key executives who combined their talents to form a whole whose output far exceeded the sum of the input of its individual members—a sort of intellectual synergy. Carnegie reportedly knew little of the technical end of the steel business; his greatest strength was his ability to get others to work together in perfect harmony toward achieving a common goal. That talent made him a very rich man.

Hill so valued the Master-Mind concept that he opened his tome, *Law of Success*, with a lengthy dissertation on the subject. According to Hill's account, much of Ford's gigantic success was the result of his astute application of the

Master-Mind principle, a dramatization of which unfolded in a Chicago courtroom.

According to Hill's account, a *Chicago Tribune* article labeling Ford an "ignoramus, an ignorant pacifist" during World War I prompted Ford to file a libel suit against the paper. *Tribune* attorneys, basing their defense on the maxim that truth is not libelous, attempted to prove that Ford really was an ignorant person. They quizzed him on subjects which ranged from the historical to the technical. Ford patiently answered the questions for more than an hour.

Finally, exasperated over what he considered a particularly silly question, Ford let go "If I should really wish to answer the foolish questions you have just asked, or any of the others you have been asking, let me remind you that I have a row of electric push-buttons hanging over my desk, and by placing my finger on the right button I could call in men who could give me the correct answer to all the questions you have asked and to many that you have not the intelligence either to ask or answer. Now, will you kindly tell me why I should bother about filling my mind with a lot of useless details in order to answer every fool question that anyone may ask, when I have able men all about me who can supply me with all the facts I want when I call for them?"[1]

The case dragged on for months, creating quite a stir in the tiny Macomb County courthouse in Mt. Clemens, Michigan, where the trial was held. Ford's views reverberated around the world as journalists filed daily reports by telegraph to 15,000 weekly and 2,500 daily newspapers.

Although he had sued for $1 million in damages, Ford had to be satisfied with a moral victory. The jury found in his favor, but awarded him only six cents in damages and six cents in court costs. Nevertheless, he certainly made an impression on the attorney questioning him, and vocalized on the record his ardent belief in the abilities of his management team—his Master-Mind Alliance.

Since the introduction of the master-mind idea years ago, the concept has taken a lot of twists and turns, but the principle has remained essentially the same. Call it what you will, but when you assemble the right people under the right conditions, the results can be impressive.

Perhaps you've seen it at work yourself. In a meeting or brainstorming session when everything just clicks, ideas build on each other with each member of the group actively contributing until out of the group activity comes the best possible solution to the problem, a fantastic marketing campaign, or a revolutionary new product idea.

Take that concept—the strength of an idea that represents the highest order of thinking by a group of knowledgeable people, each contributing according to his own ability, expertise, experience, and background—raise it to the tenth power, and you've just begun to glimpse the energy that can be generated and sustained when a group of like-minded people work together in perfect harmony toward a single objective.

In recent years we have seen the institutionalization of the Master-Mind Alliance under a variety of different labels. We've seen computer consortiums sharing research, domestic automobile manufacturers aligning themselves with foreign companies to leverage manufacturing and marketing strengths, multinational conglomerates forming partnerships with small, emerging, high-technology companies, and accounting firms forming strategic alliances with public relations and marketing firms.

Perhaps the best known of these is Microelectronics and Computer Technology Corporation (MCC), a research consortium of U.S. semiconductor and computer companies headquartered on the campus of the University of Texas in Austin. Organized in 1983, the consortium was the brainchild of William C. Norris, founder and for many years CEO of Minneapolis-based Control Data Corporation.

The original 11 founding member companies have grown to 21, including such luminaries as 3M, Bell Communications, Rockwell, RCA, Motorola, Eastman Kodak, and Honeywell. Each pays approximately $1 million per share for the privilege of participating in program areas that center on software development, semiconductor technology, computer-aided design for large-scale systems, and artificial intelligence. MCC's budget for the consortium's expected 10 year life is close to $700 million.

In a country founded on the principles of competition and free enterprise, such cooperation represents a major change in attitudes among competing companies. Participating firms supply about a third of the talent; the remaining two-thirds of the research staff was recruited directly by MCC. All share in their results of programs in which they participate.

At this writing, it's too early to predict the outcome of this brain trust, but Admiral Bobby Inman, who until recently headed the consortium, told *Chief Executive* magazine in 1986 that MCC was churning out reports on advanced technology in several areas and "talking to patent attorneys in a couple of areas." The consortium was already gearing up to transfer the technology to member companies, working out the kinks in licensing agreements in anticipation of the breakthroughs to come.[2]

Other examples of sophisticated alliances abound. To expand its interests in bionics and biotechnology—the next high-tech boom area according to some experts—W.R. Grace & Co. recently formed a joint venture with Cetus, a genetic engineering company, to develop sturdier plant strains, and cemented an alliance with Symbion of Salt Lake City with a 5.3 percent investment in the firm. Symbion makes such exotic health-care devices as the Jarvik-7 artificial heart which was designed by the firm's founder and president, Dr. Robert K. Jarvik, and an artificial ear which is capable of bringing hearing to the "profoundly deaf."

Commercialization of high technology products has fathered many unlikely alliances. The intent, of course, is to capitalize on the marketing and financial prowess of large multinationals paired with the flexibility and rapid response ability of smaller technology-driven companies. An effective combination can be a formidable force in the marketplace.

New versions of the Master-Mind Alliance are not limited to so-called high technology companies, though. As the industry has become increasingly competitive, alliances between automobile manufacturers span the globe. Foreign manufacturers build cars here, American manufacturers assemble cars in other countries, and alliances have become so numerous and so exotic that one needs a scorecard to keep up with the players.

Change—profound and painful—has rocked the industry and will continue to do so for years to come. According to *Time Magazine,* the big three automakers in the past decade "have sunk an estimated $20 billion into new, high tech plants and other firms of modernization to cut costs and raise efficiency. They have also fashioned new agreements with labor unions to boost productivity and taken critical aim at inefficient white-collar bureaucracies. By sending increasing numbers of parts orders abroad, they have drastically reshaped their traditional supply networks. The big U.S. automakers have redesigned many of their offerings, sometimes radically and often with the help of new foreign partners, and have marketed them with new aggression and esprit."[3]

One old-line company that took a cue from its high tech brethren is Ore-Ida Foods Inc., a Boise, Idaho subsidiary of H.J. Heinz Co. Ore-Ida introduced a "Fellows" program, patterned after similar arrangements at IBM and Texas Instruments, that is designed to capitalize on the good ideas employees come up with. The company allocates $50,000 to employees who volunteer to be Fellows in addition to their regular jobs. The men and women who are selected to serve as Fellows are people other workers know and feel comfortable with. Out of their $50,000 annual allotment, the Fellows fund employee ideas they think have merit without going through the normal bureaucratic channels.

The program has already paid big dividends. Out of it came frozen potato skins, which the $1 billion company expects to be one of its best-selling items ever, new computerized scales (funding: $15,000) that have already saved the company over $2 million, and several other cost-cutting and productivity improvement measures.

More fundamentally, the program has been influential in affecting a significant change in the way the company operates. President and CEO Paul I. Coddry told *Business Week* that before instituting the Fellows program, the firm was "doing a fairly classic method of assigning a given new product to Research and Development and then parceling out various development aspects to specialists. For a new potato product, one part would go to the guy who was good on frying and another to the guy good at recipes.

"This fragmented system was replaced by a team approach that coordinates each individual's responsibilities and generates group commitment to completing a project."[4]

Among big businesses, master-mind alliances are sweeping the globe in exciting new forms, bringing with them entirely new ways of making and selling products. The principle of the master-mind still works in traditional, old fashioned ways as well. All you really need to form a master-mind alliance are two compatible minds working in harmony toward a common goal.

Dick and Jinger Heath's master-mind alliance took BeautiControl Cosmetics, Inc. (of Carrollton, Texas, a suburb of Dallas) from a loss of $65,000 in 1981 to a record-breaking net income in 1986 of $3.3 million or 87 cents per share on sales of $23 million. The fiscal 1986 results were 63 percent over budget in net income and 43 percent over the sales budget for the year.

Company growth has slowed some recently, reflecting the economic downturn in energy-producing states which account for 36 percent of the company's revenues. To keep sales and profits up, Dick Heath says, management has installed cost control programs, and initiated an aggressive territorial development program to increase market share in states outside the energy belt and developed an exciting new marketing concept that will be backed by a major national advertising campaign.

The dynamic duo that heads this thriving enterprise is a husband and wife team (which Napoleon Hill considered ideal for the development of a master-mind alliance) that combined their strengths and energies in pursuit of a common goal. It was Jinger's idea to offer free color analysis supported by color-coded cosmetics to be marketed by a sales force of career-oriented women. Her most recent and successful development is a Personal Image Profile which provides an accurate computer-assisted analysis of a woman's body type, face shape, clothing, and makeup personalities, and teaches women "how to put their best image forward." She serves as chairman of the board, manages product and concept development and quality control in the company's cosmetic and clothing lines.

Dick, who serves as president and CEO, brought 20 years of direct selling experience to the partnership. It was his marketing, recruitment, and management strategies that have made BeautiControl one of the 100 fastest growing public companies in America over the past five years. For their efforts, both are paid the exact same salary (well into six figures), with a bonus plan based on pre-tax profits and other assorted perks that come with top management jobs.

The Heaths start each day with a jog around the neighborhood where they recently bought a new $1 million home. They have breakfast together, then Jinger is off to carpool the kids to school in her new Mercedes, before joining Dick at the office.

The office is a 60,000-square-foot building in Carrollton

that houses the executive offices of the company as well as its manufacturing, distribution, and storage facilities. There, BeautiControl manufactures its makeup base in 17 shades, lipstick in 14 shades, eyebrow pencils in 11 shades, and a host of other cosmetic, skin care, and toiletry products for women.

Products are sold primarily at home "clinics" by over 10,000 BeautiControl trained consultants who help the company's 410,000 customers find just the right shade of colors that harmonize with their own natural coloring.

In March 1986, the company "went public" on the NASDAQ exchange, and in August of the same year issued a prospectus to issue an additional 10,000 shares to be used as incentive awards for consultants under a program called "Ownership through Leadership."

How is it that some people seem to have a knack for forming alliances and getting the most out of a partnership or group while others are always at loggerheads? Some researchers think it begins in childhood. In any group of children, there always seems to be one who is the mediator of disputes, who somehow sees both sides of differences that lead to confrontations, and who good-naturedly resolves the conflict.

Those children, says a *New York Times* report on the subject, grow up to be successful: "One of the most important skills, the research shows, is seen in people who have an unerring ability to understand the motives and desires of others regardless of whatever is being said or done on the surface." These same people seem to understand themselves, to know what they are really driving at, regardless of what they find themselves saying.

"This kind of empathy combined with self-understanding," the research suggests, "is often joined with self-confidence and a desire for power. The result is a person who is able to reconcile his motives with those of others to move toward a solution to a problem that in fact has never been stated."[5]

What these people seem to have as adults, the report says, is a natural ability to identify individual members' hidden agendas, and keep the group moving in a productive direction by reconciling the motives of each individual with the overall objectives of the group.

While it's a skill that some people seem to be born with or intuitively pick up somehow in childhood, it can be learned, according to W. Clement Stone. He offers the following advice for developing a master-mind group:

1. Begin by attuning yourself to every member of the group. Try to imagine how you would react in a given situation if you were in his or her shoes.
2. Pay attention to body language. Sometimes facial expressions and movements say far more about what a person feels than the words that come out of his mouth.
3. Be sensitive to what is not being said. Sometimes what's left out is far more important than what's included.
4. Make sure your Master-Mind Alliance has a definite purpose and that every member of the team fully understands the group's objective.
5. Choose individual members of the alliance whose education, experience, and influence best suit them for achieving the goals.

6. Decide what each member of the group will receive in return for participation. Be fair and generous, and remember that in such partnerships the principle of Going the Extra Mile is especially important. As the leader, you should set an example for others to follow.
7. Create a non-threatening environment. Explore all ideas with equal interest and concern for the originator's feelings.
8. Know when to move the group along. When one person begins to monopolize the conversation, sum up the discussion and move to the next point.
9. Set a definite meeting time and place, report back to the group, and stay in regular communication.
10. Establish specific responsibilities and action steps to be taken.
11. Remember that it is your responsibility as leader of the group to keep the peace and make sure that all members of the group are working collectively and individually toward achieving a common goal.
12. Limit the size of the group to the number of people necessary to get the job done given its complexity and magnitude. Generally, the smaller the group, the more productive it is likely to be.

Additional advice on directing group efforts comes from Dr. Sheldon D. Glass, assistant professor of psychiatry and education at Johns Hopkins University and author of *Life Control*, a study in group dynamics. Glass doesn't attempt to explain why groups behave as they do. Rather, he concentrates on the process that any group goes through (he defines a group as anything from a husband and wife to the United Nations) in pursuit of a common goal.

There are four phases. The first is the introductory phase—the time when new goals are worked out and agreed upon. It is characterized by excitement, even euphoria. No doubt you can recall a time when you or someone else in your group proposed an idea that seemed terrific at the time, but was later tabled and finally discarded.

The second phase, Glass theorizes, is resistance-testing. When the group reacts anxiously to the change the new goals require, it may inherently resist the change, or it may merely test the leaders to see if they are up to the process. In any event, in resistance-testing, members of the group (sometimes under the guise of playing devil's advocate) question the cost, the timing, the willingness of some larger group to accept the idea, or bring up any number of other reasons why the idea won't fly.

In the third, or productive, phase, the group gets down to business. After the resistance-testing is out of the way, timetables are set, responsibilities are fixed, and the next meeting date is set. Whatever steps are necessary to get the job done are completed in the productive phase.

The final phase, termination, is when the project is wrapped up. Temporary committees are disbanded or the project is handed over to another department (from Research and Development to Production, for example). Although it might not seem as important as the other phases, Glass believes that without the termination phase the group is left with a nagging feeling that something was left undone, that loose ends were never tied up.[6]

Of course, this is a simplification of a very complex subject, but Glass's point is that most groups will go through this process. If a leader tries to force the group along too quickly—from the introductory to the productivity phase, for example—someone in the group will usually circle back to resistance-testing. To be an effective leader of your Master-Mind Alliance, you must learn to read the group and steer it though the phases until you reach your common objective.

Understanding the process that the group is going through will enhance your effectiveness and make you more tolerant of objections. You know that once the resistance-testing is over the group will get on with the job. You can then mold the group into a cohesive unit with harmony of purpose that will become a powerful force in achieving your common objectives.

No doubt you will notice some similarities between the principles of Teamwork and the Master-Mind Alliance. It might have been possible to combine the two into one principle, but to do so would have the effect of diminishing important differences between the two.

Teamwork can be achieved by any group—even one whose members have disparate interests—because all it requires is cooperation. Napoleon Hill made a distinction between *willing* and *unwilling* cooperation. He said that willing cooperation "leads to constructive ends and insures permanency of power through coordination of effort." Team members who cooperate unwillingly, Hill added, "do not continue their effort any longer than it takes them to eliminate the motive that impelled it."

Fred C. Lickerman, executive director of the International Federation of Keystone Youth Organizations and a longtime associate of W. Clement Stone, observes that teamwork may be either voluntary or hired. Voluntary teamwork may occur for a variety of reasons, not necessarily having to do with the goal sought. People might simply be cooperating because they like the leader, for example, or because they feel duty-bound. Examples of hired cooperation are everywhere. Professional sports teams cooperate with a high degree of skill and dedication to winning but few of the members would continue playing if they weren't paid to do so.

Master-Mind Alliances, on the other hand, are formed of individuals who have a deep sense of mission, a personal commitment to achieving the goal. Such a group is distinguished by its unity of interests and the harmony with which its members work together toward the common goal. Their efforts are creative rather than merely cooperative. At its best, a Master-Mind group reaches a level of intensity that truly does make two-plus-two equal five. The synergistic effect of like minds working in harmony is capable of generating accomplishments of enormous proportions.

Arthur E. Bartlett, founder of the giant Century 21 Real Estate Corporation, says the Master-Mind principle was essential to his company's success. "We had 30 regional directors across the U.S. and Canada," he says:

"Many of them owned their own regions; others had large stock positions within the regions. Needless to say, they all wanted success.

"We met—all of us—every 90 days in what I consider the epitome of a master-mind group: thirty entrepreneurs, all working to the same plan, having the same desires, the same dedication, the same values, working to the same purpose—to build the largest real estate organization in the world. But we all worked in harmony. We certainly didn't agree on everything. Not by a long shot. But we respected one another, we cared about one another, and the group concentrated on solving problems.

"This was truly one of the most memorable experiences of my life—working with these 30 individuals, all extremely intelligent, all very outspoken, all working in harmony for the success of the company. Without them, Century 21 would not have been possible."

Chapter 13

Teamwork

In the baseball world, 1986 was the year of the Mets. Dubbed "Destiny's Darlings" by the media, the New York Metropolitan Baseball Club made impossible save after impossible save. In the regular season, the team came from behind to win no fewer than 108 times, finally winning the National League championship.

Pitted against the American League champions, the Boston Red Sox, the story was the same. Down three games to two, the Mets tied it up at three apiece with the seventh and final game to be played at Shea Stadium in New York on October 27. Behind again earlier in the game, the Mets rallied in the fifth inning to tie the score at three all.

In the seventh inning, third baseman Ray Knight stepped to the plate. Earlier in the season, many doubted that Knight would play at all in 1986. He'd been plagued with injuries, and his first two years with the Mets had been lackluster at best. But this day belonged to Knight. On the two-one pitch, he connected with a high fast ball, to be named the World Series Most Valuable Player considering the earlier speculation that he might not play that year.

"It's been a great season for me," Knight responded. "You know, David, you can judge talent, but you can't judge heart, and I have a big heart and I'm a winner, and I know that. I've never been a great player, but I'll find a way to win, and I want to win. You know, it's easy to explain. You go out there and you play hard every day and you do the best you can, and if you try hard enough, things usually turn out for you, and that's just my case. I try as hard as anybody, every day, as long as I can, as hard as I can, and that's why I've been a success in the game and that's why it hurt me not to play, 'cause I love to play so much."

On other days, in other games, other players shared the limelight, but it was the collective efforts of the members of the team that made it work for the Mets. In the same broadcast, Los Angeles Dodgers coach Tommy Lasorda, who was an ABC correspondent during the series, described the World Champion Mets this way: "There are three types of baseball players, just like there are three types of teams: there's one who makes it happen, then there's one who watches it happen, and then there's one who wonders what happens. The Mets make it happen."[1]

While Americans have long recognized the value of teamwork in sports, we haven't been so quick to adopt the practice in our other endeavors. Part of the problem is our culture. We haven't completely shaken our fascination with rugged individualism, with the gunslinger who rides into town, beats the bad guys at their own game, then rides off into the sunset the same way he came in—alone.

That's something that is slowly changing, believes Bob Bookman, president of Bookman Resources Inc., a Chevy Chase, Maryland consulting firm that specializes in teaching teamwork to corporations.

"Ten years ago," he says, "the norm for getting something done in most work settings, to borrow George H. Bush's words, was to 'kick a little ass.' That norm is changing. Now it's participate, cooperate, innovate, and facilitate. It's teamwork."

Bookman attributes much of the shift in attitudes to the Japanese influence. "The undeniable success of the work-team way of thinking in Japanese industry," he says, "has great appeal here in our corporate world."[2]

As American quality and productivity began to slip in the 1970s and imports began grabbing larger and larger shares of U.S. markets, managers started to pay more attention to what Japanese companies were doing right. What they found was teamwork. Workers participated in decisions that affected them and worked with—not against—management. The result, of course, was higher productivity and better quality products.

Managers' attempts to clone the Japanese style in this country have been marginally successful at best, but the concept holds promise if it is properly implemented, according to Roland A. Dumas of Zenger-Miller, a San Bruno, California consulting firm.

The idea of a quality circle, for example, is simple and straightforward enough, Dumas says. It is really nothing more than a supervisor-led problem-solving group. It is in the implementation in this country where the concept begins to fall flat.

The Japanese, Dumas says, use the foreman as the leader of the group, and he functions as the "conduit through which the best interests of the workers merge with the best interest of the organization." In the United States, choosing group leaders is still a matter of experimentation. Some organizations use a facilitator who becomes the *de facto* leader. Sometimes the facilitator makes all the decisions, thereby eliminating the need for the group. "That," Dumas says, "is not the way it is supposed to work."

Another reason the method hasn't taken hold in the United States, Dumas believes, is that we are not a society that makes group decisions. "We tend to see the manager or the person who gets things done as a hero," he says. "That person gets points for the heroic things he or she does for the company; we don't reward for shared credits."

An obvious solution to the problem, of course, would be to provide incentives for group efforts—financial and others—and to train people better in group leadership, problem solving, and decision making, but we tend not to do so, Dumas says, because Americans are always looking for a quick fix. We want to begin a new method today and see the results tomorrow.

Another problem the quality circle importers failed to anticipate is that people who are chosen as group leaders are usually chosen for their natural leadership abilities and tend to move up in the organization, reaping the rewards for the good work of the group. This leaves the rest with little recognition and a new, untrained leader. The outcome is a foreseeable decline in the group's contribution.[3]

While quality circles are but one example of how teamwork hasn't fared too well with American managers, their evolution is a good example of how we are recognizing that old management formulas don't work so well any longer. We have finally begun to recognize that something is missing. That something is teamwork, and the implications are enormous as we begin to shift away from an individual to a group orientation.

Best-selling author Alvin Toffler believes the changes that lie ahead are "at least as massive as those associated with the Industrial Revolution," and that they threaten and will probably change our most basic institutions.

Managers will be forced to learn radical new ways of doing things; they will have to abandon the habits of a lifetime, the very ones that helped them succeed but have since become counterproductive.

"And the same is true for organizations," Toffler adds. "The very products, procedures, and organizational forms that helped them succeed in the past often prove their undoing. Indeed, the first rule of survival is clear: nothing is more dangerous than yesterday's success."

Futurist Toffler foresees a business culture devoid of corporate giants stifled by their own hierarchies and bureaucracies. It would take into account the "diseconomies of scale" that result from a company becoming too large to be managed effectively and efficiently in an environment of rapid and massive changes that are "creating a wholly new civilization based on high technology, information, and new ways of organizing for economic purposes.

"The basic shift that will be required can best be symbolized by the difference between the Great Pyramid of Cheops and the Calder mobile. Classical industrial bureaucracies are pyramidal in structure, with a small control group at the top and an array of permanent, functional departments below. The [adaptive] corporate form is more likely to consist of a slender semipermanent 'framework' from which a variety of small, temporary 'modules' are suspended. These, like the parts of a Calder construction, move in response to change. They can be spun off or rearranged as required by shifts in the outside world."[4]

In that environment, says W. Clement Stone, "teamwork will be especially critical. Cooperation and teamwork on the part of individuals, divisions or units of the same company, and even between organizations, will be tantamount to success.

"In sports, in business, or in any other activity in life, the team that pulls together, combining the talents of each individual member into a powerful whole, will win. The days of the rugged individualist who does everything his own way with little regard for others are virtually gone.

"Unless you are a hermit living on a tropical island, you need others and others need you to be successful. Moreover, whether you are a wealthy individual whose money works for you, or a professional manager who works for your money, you will go farther and earn more with the enthusiastic cooperation of others than those who choose to go it alone.

"In addition," Stone says, "the person whose philosophy of life is based on cooperation rather than confrontation will accumulate the luxuries of life more readily, and enjoy peace and happiness that others will never know. You will never leave scars on your own psyche if you achieve success through harmonious cooperation with others. That is something you can't say about fortunes acquired through conflict and unfair competition."

One who recognizes the power of teamwork and has put it into practical operation is John Lux, chairman and CEO of AMETEK. A Ph.D. in chemical engineering, Lux oversees a $600-million-plus operation that manufactures such low-tech products as wine-making machinery and stainless steel storage tanks, and such high tech products as precision instruments and unmanned undersea vehicles. In 1985, unmanned submarines built by the firm's Straza division located the flight data recorders from an Air India flight that crashed in the North Atlantic, and in January 1986, the subs were called into service to search for and photograph the wreckage of the space shuttle *Challenger*.

AMETEK's organizational structure closely parallels Toffler's "Calder mobile" vision of the future. The company has about 40 groups, each headed by a general manager who has his own finance, production, sales, and development departments. Each general manager, Lux says, is an entrepreneur in his own right since he has the ability to make the decisions to create a front-running division.

Lux is proud of the company's highly decentralized structure. He says, "Many companies seem to have a decentralized management, with operations managers who can move quickly and have the motivation and incentive to take responsibility and make decisions on their own. But at AMETEK we can *really* do this, because we know our managers and we know their businesses almost as well as they do. We have confidence in their daily, weekly, and monthly numbers.

"Faced with a major, big-money decision, an AMETEK manager doesn't avoid responsibility by filling out reams of paper, and doesn't wait for weeks, or even months, for help. If we can't handle it by phone, (president) Bob Noland and I will be there—not next month—but next week at the latest.

"That's how AMETEK is managed—with a small staff of financial experts; excellent, very timely financial controls; and a group of experienced, highly motivated operations managers who look to long-term return on investment as well as short-term earnings. It's designed to be a minimum-paperwork structure with enough personal contact to be a truly 'no surprises' management."

Lux credits Teamwork for his success in a career that has spanned over 40 years. He recalls a time in the 1950s when he was an executive with Shea Chemical. "We had a project down in Tennessee where we had to build a phosphorus furnace that was going to cost $4 million to build, and we only had $2.5 million. For us to keep the company solvent, we had to complete the furnace, so we—every member of the group—worked fifty to sixty hours a week, week in and week out. We bought used equipment and wrote contracts for the future.

"When we finally got the furnace up and started operating, we had no working capital so we had to forget about paychecks and paying bills. Finally, we got the thing running and made money and paid everybody off, but it was a project that took almost two years. It was a fantastic accomplishment on the part of the team.

"The same thing is true for Haveg Industries [an engineered plastics-manufacturer that Lux served as president for eleven years prior to its sale to Hercules, Inc. in 1964]. We took a company that was losing money, and in a period of one year we made it into a profitable company. We added other small companies, and ultimately expanded it to a nearly $40-million company. To do that in eight or nine years in the late fifties and early sixties took a real hard-fighting group."

He employed the same Teamwork principles at AMETEK. "It takes a lot of hard work by a lot of good people to take a company from $60 to $600 million in two decades while continuing to raise the dividend every year bringing a record thirty-nine consecutive years of increases," he says. "The team is not just the operating people. It is also the people who develop new products as well as a board of directors that has been with us for twenty years. It is the whole idea that makes it work; without the team, I couldn't have done anything at all."

For a team to be successful in the long run, Lux believes, team members have to support and trust each other, particularly during difficult times. "We don't win all the ball games," he says. "We've had people who came to us and said, 'This division is not going to grow and we think you should take your money out.' As a result, since 1970, we have closed down about twenty product lines or businesses. The ability to recognize and pull out of losing propositions is as important as recognizing the growing businesses and keeping them going. And pulling out takes a lot of guts on the part of the manager.

"In 1982, we had a man in Texas who was in the business

of selling fittings to the oil and gas industry. He sensed that the business was going to go downhill; he believed prices had peaked and the decline of the dollar made it cheaper to import the product. He said, 'We should close down this business.' We did, sold the inventory at a profit, and have since watched our competitors drop like flies. This is the kind of thinking we expect from our management team."

Necessity is often the mother of teamwork. It is common today for companies to form strategic alliances to take advantage of each other's strengths, and for universities to form partnerships with industry to commercialize high-technology products, and even for unions to cooperate with management to work through difficult economic problems.

It wasn't so common back in 1982 when an unlikely team of university students and professors, factory workers, and the world's largest automaker joined forces to try to save a major factory and the people it employed in Tuscaloosa, Alabama.

Faced with increasing foreign competition, a recession, higher interest rates, and declining sales, GM reluctantly concluded that it should move the Tuscaloosa carburetor assembly operation to Rochester, New York. Space was available in the Rochester facility, and the move would allow substantial cost savings through staff and overhead cuts.

The decision was not popular with community leaders, United Auto Workers members, and some GM executives. After all, the Tuscaloosa plant was one of the GM division's most productive; morale was high, absenteeism low, and the UAW had been successful with some unusual team participation programs there.

When the protests reached GM headquarters in Detroit, management agreed to rescind the decision on the condition that the plant could cut operating costs by $2 million a year. Management and labor worked together, GM sent in experts, but the best they could come up with was a cost reduction of $1.53 million per year. Finally, in a desperate attempt to save the additional $470,000 GM management required, local mangers approached the University of Alabama, the area's largest employer, with an offer to sell the 325,000 square foot facility to the university and lease it back.

University officials didn't have much use for a carburetor plant, but President Joab Thomas believed that a university should be involved in its state's economy. With area unemployment already flirting with 17 percent, Tuscaloosa couldn't afford to lose the 200 jobs and almost $7 million the plant spent on local wages and supplies. Thomas believed the university could and should help.

Eventually a financial arrangement was worked out. Community leaders put up $75,000 as seed money to get the program started. The university leased 50,000 square feet for $470,000 annually for three years on the condition that the rent would be reduced by the amount it helped save. Savings could not include employee layoffs, and all cuts would have to be agreed upon by the UAW, GM, and the university.

Some 50 salaried and 200 hourly workers reached into their own pockets to kick in an average of $53.50 each week from their paychecks. The money was to be placed in a bank trust until it reached the $470,000 figure in case the cost reduction efforts fell short. The risks were high: if the team succeeded, they kept their jobs; if not, they joined Alabama's already swollen ranks of unemployed.

Students involved in the project recognized all too well their obligation to contribute. This was no theoretical case study. To fail meant far more than a low grade on a term paper—people's lives would be seriously affected. "The key," said Roger Sayers, the university's vice president of academic affairs, "was to establish mutual trust" among the disparate members of the group. "Barry Mason [the professor of business administration who chaired the task force charged with developing cost-saving ideas] was determined to approach the venture as an equal partnership for all involved."

For his part, Mason wondered if Joab Thomas had suddenly taken on the persona of a riverboat gambler. The university's reputation, not to mention a considerable amount of its money, was at stake. It was by any measure a "trial by fire" for the principles of teamwork. Did it work?

It worked better and faster than even the most optimistic union members would have predicted at the outset. The $470,000 bogey was reached eight months into the project, and in late 1983, an average of $1,600 was returned to each employee to pay back the $53.50 weekly contributions.

In all, the GM, university, and UAW team identified close to $1 million a year in cost savings. These included such activities as buying instead of leasing copying and graphics equipment, upgrading some equipment with more efficient models, streamlining procedures, and installing a computerized inventory-control system.

Barry Mason says the GM project was so successful that the university has taken on a similar project with Stockham

Valves & Fittings, Inc. of Birmingham. The company is not in financial trouble, but wants to take advantage of the university's expertise in quality control, security, materials handling, and process layout—cost-cutting measures that can be taken without eliminating jobs. Several other proposals are pending.

GM was so encouraged by the project, Mason says, that it decided to invest $14 million to automate the Rochester plant so it could manufacture the carburetors as well as assemble them. The UAW has set aside funds to retrain the workers and is interested in using the Tuscaloosa program as a prototype for similar activities in other auto plants.

Mason offers the following formula for ensuring such successful teamwork:

1. Don't start without a commitment from the top from each participating unit.
2. Develop a broad group of supporters to provide continuity and ensure cooperation, especially during personnel changes.
3. Be flexible in contractual issues, cost-accounting procedures, sharing of confidential data, and in accepting nontraditional ideas.
4. Go after quick-kill costs early to establish credibility with supporters and doctors alike.
5. Honor "off limits" areas by focusing on non-threatening cost reduction proposals.
6. Use an impartial third party (in this case, the university) as a mediator and facilitator in sensitive areas that might lead to labor/management disputes.

7. Include each party's goals and needs in the written agreement.

That approach, Mason says, allowed the twelve-member task force (four from each organization) to quickly accept complete responsibility for the success of the project. All members of the team adopted a "we're all in this together" attitude. Ideas became "our" proposals, not the university's or management's.

Winning teams in the future may well take on a different character than those of today, and certainly managers will have to coach them differently to be successful. "The traditional idea of winning," says Stephen L. Pistner, president and CEO of Montgomery Ward & Company, a wholly owned subsidiary of Mobil Company, "entails winning at another's expense. That orientation drives a very limiting definition of who a winner should be. All of us have instinctive impressions about what 'stuff' winners are supposed to be made of: they are brash, self-confident playmakers, the highest level of individual performers.

"This notion of winning," Pistner says, "does not acknowledge the diversity of personalities, attitudes, and skills that are required to run large, complex businesses. If the creative needs of business and the human demands of our culture are to be met, managers must redefine winning to relate to the needs of varying business situations. Winning is no longer a synonym for individual aggressive behavior, no matter how skillful."[5]

Management's job, as Pistner sees it, is to put people in winning situations, jobs and projects that match their individual skills, interests, and ambitions. People want to be successful and competent, he says: "When the unique skills and chemistry of a person are permitted to excel, that's a winning situation.

"Too often, corporate America has tried to squeeze out diversity in its employees as if it were a failing to be overcome. Our job as managers is to recognize and motivate in a way that recognizes and draws upon that diversity."

It might surprise you to know that John Wooden, the winningest coach in college basketball, would agree. In an essay published by Panhandle Eastern Corporation in the *Wall Street Journal*, Wooden writes: "To me, success isn't outscoring someone, it's the peace of mind that comes from self-satisfaction in knowing you did your best. That's something each individual must determine for himself. You can fool others but you can't fool yourself.

"Many people are surprised to learn that in twenty-seven years at UCLA, I never once talked about winning. Instead, I would tell my players before games, 'When it's over, I want your head up, and there's only one way your head can be up—that's for you to know, not me, that you gave the best effort of which you're capable. If you do that, then the score doesn't really matter, although I have a feeling that if you do that the score will be to your liking.'

"I always taught players that the main ingredient of stardom is the rest of the team. It's amazing how much can be accomplished if no one cares who gets the credit."

Wooden says he was far more concerned with a player's character than with his ability. "While it may be possible to reach the top of one's profession on sheer ability," he says, "it is impossible to stay there without hard work and character.

"Your character is what you really are. Your reputation is

only what others think you are. I made a determined effort to evaluate character. I looked for young men who would play the game hard, but clean, and who would always be trying to improve themselves to help the team. Then, if their ability wanted it, the championships would take care of themselves."

You might be further interested to know that Wooden is the only man in history to be enshrined in the Basketball Hall of Fame as both a player and a coach. When he retired after 40 years of coaching, he left a record unmatched in American sports. In 27 years at UCLA, his teams never had a losing season. In his last 12 years there, they won 10 national championships, seven of them in succession. They still hold the record for the longest winning streak in any major sport—88 games in four seasons.

That's what Teamwork is all about. It makes every individual on the team a winner.

PART IV

Intellectual Principles

"One of the problems I've found with self-help books," W. Clement Stone says, "is that too often they tell you *what* to do, but they don't tell you *how to do it*." This book reflects his bias toward solid, practical, actionable information. We have attempted to include in this section on the Intellectual Principles the kind of information you can quickly grasp and apply in your unique situation.

As with Stone's other principles of success, the Intellectual Principles have a pragmatic bent. Creative Vision, Controlled Attention, and Accurate Thinking are explained in action terms. Specific suggestions and proven techniques are provided to help you develop your creative abilities and learn to think more clearly.

The Intellectual Principles are in no way to be construed as a substitute for formal education. All the PMA in the world won't get you a position that requires a Ph.D. when you only have a high school diploma.

What these principles *will* do for you is help you put into action the knowledge you already have and the knowledge you have yet to gain. When applied in concert with your formal education, the Intellectual Principles will help you become a more focused, imaginative, creative, *motivated* person.

If you need advanced degrees to move forward in your career and you are well past your school years, this philosophy will help you find the courage within yourself to do what you must to achieve the goals you have set for yourself. If you've never had much of a plan for your life, these principles will help you develop one. If your plan is rusty from disuse and inattention, these principles will help you get back on the success track.

When you combine the power contained in the Intellectual Principles with academic knowledge, you can create an intellectual force capable of solving any problem or overcoming any obstacle. The principles work; they have been successfully applied by many achievers to reach great heights of success.

They can do the same for you if only you use them.

Chapter 14

Creative Vision

In 1979, the Club of Rome, an *ad hoc* group of elite volunteers that analyzes major world and national problems and identifies positive solutions, issued a major report on learning. It was the culmination of a two-year effort aimed at helping mankind "learn how to stir up our dormant potential and use it from now on purposefully and intelligently." The project involved hundreds of people and teams of educators in three countries: Romania, Morocco, and the United States. Seminars were held in several locations around the globe, and many of the world's most prominent educators contributed ideas to the project.

The end product of this impressive application of brainpower was a persuasive argument that the future of the planet hinges on our ability to learn. Through learning, starving nations can feed themselves, industrial and service economies can become far more productive, and the worldwide threat of nuclear destruction can be minimized.

A byproduct of the study was a better understanding and classification of learning and creativity. The team identified two types of learning:

- *Maintenance learning.* This is problem solving of the type that is taught in the public school system. We are "given" a problem and told to find a solution.
- *Innovative learning.* This type of learning, according to the report, is "problem formulating and clustering." It consists of imagining totally new concepts and challenging old assumptions—in other words, broadening horizons.

The scholars also found that much of our potential for innovative thinking resides in our ability to think in images. "Images precede words," the report says. "In the process of interaction and cognition, the human mind uses images which are basic to reasoning."[1]

It is those images that often lead to radical innovations, says Dr. James Botkin, one of the report's three authors: "Many people believe the sequence is: first, science invents the product, then the technology is made available, and finally the product becomes available."

Botkin, a Boston-based writer, researcher, and consultant on technology management and learning, says, "High technology entrepreneurs would argue that the reverse is true. They would say that first it's the technology, then the commercial product, and finally science figures out what it was they invented. The real point is that the key is neither scientists nor technologists but rather 'visionaries.' And visionaries occur at least as frequently among technologists (witness Steven Jobs) as among scientists."

The author of several books on education and technology issues with a Harvard Business School doctorate in computer based systems, Botkin points out that the computer can store and manipulate information the same way the human mind can. What it can't do, he says, is generate the original idea that is visualized in the imagination.

"Once you have the idea, you can program it into the computer, so that the computer can recreate the same vision. And you can break it up into little pieces, manipulate the pieces with the computer, and make it come out different. But you have to start with the vision."

Popular folklore has it that Einstein's imagination, not his knowledge of physics and mathematics, led him to the theory of relativity. He understood the theory, the story goes, when he visualized himself riding a beam of starlight through space. When he imagined what would happen as he sat astride the beam of light, he was able to work out the mathematical formulas that proved the theory.

Thomas Edison was undoubtedly one of the greatest inventors of modern history, yet, in the most basic sense, his electric light was merely the combination of two already well-known principles. It was common knowledge that passing electric current through a wire would heat it enough to generate light; the problem was that the wire would burn up.

Edison conducted hundreds of experiments with filament materials, but it wasn't until he remembered that nothing will burn without oxygen—a principle commonly used in making charcoal—that he was able to develop a workable incandescent light. He pumped the air out of a glass bulb, heated a wire with electric current, and set in motion a force that spawned entire industries and built the foundation for today's technological revolution.

Edison's creative vision might best be defined as a combination of imagination and intuition. It has been practiced by men and women from all walks of life who dare to try something different. It has been responsible for all the great advances civilization has made from the invention of the wheel to the space age. "Every new advance in science," Thomas Dewy said, "has issued from a new audacity of imagination."

Every time you rearrange information into a new combination or order, every time you put old information to a new use, you are using your imagination. Every time you set a goal and visualize yourself as having achieved it, you are using your imagination.

The late A.N. Pritzker, patriarch of a family that controls billions of dollars in the operation of its Hyatt Hotel companies and the Marmon Group, liked to relate the story of how he got into the hotel business.

"About 25 years ago," he recalled, "my son Jay telephoned me from a hotel he was staying at called the Hyatt House at the airport in Los Angeles. He said, 'Dad, I think we ought to buy this hotel. It has to be making a lot of money.' I said, 'Well, go ahead and buy it.'

"For about 10 years, it went noplace. We bought some other hotels, but they weren't spectacular, either. Then we heard about a situation in Atlanta that was interesting. John

Portman, the famous architect, had designed a hotel, but work on it was being held up because the insurance company that was committed for the loan told the parties involved they had to get a new owner."

Portman's design exploded in Pritzker's imagination. He saw, in the architect's drawings, a new concept that would "revolutionize the world of hotels with its open-atrium lobby." (Pritzker chuckled, recalling that they used to refer to it as the *Jesus Christ* lobby, because when people saw it for the first time they would look around and exclaim "Jesus Christ!")

Within minutes, he signed a contract to take over the hotel, and the Atlanta Hyatt became the flagship of a worldwide chain of hotels. The soaring atrium lobby became a Hyatt trademark. Nothing happened, however, until Pritzker saw in his imagination the possibilities this unique design held and took the necessary steps to put his plan into action.

You, too, can develop that kind of Creative Vision by combining the powers of both your conscious and your subconscious mind—your imagination and intuition—into one powerful force.

To use your imagination to its fullest capacity, begin by gathering all available information on the subject from every possible source. Read it once superficially, just to get an overview of what you have. Then read it again in detail—slowly and with full concentration. Make notes and organize the information in the order you plan to use it.

These are routine steps that anyone can follow. The real test is not in gathering information, but in applying it. The next step in the process is critical. Review the facts again, this time looking for any unusual things that you may not have noticed before. SRI International, the California think tank, calls this "pattern recognition," and has developed a system it says can help you spot trends long before they become public knowledge.[2]

The SRI system calls for "scanners" who review publications with an eye toward anomalies—developments that surprise them in light of what they already know. The scanners then abstract the articles and submit them to experts in various fields who review the information prior to monthly meetings.

At the meetings, team members form clusters or idea tracks and apply their insight and intuition to sense change. Everyone is encouraged to say whatever is on his or her mind without fear of criticism, concern for rank, or the outcome of the discussion.

SRI Team Leader Jim Smith says these freewheeling thinkers have come up with a surprising number of correct associations. Among others, program leaders proposed opening trade with China long before President Nixon's historic visit to the country in 1972, and identified stress in the workplace long before it became a popular topic.

W. Clement Stone advocates what he calls the R2A2 Formula—Recognize and Relate, Assimilate and Apply principles from what you see, hear, think, and experience—to achieve any goal. "It make no difference what the goal is," he says, "so long as it doesn't violate the laws of God or the rights of your fellowman. You can achieve what others believe to be impossible.

"Your mind is the greatest mechanism ever created. It is so awesome that only God could create it. It is the human computer. The electronic computer is designed to function similar to your computer, your brain and nervous system. Your human computer is similar to its electronic counterpart in another way, as well: you can never get out of it more than you put into it."

In addition to gathering information from related and unrelated fields, if we are to be truly imaginative and creative, we must effectively use both sides of our brains. More than 50 years ago, Rudyard Kipling wrote the poem, "The Two-Sided Man," in which he concluded:

I would go without shirt or shoe,
Friend, tobacco or bread,
Sooner than lose for a minute the two
Separate sides of my head!

Despite the fact that mankind has known of the existence of the separate sides of the brain for some time, we have just begun to understand the inner workings of the mind. It is generally accepted today that even though both halves of the brain receive the same information, each processes it differently. The left half runs on logic; it controls language, it is analytical, sequential, and linear. The right half, on the other hand, runs on imagery. It is the "mind's eye" that helps you understand metaphors, visualize things, and create new combinations of ideas.

While we obviously need both capabilities to function effectively, most education is concentrated in left brain activities. We memorize numeric tables and mathematical formulas, we store information in memory and learn to recall it when we need it, and we are taught to think in an analytical, linear fashion. Little emphasis is placed on the emotional, the intuitive, the visualization skills that reside in the right hemisphere of the brain.

Is it something that can be learned? Betty Edwards, an art teacher at California State University in Long Beach, believes it can. In her book, *Drawing on the Right Side of the Brain*, she says, "One of the marvelous capabilities of the right brain is imaging: seeing an imaginary picture with your mind's eye. The brain is able to conjure an image and then 'look' at it, 'seeing' it as if it is 'really there.' The terms for this ability, *visualizing* and *imaging*, are used almost interchangeably, although to me the term *visualizing* tends to carry the idea of a *moving* image, while *imaging* seems to connote a still picture."

Edwards suggests a series of exercises to develop the right brain, beginning with drawing images upside down, from right to left, or in reverse. The idea, of course, is to look at things differently than you always have, to "learn the artist's mode of seeing: the key is to direct your attention toward visual information that the left brain cannot or will not process." [3]

You can apply the same technique to virtually any exercise in imagination, whether it is solving a particularly difficult problem, coming up with a new promotional campaign, or finding new customers for a stagnant product line. Use your visualization abilities by turning the idea over in your mind and looking at it from every possible direction until you see it in a way you have never seen it before. A fresh point of view may be all you need to find a creative solution to a problem you've been wrestling with.

Don't forget to write down your good ideas. Thoughts are fleeting; you may not be able to duplicate them on command. In his book, *Lake Wobegon Days*, Garrison Keillor laments a lost manuscript:

"The lost story shone so brilliantly in dim memory that every new attempt at it looked pale and impoverished before I got to the first sentence . . . I brought in Lake Wobegon as the home of a weekly monologue [for the *Prairie Home Companion,* a public-radio show he hosts], hoping that one Saturday night, standing on stage, I would look into the lights and my lost story would come down the beam and land in my head. Eleven years later, I am still waiting for it."[4]

If you listened to Keillor's whimsical monologues, you'll remember that one could never be sure what was real in them and what was fantasy. One thing is certain, however: lost ideas may be difficult to recover. Write them down when they occur to you.

The next step in the Creative Vision is a little fuzzier and a lot more abstract. It is the application of the data that reside in your subconscious mind. While your conscious mind works only when you are alert and awake, our subconscious is on the job 24 hours a day. If you learn to listen to it, your subconscious can provide some startling new ideas as well as some unlikely combinations of information that result in a new and better way of doing something. It's not very scientific, but it works.

Singer and songwriter Carl Perkins delights in telling how a chance remark overheard at a dance and part of a nursery rhyme were combined in his imagination to produce a record that sold millions of copies. A teenage boy's admonition to his girlfriend to "stay off his suede shoes" kept running through the singer's mind long after the dance was over and he was home in bed. He sat bolt upright when he thought of the line, "One for the money, two for the show..."

He wrote the words to "Blue Suede Shoes" on a brown paper bag, and the song was already a hit for him when Elvis Presley recorded it and made it a rock-and-roll classic.

Those flashes of inspiration that come to you in the middle of the night should be encouraged, not discouraged, says Rance Crain, president and editor-in-chief of *Crain's Chicago Business*.

"Your subconscious mind woke you up for a good reason," he says, "and that reason may very well be that an idea is about to be born. So let your thoughts take you where they may, and pretty soon they will zero in on the problem (or opportunity) that you've been wrestling with. And pretty soon after that, you'll have your solution."[5]

Crain, whose firm also publishes *Advertising Age*, discounts the notion that some people are creative and others aren't. He defines creativity as "a new way of looking at familiar things and concepts. The trick is to see things in new ways," he says, "and from that you may have to alter the way you operate a bit.

"It's not so much what you do that's different. But the process of thinking about little ordinary things in different ways will lead inevitably to thinking about the relationships of bigger, more substantive matters."

Crain believes that it's the process that's important, and that changing the order of the things you do, or changing how you do them, will force you to think more about what you are doing. Maybe by making such a change, you will notice something that had not occurred to you before that will suggest a new solution to an old problem.

He points to James Webb Young's book, *A Technique for Producing Ideas*. Although it was published in 1940, it describes a method that is as valid today as it was over four decades ago. Young suggested five steps to taking an idea from conception to incubation to implementation:

1. Gather the raw materials. Research the immediate problem and apply information that comes from constant enrichment of your store of general knowledge.
2. Work this information over in your mind.
3. Incubate the idea in your subconscious.
4. Recognize the "Eureka! I've got it!" stage when the idea is actually born.
5. Shape and develop the idea for practical usefulness.

Crain reminds us that all ideas involve risk, and that, if we are to truly express our creativity, we must overcome such obstacles as fear of failing, fear of rejection, or fear of appearing foolish.

No doubt the most difficult of Young's five steps is the subconscious incubation period. One who mastered it was Dr. Elmer Gates, a contemporary of Thomas Edison. In fact, he held almost twice as many patents as Edison, and was a highly paid consultant to the industry leaders of his day.

Gates developed a method of unlocking his Creative Vision that he called "sitting for ideas." When he wanted a solution to a problem, he went into a soundproof room that he designed expressly for this purpose, closed the door, sat at a table with a pad of paper and a pencil, and turned off the lights. He then concentrated his thoughts on the problem and waited to receive a solution.

Sometimes the ideas would flow quickly, sometimes not. Occasionally they never came. But Gates refined and perfected more than 250 patents by using this method.

In their book, *Higher Creativity; Liberating the Unconscious for Breakthrough Insights*, Willis Harman, Ph.D., and Howard Rheingold give W. Clement Stone's computer analogy a slightly different twist. They say the process is simply "input, processing, and output." They advocate a four-step method of tapping the powers of the creative subconscious:

1. Use visualization and imagery.
2. Program and reprogram the unconscious idea processor.
3. Achieve alert relaxation to open the channel.
4. Use your dream power.[6]

They, too, suggest regular exercise for your mind's eye to help you visualize situations more clearly. Begin with soothing, restful imagery, such as walking along a green mountaintop, drinking from a cool spring or looking at the sea. Then when you return from your mental journey, write down your impression and images or draw them.

Your first images are especially important, because they may hold clues to your deepest feelings and help you develop your visualization skills. "But sometimes," the authors caution, "the meaning of the images only becomes clear later, when other images can furnish a context.

"Don't be discouraged if nothing spectacular happens at the beginning. Simply repeat the exercise daily, until you are comfortable with it and the images grow vivid. After all, it is worth a little practice and effort to learn the language of the unconscious so that when it speaks, you can understand and communicate with it."

The second step in Harman and Rheingold's process is affirmation, by programming and reprogramming the unconscious idea processor. It is essentially the method of autosuggestion developed by Stone and Napoleon Hill that is described in Chapter 18.

Harman and Rheingold cite Maxwell Maltz, author of *Psychocybernetics*, who wrote: "The lucky or successful person has learned a simple secret. Call up, capture, evoke the feeling of success. When you feel successful and self-confident, you will act successfully.

"Define your goal or end result. Picture it to yourself clearly and vividly. Then simply capture the feeling you would experience if the desirable goal were already an accomplished fact. Then your internal machinery is geared for success: to guide you in making the correct muscular motions and adjustments, to supply you with creative ideas, and to do whatever else is necessary in order to make the goal an accomplished fact."

To arrive at a state of alert relaxation and open the channel of communication to the subconscious, Harman and Rheingold recommend the approach outlined by Dr. Herbert Benson (see Chapter 11).

They also offer some practical advice for using your dreams to advantage. "One thing is certain: when we sleep, we (usually) cease to be conscious. We are in the realm of the unconscious and it can speak to us directly with no interference from exterior distractions, the babble of thought, or the demands of the body. Is that why so many inspirations, illuminations, revelations, ideas, breakthroughs and symbols come to us 'in our dreams'?"

Don't worry about interpreting dreams according to psychological theory, the authors say; dreams are as individual as the people who dream them. They do, however, suggest remembering them. Keep a notebook or tape recorder by your bed, note the date of the dream, and review the dream as soon as you awaken. Analyze your dreams over the course of time, discuss them with others, attend classes and seminars on the subject, but don't expect immediate miracles. You may master the relaxation techniques long before you begin to understand your dreams.

Despite years of research, scientists are just beginning to understand how the human mind works. We may make quantum leaps in the near future, or it may take centuries of deliberate progress before we can begin to effectively release the vast potential of the human brain. No one knows what answers the future holds.

What we do know is that various techniques for tapping the subconscious have been successfully applied to enrich the personal and professional lives of many achievers. They have used these methods to help them develop and refine the Creative Vision we all possess. You can do the same.

Never has the demand for creative vision been more urgent than in today's increasingly information-driven society. The winners in a marketplace that changes with dizzying speed—where products and entire businesses have shorter and shorter life cycles—will be those who have the creative vision to anticipate market needs even before customers themselves know what they want.

Chapter 15

Controlled Attention

For ten years, Michelangelo labored to build St. Peter's Cathedral, combating bureaucracy and politics, struggling against the vicissitudes of age and infirmity. At age 82, after being bedridden for several months with a severe attack of kidney stones, he returned to the project to discover that a new superintendent of construction had misread his plans, making several errors in construction. One of the chapels would have to be pulled down.

He went to see Pope Paul, only to find that his critic, Baccio Bigio, had already been there, urging the Pope to remove Michelangelo as architect of the cathedral. As the great artist and the Pope talked, Michelangelo reflected, in a scene written by Irving Stone in *The Agony and the Ecstasy*:

"Holiness, for thirty years I watched good architects pour

foundations. They never got St. Peter's off the ground. In the ten years I have been the architect, the church has risen upward like an eagle. If you dismiss me now, it will be the ruin of the edifice."

"Michelangelo, as long as you have the strength to fight back, you shall remain the architect of St. Peter's," the Pope replied.

But it was painfully apparent that Michelangelo must complete the sketches for the magnificent dome. If anything should happen to him, no other living soul could imagine his vision of it. The church could not be completed without him.

Faced with the ultimate deadline, Michelangelo knew he must complete the dome design. "He was after absolute balance, perfection of line, curve, volume, mass, openness, density, elegance, the profundity of endless space," Stone writes. "He aspired to create a work of art that would transcend the age though which he had lived."

Michelangelo had already made several drawings and models, but none met his expectations. He discarded them all. Finally, one night soon after his conversation with the Pope, it came, Irving Stone says, "After eleven years of thinking, drawing, praying, hoping and despairing, experimenting and rejecting: a creature of his imagination, compounded of all his arts, staggering in size, yet as fragile as a bird's egg in a nest, soaring, lilting heavenward, constructed of gossamer which carried effortlessly and musically upward its 335 foot height, pear-shaped as was the breast of Medici Madonna . . . It was a dome unlike any other."

When Michelangelo's old friend Tommaso saw the drawings, he murmured, "It has arrived. Where did it come from?"

"Where do ideas come from?" Michelangelo replied. "Sebastian asked that same question when he was young. I can only give you the answer I gave him, for I am no wiser at eighty-two than I was at thirty-nine: ideas are a natural function of the mind, as breathing is of the lungs. Perhaps they come from God."[1]

In a single night, Michelangelo accomplished what he had been struggling to perfect more than a decade.

That state of heightened concentration brings with it a mental efficiency that researchers have likened to a sense of euphoria similar to drugs, sex, or a runner's high. It is, says a *New York Times* piece on the subject, an altered state "in which the mind functions at its peak, time is often distorted, and a sense of happiness seems to pervade the moment.[2]

"One team of researchers describes these moments of absorption as 'flow states.'

"According to Mike Csikszenthmihalyi, a psychologist at the University of Chicago," the *Times* goes on, "'flow' refers to 'those times when things seem to go just right, when you feel alive and fully attentive to what you are doing.'"

Dr. Mihaly Csikszenthmihalyi studied 82 volunteers, ranging from hourly workers and clerks to engineers and managers, who recorded at various times throughout the day how they felt and what they were doing. Interestingly, the researchers found that somewhere between boredom from unchallenging work and anxiety from overly demanding work is a zone where concentration seems to peak. Dr. Csikszenthmihalyi labels it a "sort of mental overdrive," in which we are able to extraordinarily focus our concentration.

The results of such concentration can be remarkable. The

late syndicated columnist and author Sydney J. Harris used a sports analogy to point out that just a little more concentration can yield significantly greater results. "Consider two major league baseball players," he said. "One hits .275 for the season. The other hits .300. The one hitting .300 may easily have a contract awarding him twice as much as the one hitting .275. Yet the difference between the two, over the season, is only one extra hit in forty times at bat."[3]

The comparisons are endless: a racehorse that wins by a nose, a marathon runner who wins by a step, a field goal kicker who carries his team to victory on the strength of a single point, or the basketball player who hits the winning shot at the buzzer.

Harris used the analogy to illustrate the point that in any field where there are a lot of skilled, highly trained competitors, nobody is twice as good—or even half again as good—as everyone else. You don't have to be; a five or ten percent advantage will put you far ahead of the pack.

It's like the story of two hikers deep in the woods who see increasingly frequent signs of bears. As they become more and more anxious, one of the hikers sits down on a stump, takes off his hiking boots and begins putting on his running shoes.

"What are you doing?" his friend asks.

"I'm putting on my running shoes," is the reply.

"Are you crazy?" his buddy asks. "You'll never outrun a grizzly bear."

"I don't have to outrun the bear," the first runner says, standing up and dusting himself off. "I just have to outrun you."

In that situation, a five or ten percent advantage would

certainly be welcome, and more than enough to get the job done.

The question is, of course, is it possible to train yourself to easily reach heightened levels of concentration, or is the flow, as Michelangelo suggested, the work of God? The answer may be that it is a combination of both.

In likening the brain to a computer, W. Clement Stone points out that while the human equipment has a marvelous capacity to store and process information, there is a major difference in capacity. The brain has far more "bytes" of memory, much more rapid processing times, and it can be much more easily programmed than its electromechanical counterpart.

It begins with the "data base" of your human computer. Most of us in our lifetimes will use only a small percentage of the capacity of our brains, but it is possible to expand its use, believes Orlando Battista, president of Knowledge Inc. and O.A. Battista Research Institute.

Battista, who has been granted 80 United States patents and more than 500 foreign ones, "stretches" his mind with constant reading: "I cull maybe thirty magazines and only keep what is absolutely new. The minute I find something that is new to me, I want to read it. This helps stretch your intellectual cells and develops your memory. I believe that developing brain power is not a repetition of things that are 'old hat' to you. Where you really make progress is by forcing the brain cells—thirteen trillion of them, I'm told—to work a little harder. To make them work harder, you've got to put in new information. When you add a new bit of information, you are causing those cells to become more efficient in their ability to be intellectually powerful."

A recipient of countless awards, author of 22 books, more than 100 scientific publications, and more than 1,000 articles for national magazines, Battista says: "If I read something new, I never let go until I clearly understand it. Most of us read something new and it's only a passing flicker. That's the easy way out. I go back and reexamine and reexamine until I have it clearly in my mind.

"We are, by nature, very superficial intellectually. Therefore, you have to discipline yourself like an Olympic runner or high jumper. He doesn't do it on the first shot. He's got to force himself to put out that extra effort to shave a second on swimming a mile or something. That doesn't come easy.

"The same thing occurs with brain cells, I'm convinced. You can train them, just like you can learn to play the piano. You can learn to play your intellectual brain cells to the advantage of humanity—not just yourself. We haven't begun to even scratch the surface of the potential. It makes everything else I can think of fade into mediocrity by comparison."

If you think intellectuals like Battista were born under a different star or have some kind of special genetic advantage, you're wrong. He attributes his love for knowledge to his father, an immigrant laborer, a stonemason who could barely read. "He always told us when we were little children—all eight of us— 'As long as I see you with your nose in a book, I will never ask you to do manual labor.' As a result, all of us were constantly reading! I remember my brother, Arthur, who is one of the world's most famous neurosurgeons, reading *Microbe Hunters* at thirteen. He closed the book in our very modest living room and said to me, 'Landy, I'm going to be a neurosurgeon if it takes me thirty years.' And it took him thirty years before he was really there.

"My father had the wisdom to appreciate the importance of studying, not for himself, but for us."

It may not be easy to force yourself to study, no matter how interested you are in the subject or how important it is to you. Sigmund Freud, in the developmental stages of his theories on the subconscious mind's influence on dreams, so struggled with then-current books on the subject that it became an affliction with him, says Irving Stone in his biographical novel on the great psychologist. It seemed that the literature stretched endlessly.

When his wife saw how reading the 80 volumes irritated Freud, she asked, "Why must you read every word of these books?"

"Because I cannot risk the chance of having neglected any of this work, fragmentary as it may be."

The discussion continued about the futility of quoting half a hundred authors only to prove that "they led themselves down the garden path," until Freud said, "It is the scientific way: summarize everything that has already been written on the subject, and analyze its value."

"But what happens to the reader if he gets lost in the thicket?" his wife asked.

"Sigmund smiled ruefully. 'He will never get to see the Sleeping Beauty within. It's a kind of ritualistic ground clearing, the way farmers burn off last year's stubble before plowing.'"[4]

Even Einstein had his problems. A lackluster student, when he first applied to the famous Federal Institute of

Technology in Zurich—the Polytechnic, as it was popularly called—he failed the entrance exams. In elementary school, he resented the then-prevalent harsh methods of rote instruction and refused to cooperate with his teachers. Years later, he wrote to an inquirer, "As a pupil I was neither particularly good nor bad. My principal weakness was a poor memory and especially a poor memory for words and texts." Indeed, his Greek teacher, according to one of his biographers, said to him, "You will never amount to anything."[5]

Whatever his weaknesses in literature and memory, Einstein, of course, found his niche in mathematics and physics. His discoveries remain unsurpassed.

Even in areas in which you excel, intense concentration can be difficult, but it's worth the effort. In his book, *Managing*, Harold S. Geneen, a former accountant and for 17 years the CEO of ITT, writes:

"If you are running a well-managed company, most of the numbers will be those you expect. That makes them even more mundane and dull. But you cannot skip over them; you dare not allow your attention to flag. Those numbers are your controls, and you read them, on and on, until your mind reels or until you come upon one number or set of numbers which stand out from all the rest, demanding your attention, and getting it."

Geneen's attention to detail, his forced concentration on the numbers, led ITT to 58 consecutive quarters of growth at an annual rate of 10 to 15 percent; yearly sales swelled from \$766 million to \$22 billion.[6]

"Regardless of what you are or what you have been," says W. Clement Stone, "you have the capacity to be *what* you want to be.

"In very rare instances an individual may be born with such remarkable inherited tendencies that he could be considered to be a natural genius, but as a rule, gifted persons are made, not born. Every normal person is, in fact, potentially gifted, for he or she has inherited enough from the vast reservoir of the past to become outstanding in achievement.

"Genius, talent, aptitude, gifts, and ability are faculties which can be developed and grown. They lie dormant in every normal child at birth, and they can be educed at any given point in his development when he is ready. Furthermore, he can be made ready if he is taught—and he learns and applies—the Art of Motivation with a Positive Mental Attitude.

"Although you may have the capacity for greatness, however, your talents or gifts will be evaluated only by virtue of your achievements. And great achievement is the result of persistent effort that begins with the desire to achieve definite goals.

"I have often quoted J. Milburn Smith, former president of Continental Casualty Company, who taught me: *'The burden of learning is upon the person who wants to learn, and the burden of teaching is upon the person who wants to teach.'* It is the responsibility of the parent, the teacher, and the minister to motivate the child to want to learn. However, it is always the individual's responsibility to motivate himself.

"'Genius is one percent inspiration and ninety-nine percent perspiration,' Thomas Edison said. Without that one percent inspiration, you will never persevere; you'll always remain only a *potentially* gifted person.

"Remember: you are the product of your heredity, environment, physical body, conscious and subconscious mind, experience, position and direction in time and space, and something more...powers known and unknown. And you have the potential power to affect, use, control, or harmonize with all of them.

"Regardless of what you are or what you have been, you have the potential power to be what you want to be... if you are willing to pay the price. What is the price? TIME. Spend a half hour every day in creative thinking time and concentrate on your major definite goals in life. During this time, keep your mind on what you want and off what you don't want.

"Thomas Edison devoted many hours each day to creative thinking. Remember his words, 'Genius is one percent inspiration and ninety-nine percent perspiration,' and remember that creative thinking time always precedes the work or preparation time."

Knowledge is essential to personal growth. We are products of a system that teaches us that we go from kindergarten through high school, possibly on to college, and if we are extremely dedicated and/or fortunate, on to graduate school. Then our education is finished. In reality, that is far from true. As the technological revolution continues to sweep the world, it becomes increasingly necessary to continue learning.

It's been said that today the half-life of an engineer in our high-tech society is five years. That means that half of what a bright, young engineer graduating from MIT this semester has learned in his college career will be obsolete in five years. Formal education only provides the qualifications to enter the job market. Our future success will depend on how well we apply that knowledge and how frequently we supplement it.

Nowadays, billions are being spent on continuing education; big corporations have training centers that rival universities in size and scope of offerings. Indeed, in many locations, universities themselves conduct extension courses for college credit in corporate offices, in hospitals, on military bases, and in other locations wherever interested, motivated adults congregate.

Seminars, self-help courses, and books abound on virtually any topic you can imagine. It's all there, and it's waiting for you. Is controlled focused knowledge and attention really important? R. Buckminster Fuller pointed out in his massive tome, *Critical Path*, that there are two fundamental realities in our universe: the physical and the metaphysical. Physical assets are tangible, patentable, and are carried on the books as assets, but only in special cases can the metaphysical assume the same status. The metaphysical is considered to be insubstantial; in Latin, Fuller observes, it means "nothing on which to stand."

"The large issue today," Fuller wrote, "is the technical know-how that governs the transformations of energy between its two states. 'Know-how' is metaphysics. Metaphysics now rules. When the head of one of the U.S.A.'s largest banks was asked what 'commodities' were involved in that bank's import-export dealings with the rest of the world on behalf of the Chinese government, he answered that know-how was the prime commodity being acquired by the Chinese through that bank." [7]

However the debate between governments about the value of knowledge is resolved, it remains that knowledge applied through Controlled Attention is an essential success principle.

As the nineteenth-century English literary historian Robert Eldridge Aris Willmott once observed, "Attention makes the genius; all learning, fancy, science, and skill depend upon it. Newton traces his great discoveries to it. It builds bridges, opens new worlds, heals diseases, carries on the business of the world. Without it, taste is useless, and the beauties of literature unobserved."

Chapter 16

Accurate Thinking

"Thinking," Henry Ford said "is the hardest work there is, which is the probable reason why so few engage in it."

Accurate Thinking in the context of W. Clement Stone's principles might be described as the evaluation and application step of the intellectual process. Ideas are conceived in the imagination through Creative Vision, nurtured and developed through Controlled Attention, and evaluated and applied through Accurate Thinking.

Accurate Thinking is critical to the successful application of the other principles. Unless you test the validity of ideas rationally and build your goals on a foundation of accurate thought, it will be virtually impossible to achieve them. And you certainly cannot inspire others to follow your vision if your logic is faulty.

In the contemporary analyses of the left brain/right brain functions, Accurate Thinking would reside in the analytical left brain while Creative Vision would be the product of the imaginative right brain. Accurate Thinking would help logically solve problems that have been identified by intuitive Creative Vision.

The real key to success, says Dr. James Botkin, is how well you integrate the two. One of the principal authors of the Club of Rome report *No Limits to Learning* (see Chapter 14), Botkin says innovation occurs when Creative Vision and Accurate Thinking are integrated, "despite popular literature to the contrary. I would define innovation in an industrial or business sense as the successful commercialization of a new idea," he says. "Of course, there are other interesting definitions. According to Nobel Prize winner Herbert Simon of Carnegie Melon, innovation and creativity are nothing more than the mastery of 50,000 "chunks" of information. According to his theory, anyone who can master 50,000 chunks of information in his or her own field will become a creative thinker. (In this context, a chunk of information would compare to one move by a chess master—moving a particular piece under a certain set of circumstances will result in a certain situation.)

"Simon goes even further to state that 50,000 chunks of information are masterable in ten years. So, it takes you ten years to become innovative. Simon says that creativity is 'thinking writ large.' I don't believe that; it's almost a formula approach.

"Creative Vision comes from some source other than Accurate Thinking. It comes from the driving force within each of us that is referred to as our spirit. In a business sense, that is the life force that makes you work, think, be alive. That's where Creative Vision comes from, and your ability to tap into that life force gives you imagination. After you get the creative vision—the big idea—you can go back and rationalize it, cut it up, and work out the formulas. But it doesn't work the other way; you can't start with accurate thinking and fit it into little formulas.

"Accurate thinking," Botkin says, "is not only the ability to identify what's true and what's false, but more importantly, it is the ability to identify what's relevant. Only the best schools today teach this point. Most schools, unfortunately, do not. They are stuck on 'critical thinking'—sharpening a person's ability to critique an agenda set by someone else. But what's really important is the ability to create a new agenda where none previously existed. In other words, we may say that attacking a problem is only a mop-up operation; the real creative genius comes in foreseeing and avoiding the conditions that lead to war."

The author of several books on technology, education, and innovation, Botkin says that truly innovative learning and thinking is "anticipatory and participatory." It consists of anticipating problems before they occur—in time to do something about them—and in working together to solve them.

These things don't happen in school systems in the United States "There 'ain't' no such thing, as teamwork in the schools," Botkin says, "It's un-American; it's called cheating. Nor do schools spend any time on thinking about or identifying things that aren't here yet. And yet, these are the very things that make you successful when you enter the real world. If you were in the business world and faced with a new situation, which would you do—go alone to consult a book or call some business associates on the phone? I think small executives do the latter—they seek help from others to learn to straighten their own shortcomings."

Another wrong lesson we learn in school is to minimize risk. "We live in terror of doing the wrong thing instead of in hope of finding the right," said the British educator Harold Joseph Laski. Roger von Oech, president of Creative Think, a California-based consulting firm, points out that our school system is one in which you get a C if you are wrong just 22 percent of the time. What this does for us, von Oech believes, is to teach us not to put ourselves in situations where we might fail.

"The problem is," he says in his book on creativity entitled *A Kick in the Seat of the Pants*, "this leads to conservative thought and action patterns. These may be okay for much of what you do, but if you're trying to get a new idea into action, they're inappropriate. If there's only a fifty percent likelihood of success, but a ten to one payback if successful, then (you are) a fool not to go with it."[1]

Von Oech quotes Charles Kettering of General Motors who said, "An inventor is simply a person who doesn't take his education too seriously. You see, from the time a person is six years old until he graduates from college he has to take three or four examinations a year. If he flunks once, he is out. But an inventor is almost always failing. He tries and fails maybe a thousand times. If he succeeds once, then he's in. These two things are diametrically opposite. We often say that the biggest job we have is to teach a newly hired employee how to fail intelligently. We have to train him to experiment over and over and to keep on trying and failing until he learns what will work."

When you evaluate your ideas, von Oech says, you function as a judge. "When you adopt this role, you decide what to do with the idea: implement it, modify it, or discard it completely. In carrying out this task, you should recognize imperfections in the new idea without overstating them. You should also be open to interesting possibilities and use your imagination to develop these without losing your sense of reality and perspective."

Joseph Cygler, managing director of Kepner-Tregoe, Inc., a Princeton, New Jersey consulting firm with an international register of clients, has developed a "formula" for effective decision making.

First, Cygler says, make sure you understand the scope of the decision. Make sure you consider all possible alternatives. Don't narrow the focus of your thinking so much that you overlook options that might be successful. "Too often," Cygler says, "decisions become a matter of should we or shouldn't we, instead of taking a broader look at what might be accomplished."

Next, specify your objectives. Make sure you know what you are trying to accomplish. While this may on the surface appear to be a simple task, the answer is not always obvious, Cygler observes. He says that one of his clients, a manufacturer, established a goal of expanding corporate sales through acquisition, but after thinking the decision through, he realized that his real objective was to increase profitability. That realization led to a number of possibilities in addition to mergers and acquisitions.

The third step in effective decision-making, according to Cygler, is to evaluate the alternatives. He cautions that using a consistent evaluation system is essential to avoid bias, and he warns that often decision-makers unconsciously define objectives to put a favored alternative in a good light. Consistent evaluation techniques will minimize the danger of such distortions creeping into the decision-making process.

Finally, evaluate the possible adverse consequences of each alternative. Identify the risks associated with your preferred solution and assess the negative impact this course of action might have on the organization. Decide in advance how you plan to deal with such problems.

Cygler believes that executive commitment to a systematic decision-making process will encourage accurate thinking throughout a company. He advises managers to help subordinates assess their decision-making processes whenever they ask for approval of decisions they've made. He urges: "Help them identify their objectives and analyze the risk/reward relationships of the various alternatives."[2]

One who benefited from Cygler's approach was John Folkerth, president of Shopsmith, Inc., an Ohio manufacturer of a multipurpose home woodworking tool. When he acquired the company 15 years ago, it was barely selling enough units through its hardware store dealer network to survive. Something needed to be done quickly to get more exposure to potential buyers.

Folkerth and his staff analyzed the problem, and decided to risk trying to market the Shopsmith through shopping-mall demonstrations—an unorthodox approach to selling a product that retailed for more than $1,000.

Before scheduling the first demonstration, Folkerth calculated the cost of constructing a mobile sales booth, hiring a demonstrator, renting mall space, and advertising. He knew exactly how many sales he would need to break even, and built the cost of follow-up with prospective customers into the plan. He also took into account the consequences of a potential conflict with hardware store dealers.

His approach to making this decision paralleled the type of analysis he did in deciding to buy the company in the first place. Although Shopsmith had been out of business for four years at the time Folkerth believed he could breathe new life into it.

He called 50 former dealers to get their advice, talked to the original owners, and interviewed several potential investors. His business plan—four months in the making—covered the business from top to bottom, from cash-flow projections to customer credit.

Folkerth's goal was to take the gamble out of the venture. "I think you will find most entrepreneurs are not particularly gamblers," he says. "They're risk takers. What that involves is digging out all the information you can and analyzing the situation to—as much as possible—take the gamble out of the risk.

"I have found, over the years, that although I always try to be very prepared and thorough, most of the mistakes I've made have occurred because I didn't sit down and go through the process of thinking out a decision—asking what results I am looking for, and analyzing the risks."

In the case of the shopping mall demonstrations, the results more than validated Folkerth's decision. The first demonstration in Dayton, Ohio, generated 40 sales and set in motion a nationwide sales demonstration program that five years later earned Shopsmith a spot on the list of the fastest growing public corporations in America.

Kenneth A. DeGhetto, chairman of the board of Foster Wheeler Corporation, a multinational design, engineering, construction, and management-services firm, attributes much of his success to his engineering education, which taught him to study and to think.

Like the other innovative, creative, accurate thinkers profiled in this book, DeGhetto has an insatiable appetite for information. As a young midshipman in the merchant marines during World War II, he spent evenings in the engine room of his ship reading and studying. It's a habit he has continued throughout his career. After 35 years with Foster Wheeler, he still reads trade and professional journals in the evenings—despite workdays that often stretch from seven in the morning until seven at night—to keep current in the field.

"I came from a hardworking New Jersey family," he says. "In our house, it was almost a sin *not* to work. My father taught me that nothing was going to be given to you; if you wanted something, you had to work for it.

"Sometimes I'm accused of being a workaholic, but I don't think of myself that way. When you like what you are doing, it's easy to spend the time necessary to get the job done right. And in a job like mine, if you want to get something done in peace and quiet, you have to get it done early or late.

"We try to treat our people with respect and respect their need for personal time, but it's not unusual for us to schedule meetings for seven in the morning or five in the evening. The fact that our people don't hesitate to come to meetings at those times is a testimonial to their desire and their belief in what we are doing."

Believing in what you are doing is critical to accurate thinking, DeGhetto believes. "You have to believe in what you and the company are doing if you ever hope to be successful. Pessimism becomes a self-fulfilling prophecy. If you think you are going to fail, you will.

"The best approach is to say, 'Here is the problem; how do I solve it?' At Foster Wheeler, we don't dwell on mistakes. Everyone who is doing anything makes mistakes occasionally. I have never been in a meeting when we tried to determine who made the mistake and nail the guy to the cross.

"Rather, we try to find out how we made the mistake and figure out how we are going to turn it around. You can't let someone having made a mistake interfere with fixing it and changing direction if you need to. Affixing blame doesn't solve the problem. It doesn't go away. You have to find a solution.

"You have to learn to learn from your mistakes. I have always believed that when you have to make a decision, you get the facts, and you make the decision. If you make a mistake, try not to make it again. But don't put off a decision for fear of making a mistake. In most cases, no decision is worse than a wrong decision.

"When you are making an important decision, it's important to involve the whole project team in it. We never, for example, ask for the data then go off in a corner by ourselves and make the decision.

"You can't run a company by committee, although I am a firm believer that one of the advantages of involving a committee or group in the decision-making process is that people need to feel they are part of it.

"I spent all day yesterday with a group of managers going over a contract on a potentially very risky new job. We all felt free to give our honest opinions. We encourage people to tell us what's on their minds, not what they think we want to hear. It's not uncommon for a lawyer with only two years of experience to say, 'I don't agree with that.' Anybody in the room has the right to say what he or she thinks. We want that. That's what they are getting paid for.

"I developed the philosophy long ago that if everyone tells you what they really think, once the decision is made, they support it as their own. It then becomes a team effort as you move forward to implement the decision."

The willingness to listen and learn from others has added benefits as well, DeGhetto believes. "You never know when you might learn something from someone," he says, "if you only pay attention to what they say. A really good idea might come from a very unlikely source if you take the time and trouble to encourage participation and listen to what they have to say."

DeGhetto's approach to accurate thinking is not just a collection of pretty words from the chairman. It's the substance of a plan to lead the company out of a downturn brought on by depressed demand in energy-related industries, traditionally the mainstay of Foster Wheeler's business, and to return the firm to the glory years of the late 1970s and early 1980s.

The company, which posted 1985 revenues of $1.23 billion—down from almost $1.7 billion in its banner year of 1979—has embarked on an ambitious acquisition and diversification program to shore up the declining demand for its engineering and management services in refinery and petrochemical processing plants and in energy equipment design, construction, and installation.

"Our traditional markets will probably remain soft and will remain low for some time to come, but we have already begun to see the results of improvements resulting from our diversification activities," DeGhetto says. "We don't expect it to be easy, but we do expect it to be successful."

Years ago, in their "Science of Success" course, W. Clement Stone and Napoleon Hill told the story of Milo C. Jones, a farmer who lived near Fort Atkinson, Wisconsin:

"Although his physical health was good, he seemed unable to make his farm yield more than the bare necessities of life. Late in life he suffered a paralytic stroke and was put to bed by relatives who believed him to be a helpless invalid.

"For weeks he remained unable to move a single muscle. All he had left was his mind, the one great power he had drawn upon so rarely because he had earned his living by the use of his brawn. Out of this sheer necessity he discovered the power of his mind and began to draw upon it!

"Jones called his family together and told them: 'I can no longer work with my hands, so I have decided to work with my mind. The rest of you will have to take the place of my hands. Please plant every acre of our farm you can spare in corn. Then start raising pigs with that corn. Slaughter the pigs while they are young and tender, and convert them into sausage. We will call them *Jones Little Pig Sausages*.'

"The family went to work as directed. In a few years the trade name of *Jones Little Pig Sausages* became a household byword throughout the nation. And the Jones family became wealthier than they had ever dreamed possible. Milo C. Jones lived to see himself possessed of a fortune earned on the same farm which previous to his misfortune had yielded him only a scant living. He had switched from the failure side of the River of Life to the success side of the stream—voluntarily—*by the power of thought*."[3]

Recently, Milo "Mike" Jones, great-grandson of Milo C. Jones, recalled for *Good Housekeeping* magazine some of the business techniques the Jones family pioneered. Jones Dairy Farms, as the company is now known, was the first to raise hogs specifically for producing premium sausage. Prior to this innovation, sausage had always been thought of as a byproduct.

Jones Farms was also the first in its field to rely heavily on mail-order sales and an aggressive national advertising program to promote its products. "They were farmers," the 55-year-old Mike told *Good Housekeeping*, "but they also turned out to be surprisingly shrewd businessmen." The company now posts sales of more than $50 million annually.

Mike Jones literally grew up in the family business. He was raised in the historic red-roofed farmhouse pictured on every Jones Farm product, and he has "more or less lived over the store" since he was married right after graduation from Harvard Law School; his house is a three-minute walk from the office.

He has continued the family tradition of innovation through accurate thought, and recently introduced Jones Light Breakfast Links, a leaner sausage aimed at health-conscious American consumers. It's now in supermarket freezers nationwide, *Good Housekeeping* reports, and "brisk sales indicate the idea will pay off handsomely." The article concludes with Jones's observation that, "Whichever way you slice it, our competitors will be trying to keep up with the Joneses for a long, long time."[4]

Thinking always involves risk. Every decision carries with it the chance of error, yet inaction is almost always worse than the wrong action. Nothing will destroy morale or cause an organization to stagnate faster than an indecisive chief executive.

No one can do your thinking for you; in the final analysis you alone must decide which course of action you will take. Any thoughtful person will solicit advice—indeed, the success of most executives hinges on their ability to surround themselves with compable people who can provide meaningful advice. But all too often the advice of one expert conflicts with that of another, and frequently the most difficult problems are those about which very little is known.

The best approach is to gather all the information available on the subject, listen to the advice of the experts, then make a decision based on hard information tempered with your own knowledge and experience.

Don't look for facts to support a decision you have already made. Begin the problem-solving process by objectively reviewing the relevant information with no goal in mind other than making the best decision possible in the circumstances—based solely on relevant facts.

The accurate thinker learns to be objective, and to separate emotion from real information. He knows that if the emotions of others are unreliable, so are his own. Every person has biases and prejudices, likes and dislikes that influence his thinking. Only through reason and logic can you overcome the temptation to be influenced by emotion.

This is not to imply that there shouldn't be an emotional commitment to the idea. Dr. James Botkin says, "In my world, the successful entrepreneurs are the ones who fail to recognize risk. If you talk to world class entrepreneurs at the point at which they are taking the step of investing their life savings to support a 'pie in the sky' idea, they do not see it as risk-taking.

"The banker perceives it as risky as hell; the accountants will say, 'You've got to be kidding me.' But the entrepreneur will be so convinced that his ideas are right that he doesn't see any risk at all. He's 100 percent sure that it is going to work. I have not met many high technology entrepreneurs who have done a risk analysis. I went to the Harvard Business School, where I was taught to do a risk analysis with decision trees that list the probabilities for each step of the decision, but I have never met a successful entrepreneur who did that. It has much more to do with the spirit and the soul and how you feel in the stomach—the gut stuff.

"When the idea is right, you *know* it. Each of us has had the feeling when you just know in your gut. You don't have to write it down on a piece of paper; you just know when you're on to something. It's the same feeling you get when you are on a team when everything just works—like the Boston Celtics in 1980. They couldn't make a mistake. The right man was always in the right place at the right time. Or it's like singing in a musical. The notes and words just come out perfectly at the right time. You can just *feel* it."

Botkin cautions against getting too bogged down in information for its own sake. "This flies in the face of the popular way of thinking about the information revolution," he says. "Everybody say that the more information you have, the more accurate your decisions will be. That's not true. It's the reverse. It's the ability to have the information filtered that gets rid of the information overload and makes clear the problem formulation—that a problem exists in the first place, or that it will exist some time in the future. That is really accurate thinking."

Many years ago, Napoleon Hill said, "The motto of the accurate thinker must be: 'I do not believe that I can afford to deceive others—I know I cannot afford to deceive myself.'"

It is within your power to control your thoughts, and it follows that it is your responsibility to determine what your thoughts will be.

You alone must decide whether you will base your career and management decisions on sound, accurate thinking and careful planning, or merely react to events as they occur. It's your decision.

PART V

Spiritual Principles

Man is inherently spiritual. Religious artifacts date from crude caveman drawings to exotic Inca icons to ornate Victorian cathedrals. Modern chrome-and-glass temples, unorthodox denominations, and television and radio ministries typify New Age approaches to spirituality; our search for "truth" is endless.

Perhaps it's ego-driven. We simply can't accept the possibility that our spirit—the essence of our uniqueness—will, like the physical entity that houses it, one day turn into dust. We are compelled to believe that there is a grander, nobler purpose for our lives than this short span on earth.

It may be part of the mystery of life itself, the ultimate

understanding of which has eluded scholars, theologians, and philosophers for centuries. We know what the elements of life are; indeed, we can now create life in a laboratory test-tube. But no one can satisfactorily explain what the soul is, where it resides, or why life exists in a body one minute and the next, it doesn't.

Perhaps religious faith flourishes with the acquiescence of society. We fear that without religious underpinnings, the moral fiber of society would ultimately unravel. It may be, as some have suggested, that our pursuit of things spiritual represents the best part of ourselves, the belief that it is possible to overcome evil with good.

It may be all of these things, or one of these things; it doesn't matter. The fact remains that spirituality is an essential part of the human animal. Without it, we lack purpose and meaning for our lives.

The Spiritual Principles outlined in this section make no attempt to persuade you that any one religious doctrine is preferred over another. We don't even attempt to persuade you that religious faith is essential for success. What we do tell you is that faith in yourself, others, and God will lead you to a richer, fuller, happier life.

The Spiritual Principles will also help you better understand the laws of the universe and how you can use them to your advantage. This is not black magic, occultism, or even astrology. It is simply the recognition that working in harmony with the forces of nature can help you develop the habits that will make you successful at whatever you choose to do.

It's that simple.

Chapter 17

Applied Faith

"I know I can never be a success on this earth unless I am on good terms with God," says Domino's Pizza founder and CEO Tom Monaghan. "My background makes concern about spiritual matters as natural to me as breathing. I grew up in a Catholic orphanage, and for a short time I attended a seminary, with every intention of becoming a priest."

Monaghan attributes much of his success to his strong religious beliefs. He writes in his autobiography, "I know I would not have been able to build Domino's without the strength I gained from my religious faith. In the earlier years, I was hit by a long series of difficulties. Each one seemed like a knockout blow. But I was able to get off the floor every time and come back stronger than ever. That's the power of faith. I use it every day. No matter how tense or tired I get, I can take time out to pray or say a rosary and feel refreshed. That's a tremendous asset."[1]

Faith, perhaps more than any other characteristic, represents a triumph of the human spirit. Without it, we could accomplish nothing. Without a strong belief in our ability to reach our goals, it would be futile to even begin. Without faith, all the great religions of the world would crumble, for we can no more prove the existence of a Supreme Being than we can prove the existence of electricity. We can't see, smell, or touch either; we can only see the *results*. The existence of either must be taken on faith.

Applied Faith is the means of directing the forces that are contained in ourselves and those that exist throughout the universe to the achievement of our goals. Applied Faith is not a passive acceptance of our spiritual existence; it is an active, positive application of our faith in ourselves, our fellowman, and God.

W. Clement Stone is a deeply religious man. He is firmly convinced that no one can realize his or her full potential or maintain success for an extended period of time without an overriding belief in the Infinite Intelligence that man has known as "God" since the beginnings of civilization. Whether or not you share his religious beliefs, you must accept the success principle of Applied Faith.

Even the simplest business transaction couldn't be completed without all parties involved having some degree of trust or faith in each other. We do have laws to ensure that all parties involved will live up to their part of the bargain, but it has been pointed out *ad nauseam* that justice is expensive. Doing business with trustworthy people will save you much grief later.

But faith in others is even more fundamental than contracts and agreements. Without some degree of faith in the manufacturer, you couldn't even risk eating a box of cereal. You assume that the contents of the box are what the label promises and not something that could harm you. Now and then some cruel, sick person tampers with merchandise and manages, by taking advantage of this trust, to hurt or even kill others. Media attention generates public fear of the product for a time, but eventually we return to our former buying habits, confident that appropriate corrective action has been taken to ensure our safety.

"Faith is very important," says Dr. Norman Vincent Peale. "I live in New York City. Here, if you don't have faith, you would be afraid to even go out in the morning. When you step out on the streets, you face a lot of hazards. The only way you can get through the day is the faith that you won't be killed or suffer an accident. You live by faith."

In addition to faith in ourselves and others, religious faith can be an integral part of the formula as well, says Dr. Peale. "When it comes to God or Jesus Christ," he says, "faith is very vital. People are perfectly free to go through life with no religious faith, but in my opinion they miss the deeper essence of life. I have noticed that the great people in almost every business or profession are those who have been reared to have religious faith."

Dr. Peale believes that religious faith will not only help you achieve material success, it will help you better cope after you have become successful: "In my experience, I've run across a lot of people who have achieved success in business, and maybe they feel guilty about it. Late in life they decide there should be more out of life and they decide the ministry is for them.

"A man came to me recently and asked: 'Was I born to manufacture this product?'

"I said, 'Maybe you were. In manufacturing this product, you are rendering a service and you have come in contact with a lot of people who have been influenced by your good moral character. But now you want to be a preacher, right?'

"He said, 'How could you have known that?'

"I said I had been thinking about it, you see. When you get to feeling that life is dull and the taste is gone out of it, the best thing is to go back to when you had enthusiasm and zest for life, and recapture that feeling. If your spiritual life has been inadequate, just step it up. You don't have to change your whole life.

"'If you decide to be a minister, you will have to go back to school for another three years to get a ministerial degree. There's no sense in that. You can do far more good by doing just what you're doing, by positively influencing by example the others you come in contact with. Maybe you should do some good with all that wealth you have accumulated so you don't have to feel guilty about it.'"

"Even the skeptical historian," say Will and Ariel Durant, "develops a humble respect for religion, since he sees it functioning, and seemingly indispensable, in every land and age. To the unhappy, the suffering, the bereaved, the old, it has brought supernatural comforts valued by millions of souls as more precious than any natural aid. It has helped parents and teachers to discipline the young. It has conferred meaning and dignity upon the lowliest existence, and through its sacraments has made for stability by transforming human covenants into solemn relationships with God. It has kept the poor (said Napoleon) from murdering the rich."[2]

Throughout history, the Durants say, religion seems to alternate with skepticism or paganism "in mutual reaction. Generally religion and puritanism prevail when laws are feeble and morals must bear the burden of maintaining social order; skepticism and paganism (other factors being equal) progress as the rising power of law and government permits the decline of the church, the family, and morality without basically endangering the stability of the state.

"In our time the strength of the state has united with [these] several forces to relax faith and morals, and to allow paganism to resume its natural sway." In 1968, the Durants accurately predicted, "Probably our excesses will bring another reaction; moral disorder may generate a religious revival; atheists may again (as in France after the debacle of 1870) send their children to Catholic schools to give them the discipline of religious belief. Hear the appeal of the agnostic Renan in 1866:

"'Let us enjoy the liberty of the sons of God, but let us take care lest we become accomplices in the diminution of virtue which would menace society if Christianity were to grow weak. What should we do without it? ... If Rationalism wishes to govern the world without regard to the religious needs of the soul, the experience of the French Revolution is there to teach us the consequences of such a blunder.'

"Does history warrant Renan's conclusion that religion is necessary to morality—that a natural ethic is too weak to withstand the savagery that lurks under civilization and emerges in our dreams, crimes, and wars?" the Durants ask. They answer the question with the words of Joseph de Maistre, who said, "I do not know what the heart of a rascal may be; I know what is in the heart of an honest man; it is horrible."

The power of faith can sometimes be demonstrated in strange or unexpected ways. Paul Zuromski, publisher of *Psychic Guide*, a magazine that explores parapsychological phenomena in an attempt to facilitate "understanding and improving body, mind and spirit," recently conducted a highly unusual test.

Charmed by the so-called psyche kinetic metal bending of Uri Geller in the 1970s and others who followed, Zuromski decided to test the possibilities on a psychic development class. "I figured," he says, "because these people are in tune with what I was trying to do, twisting the spoons (cheap K-Mart specials) would be simple."

Zuromski's first attempt ended in failure. He consulted with a friend more experienced in such phenomena, who helped him refine the procedure, and tried it again with a group of 18 people. He reports in his magazine: "Again, nothing happened. I began to see my future as a spoon-bending facilitator twist and turn away.

"Then one woman yelled. She was holding her spoon upright by the tip of the handle. Her spoon had fallen over by itself—it bent where the bowl meets the handle.

"Then most everyone else's spoon started bending. In fact, about fifteen of the people there bent their spoons to some degree. Evidently, they needed to see a spoon bend to give their own belief system the proof it needed to transcend the ingrained 'I can't do this' to 'I can.' The 'can't' became no longer valid because of what their eyes had seen."

Whether or not you believe the account of Zuromski and his 18 witnesses—indeed, you may write it off to group hypnosis or a magic trick—is beside the point.

Zuromski asks: "So what does metal bending mean? I often speak until my vocal cords crack about our wonderful potential and how we can create our personal reality. But nothing can prove this potential like a graphic demonstration of an ability the earth's mass consciousness says cannot be done. Bending a spoon is an exercise in transcending this reality. It's exhilarating. It demonstrates that a person is truly unlimited and helps them know it. Most of us rarely go beyond a familiar set of limitations until we do something like bend a spoon, walk on fire, or create a new job or relationship by visualizing what we want.

"The key is simple: thoughts are things. You are what you believe. Change your thoughts and your beliefs—and you can change your life.

"Or at least ruin some silverware."[3]

It's been said many times, many ways, but the truth still holds. The only limitations we have are those we set up in our own minds.

Faith is essential even in science and mathematics. The ancient Greek philosopher Aristotle pointed out that every science begins with assumptions or axioms that can't be proved. They must be accepted on faith, perceived intuitively to be true.

"Without some such assumptions as foundation stones," Louise Ropes Loomis writes in her introduction to translations of Aristotle's essays *On Man in the Universe,* we could never start to build anything. A student must accept the axioms of Euclid's geometry before he can go on to prove the theorems in the textbook. A doctor must believe there is such a thing as natural bodily disease before he can cure it by appropriate drugs and treatment. He cannot positively prove his assumption so as to convince a savage, who is sure that all sick persons are possessed by devils. But, on the basis of his assumption, the doctor erects his system of medicine, while the savage, on his, resorts to exorcism and magic.

"Beginning then in each case with certain assumptions that are to the holders so evident that they can dispense with logical proof, men proceed to construct their systems of knowledge and science. They add to what they already know something more that is both new and sure. To do this they may reason in the pattern of what Aristotle calls the *syllogism*. By it, 'certain things being stated, something else follows of necessity,' without need of further testimony."[4]

So it is with W. Clement Stone's success philosophy. You must begin by accepting the idea that if you follow principles that have worked for others, they will work for you—as long as your goals do not violate the laws of God and the rights of everyone. "The more worthwhile your goal is," Stone says, "the easier it is to apply the principles of success in achieving it. It is virtually impossible, for example, not to be enthusiastic about achieving a noble goal. You will become more focused, your goal will become a burning desire, and you will be willing to pay the price to reach your objective. Faith is a sublime motivator, and prayer is an expression of that faith. It accentuates the driving force of one's emotions."

Stone recalls the time when he and Napoleon Hill were holding a series of "Science of Success" seminars in San Juan, Puerto Rico. On the second evening of a three-evening course, as homework for the following day they encouraged participants to apply the principles they had learned, and report the results back to the group.

The next night, one of the participants—an accountant—gave this report:

"This morning when I arrived at work, my general manager, who is also attending this seminar, called me into his office and said, 'Let's see if a positive mental attitude works. You know, we have that $3,000 collection that is months overdue. Why don't you make the collection? Call on the manager, and when you do, use PMA. Let's begin with Mr. Stone's self starter: *Do it now!*'

"I was so impressed by your discussion last night about how everyone can make his subconscious mind work for him that when my manager sent me out to make the collection, I decided to try to make a sale also.

"When I left my office, I went home. In the quiet of my home I decided exactly what I was going to do. I prayed sincerely and expectantly for help to make the collection and a large sale.

"I believed I would get specific results. And I did. I collected the $3,000 and made another sale of over $4,000. As I was leaving my customer's office, he said, 'You certainly surprise me. When you came here, I had no intention of buying. I didn't know you were a salesman. I thought you were the head accountant.' That was the first sale I had ever made in my business career."

"That man," Stone says, "had experienced firsthand the

power of Applied Faith. He believed he could do it, and he did it. Plus, he took time for reflection. He prayed sincerely, reverently, and humbly for divine guidance. He believed he would receive it, and because he believed, he did receive it. When he did, I might add, he didn't forget to give a sincere prayer of thanks."[5]

Throughout their writings, Napoleon Hill and W. Clement Stone emphasized the importance of the application of the Golden Rule in all aspects of life, but particularly in business dealings. Simply stated, the Golden Rule says that we should treat others like we would like to be treated if our positions were reversed. It is a good rule of ethical conduct, and it makes good business sense. Excellence guru Tom Peters and other productivity and customer service consultants have spent a great deal of time and effort persuading managers that if they are simply courteous to their customers—serving them as they themselves would like to be served—they can run away from the competition because most companies don't do it. What they are doing, essentially, is helping modern managers rediscover the Golden Rule.

Domino's Tom Monaghan says, "I've always told Domino's employees and franchisees that all they have to do to be successful is have a good product, give good service, and apply the Golden Rule. I've often remarked in speeches that my objective is to have everyone say that Domino's Pizza people are nice. Not brilliant or charming or models of efficiency, *just nice*. To be nice to others, to think of the needs and interests of others, is the way to start putting the Golden Rule into action."[6]

The benefits that can be derived from practicing the Golden Rule are enormous, Stone says. It is far more than a guide for ethical conduct. Each of us comes in contact with hundreds of people in our personal and professional lives. If we demonstrate our honesty and integrity in all our dealings, we inspire others by our example, often without even knowing it. When we deal justly with our employees, we help shape a generation of fair and just managers. The results of that influence, multiplied by the number of people we know and the number they know and on and on, are simply incalculable.

When we treat our customers and clients as we would like to be treated, the same potential exists. But besides the number of people we can directly and indirectly positively influence, word spreads quickly and we will prosper in direct proportion. If we develop a reputation for courteous, honest, reliable service, our customers tell their friends and relatives, they tell their friends and relatives, and they send us customers and clients. No amount of television time or display advertising can compete with the effectiveness of a satisfied customer who tells others about us.

There's another advantage. When we deliberately set in motion a force for good, we mold our characters accordingly. When we have chosen to treat others kindly and fairly, we condition ourselves to behave in a certain way. We become fair and honest, and we attract others of like mind. We reinforce our behavior and geometrically increase our power by associating with others who are equally successful. The net result is that we help those we come in contact with, and they help us. It's a win/win situation all around.

Sadly, since Stone and Hill first began advocating the application of the Golden Rule in business several decades ago, we have seen a shift in the basic moral structure of society. The emphasis is on success at all costs, with little or no consideration for those we step on or step over on our way to the top. For example, Wall Street has been rocked by scandal after scandal following admissions by top executives that they traded stocks based on inside information, a process that is not only illegal but cheats investors as well.

Managers driven to show bottom-line results turn a blind eye to the lives and careers that may be ruined in the company's constant quest for higher and higher profits. We seem to view ethical behavior as something that can be conveniently dispensed with when it gets in the way of temporary success. The key word here is *temporary*. We may come to realize, the Royal Bank of Canada says in an essay on morality: "that immoral or unethical behavior is nothing but short-sighted [Those who cut moral corners] may learn the lesson that today's gratification is sometimes tomorrow's grief.

"They may discover, too, that decent and honorable treatment of others is returned in kind—that the moral course is not a hard and narrow road, but the way to broad new emotional vistas. For in its unadulterated form, morality is compounded of understanding and generosity.

"It is also a force in human progress, because it enjoins us to add value to our own lives and to those of others. It brings out the finest qualities in the human spirit. To consistently follow the moral course, you must be courageous, unselfish and thoughtful to others; to use an old-fashioned word, you must be a *noble* human being."

The morality of society, the essay points out, is the "sum of the conduct of every citizen, every day. 'The great hope of society is individual character,' wrote Lord Acton. Note the word 'hope,' with its implication that life on earth can be improved. The question we must ask ourselves as individuals is: would I want to live in the kind of world we would have if everyone acted as I do? If the answer is no, then we should be actively considering what we can do to better our ways.

"'In vain do they talk of happiness who never subdued an impulse to a principle,' wrote Horace Mann. 'He who never sacrificed a present to a future good, or a personal to a general one, can speak of happiness only as the blind do of colors.' So perhaps there is a selfish motive for being good after all."[7]

Perhaps the most persuasive argument for faith comes from the American journalist and clergyman, Frank Crane, who said: "You may be deceived if you trust too much, but you will live in torment if you do not trust enough."

Chapter 18

Cosmic Habit Force Universal Law

Our universe thrives on order and despises chaos. As scientists learn more about the composition of our solar system, it becomes increasingly apparent that seemingly random events, when studied over time, show a universe constantly reorganizing itself. Energy emitted from stars isn't lost; it's recycled into other stellar bodies. Of course, the whole process may take billions of years, but the point is: everything is in a constant state of change—orderly change.

The process is more readily apparent in nature. All plants, animals, fish, and fowl go through an organized process of birth, growth, maturity and death. A seed germinates, bursts forth into life, matures, propagates, and dies. Even in death, plants give life; decaying plants fertilize future seedlings.

Charles Darwin theorized that every living thing is in an endless quest for survival. Every species develops and passes along traits that help the next generation cope with a changing environment. Animals that evade predators through speed or cunning genetically pass those traits along to their offspring. As a result, the strongest and cleverest survive. Predators evolve too, of course, becoming better hunters in their quest for survival. All of nature seems to be continually engaged in a massive self-improvement program.

We have no intention of wandering into the divine creation/evolution fray. For our purposes, the origin of the species does not matter. Our only interest is in establishing the fact that change is constant. It may be negligible in our lifetime, and it may take several generations before the slightest change is perceptible, but change occurs. Constantly. Today, we *homo sapiens* are taller and healthier than our ancestors; we eat better and live longer than our forefathers. Part of the change can be attributed to the gradual evolution of our species as we adapted to a changing environment; part can be attributed to our expanding knowledge. We know more about diseases and their effects, and we have a far wider range of sophisticated treatments available to us.

Whatever the reasons, change is going on all around us as it has for millions of years, and will likely continue as long as the universe exists. Against this backdrop, each one of us tries to find our own unique niche in the cosmos. It's not an easy undertaking.

Just as nature uses repetitive patterns to bring order out

of chaos, so do we. To simplify our lives, we form habits. We do things a certain way— without even thinking—for no reason other than that we have always done them that way. We shave our faces or put on our makeup in the same order because when we were first learning how, we formed the *habit* of doing things that way. Then we no longer have to think in great detail about everything we do.

The habits we form and the way we form them has to do with the way we learn. Psychologist Clark Hull said, "Learning is dependent on a stimulus and a response," with the amount of learning being measured in what he called "habit strength." He went on to postulate that "the learned connection between a stimulus and a response is assumed to increase in magnitude gradually and continuously as a function of reinforced practice and to represent a relatively permanent change in behavior."[1]

Hull also stated that whether or not learned habits will be performed on certain occasions will depend on such external factors as the level of drive and the magnitude of the goal or reinforcer. Detracting from the performance of the habit will be such negatives as fatigue and the amount of effort required relative to the reward.

B.F. Skinner simplified the process. If you remember your basic psychology, Skinner is the guy who taught pigeons to dispense food to themselves by pecking at a key. He placed hungry animals in a specially designed box with a food dispensing lever. After at first accidentally tripping the lever, the animals eventually figured out that a certain action brought a desired result. When hungry pigeons pecked a certain key, they were fed. As a result, they learned to peck the key whenever they wanted to eat. Psychologists call it "operant conditioning" when behavior is modified by the consequences of the behavior.[2]

Of course, people are far more complex than animals. We have the ability to *think* and to *feel*. Our genetic makeup may have been determined by our ancestry, but each of us has developed a whole range of thoughts and emotions that come into play when we do anything including forming habits.

Despite our sophistication, however, we seem to form habits based on the degree of reinforcement we receive. If we try something and like the results, it is very likely that we will repeat the action. The more we like it the more often we do it.

Habits themselves make no moral judgments; they can be either good or bad. Both are formed the same way through repetition. It's Skinner's operant conditioning at work. We try something, like it, and keep doing it, probably in the exact same way.

The one thing that sets humans apart in the grand scheme of things is that we can decide for ourselves what habits we would like to develop. We can use to our advantage the knowledge that everything in the universe strives to maintain order and that habits are formed through repetition and reinforcement. By deciding for ourselves the habits we would like to develop, we can condition ourselves to change our behavior and become the people we would like to be.

Napoleon Hill identified three things that affect the voluntary formation of a habit:

1. *Plasticity.* By this he meant the ability to be molded. The term also implies that the shape will be retained

until something comes along that is powerful enough to change it. Man's plasticity can be influenced by external forces or the conscious control of his behavior. Through reason and logic, we decide how we would like to behave, and through willpower and self-discipline we force ourselves to do it.

2. *Frequency of impression.* Just as repetition is the mother of memory, it is the mother of habits. The more often we do something, the more it becomes a part of us. How quickly something becomes a habit depends on the individual situation but, generally speaking, the more frequent the repetition, the faster a behavior becomes a habit.
3. *Intensity of impression.* A strong, compelling motive and a burning desire are essential, Hill said. If an idea is impressed on the mind and backed with all the emotional desire you are capable of, it will become an obsession with you. The intensity of impression clearly affects the speed with which a habit becomes affixed.[3]

What all this means to the achiever is that you can decide what habits you would like to develop, then do so. You can replace bad habits with good ones through repetition and reinforcement. You can replace negative thoughts with positive ones, and you can replace inaction with action; you can form any habit you choose.

Let's say you have a problem maintaining a positive mental attitude. How can you use this principle to change the way you think? W. Clement Stone says: "I use self motivators. A self-motivator is an affirmation—a self-command or symbol—that you deliberately use as a self-suggestion to move yourself to desirable action. You merely repeat a verbal self-motivator fifty times in the morning and fifty times at night for a week or ten days to imprint the words indelibly on your subconscious.

"You do so with the deliberate purpose of getting into action when the self-motivator flashes from your subconscious to your conscious mind in time of need—for example, when you wish to eliminate or neutralize fear, meet problems more courageously, turn disadvantages into advantages, strive for higher achievement, solve serious problems, or control your emotions.

"When I have a problem, because I have prepared myself, one or more self-motivators will automatically flash from my subconscious to my conscious mind. Some of the ones I use for business problems are:

- You have a problem—that's good!
- With every adversity, there is a seed of an equivalent or greater benefit.
- What the mind can conceive and believe, the mind can achieve for those who have PMA and apply it.
- Find one good idea that will work—and work that idea!
- DO IT NOW!
- To be enthusiastic, act enthusiastic!

"When I have a personal problem, I use this one:

- God is always a good God!

"Actually, there is very little difference in how I meet business or personal problems, but there is a difference. If a personal problem involves deep emotions, I always use man's greatest power immediately: the power of prayer. In solving business problems, I also pray for guidance."

What Stone is advocating is a form of autosuggestion or self-talk that reinforces your habit-forming efforts. It is a fact that if you repeat something often enough you will eventually believe it. It's the principle of repetition and reinforcement.

Stone also recommends that you repeat it aloud with conviction. Whatever phrase you are trying to imbed in your subconscious, whether it is a self-motivator to help you in times of need, or a goal that you wish to turn into a deep, burning desire, you can persuade your subconscious that this is reality through convincing repetition.

Quietly talking to yourself won't have the same effect. If you want your subconscious to jump on the bandwagon, you have to show a little enthusiasm. There's another advantage to repeating it aloud: because you are using more than one of your senses, you intensify the impression.

Napoleon Hill said that the subconscious, through Cosmic Habit Force, "picks up on one's mental attitude and translates it into its material equivalent. You do not have to worry about fully understanding how the principle works, for it works automatically. All you have to do to gain the benefits of the law is to take possession of your own mind, make it predominantly positive through your daily thought habits, and plant in it a definite picture of your desires.

"The nucleus of the entire philosophy of individual achievement lies in Cosmic Habit Force. Control your mental attitude, keep it positive by exercising self-discipline, and thus prepare the mental soil in which any worthwhile plan, purpose, or desire may be planted by repeated, intense impression, with the assurance that it will grow, and find expression in its material equivalent whatever means are at hand."[4]

In today's language, Hill's idea was that if you set a goal for yourself, visualize yourself as having achieved it, and continually reinforce the message to your subconscious: "I am going to achieve this goal," your subconscious will work around the clock to help you find a way to reach it.

As we observed in the chapter on Definiteness of Purpose, the mind is goal seeking by design. Give the mind an objective and it is off and running. Combine that knowledge with the fact that the mind uses habits to make it more efficient, to do repetitive things with a minimum of effort, and you have a formula for forming any success habit you would like.

This is not to imply that changing habits is easy. Far from it. As Samuel Johnson once observed, "The chains of habit are generally too small to be felt until they are too strong to be broken." To replace an undesirable behavior pattern with a new one, we must first break a habit that we acquired gradually over a very long period of time.

Organizations that specialize in helping people break harmful, oppressive habits have learned that you don't just decide to do or not do something, and that's that. It doesn't work that way. Alcoholics give up drinking a drink at a time, an hour at a time, and a day at a time. They never consider themselves anything except temporarily cured. Smokers don't give up smoking once and forever. They quit a cigarette at a time, a pack at a time, and an hour at a time. Dieters lose weight the same way, a pound at a time, and a meal at a time. Anyone can forgo one cigarette, one snack, or one drink.

The same is true with behaviors that you would like to install in place of habits you want to break. For example, if you want to train yourself to do an unpleasant job right away instead of procrastinating, you do it once, once again, and so on until at long last you no longer think about it. You just do it automatically. If you want to eat carrots instead of Twinkies you do it a carrot at a time, and a Twinkie at a time.

John C. Maxwell, pastor of Skyline Wesleyan Church in Lemon Grove, California, and author of *Your Attitude, Key to Success*, says that once you make the choice to change your attitude, the work really begins. "Now," he says, "comes a life of continual deciding to grow and maintain the right outlook. Attitudes have a tendency to revert back to their original patterns if not carefully guarded and cultivated.

"'The hardest thing about milking cows,' observed a farmer, 'is they never stay milked.' Attitudes often don't stay changed." Maxwell identifies three stages in which you must always make the right choice if you want to change and stay changed:

- *Early stage.* "The first few days are always the most difficult. Old habits are hard to break. The mental process must be on guard continually to provide the right action."
- *Middle stage.* "The moment good habits begin to take root, options open that bring on new challenges. New habits are formed that will be either good or bad. The good news is: 'Like begets like.' The more

right choices and habits you develop, the more likely good habits will be formed."

- *Later stage*. "Complacency can become the enemy" in this stage, Maxwell says. "We all know of incidents where someone (perhaps us) successfully lost weight, only to fall back into old eating habits and gain it back."[5]

Another tough thing about behavior change is that it takes so long to eliminate a bad habit and replace it with a good one. There isn't the normal exhilaration that comes with completing a short-term goal. The thrill of victory comes long after the decision is made, and usually, by the time the new habit is firmly ingrained, you are bored with the whole thing. That's why it is important to repeat your goal to yourself often, and to congratulate yourself on small victories.

The loneliness factor (after all, we alone must change our habits) is also the reason for support groups. Alcoholics Anonymous, stop-smoking clinics, Weight Watchers, and other behavior modification groups use peer support and pressure in helping participants achieve the desired results. Go public with your goals; tell everyone you know what your plans are, so you will be embarrassed if you don't follow through. If there are no formal support groups for the success habits you plan to develop, rally your family and friends.

One schoolteacher we know uses this principle in a simple, innocuous way to get anything she wants: she sticks pictures of the things she wants on the refrigerator door with little magnets. Several times a day, when she sees the object of her desire, it reinforces the message, not only in her mind, but in the minds of her family and friends. Everyone knows what her plan is.

When she wanted a new, red sports car, she put a picture of her face over the face of the model who appeared in the advertisement. Her family and friends snickered, but every time she passed the refrigerator, she saw herself at the wheel of that sports car. The cost of the car was beyond her means, but the burning desire she instilled in herself to own that car motivated her to make extra money in a part-time direct selling job, and to cut corners elsewhere. Within six months from the time she posted the picture of the car on the refrigerator door, she owned it.

It took her a little longer to buy the house she wanted, but she used the same system. She tacked the real-estate listing to the refrigerator door in full view of the entire family. This time there were fewer doubters, but her family groused a little because they knew from experience that they would all have to work harder and save more diligently. They own the house now, of course.

Today, on her refrigerator, the teacher has a picture of the Yale and Princeton campuses, along with a news clipping about what the cost of a college education is likely to be in the year 2000. If you haven't guessed already, she's saving for her kids' tuition. There are no more doubters among her family and friends. Everyone knows that when the children reach college age, the money will be there.

Leo J. Hussey used the Cosmic Habit Force principle to stop smoking and become a marathon runner. A senior vice president of Plantation, Florida-based Burnup and Sims, Hussey tried for years to quit smoking, but in high stress situations, he says: "I would always find myself fishing in my pockets for cigarettes. Even though my father died of emphysema at an early age, I still had a very difficult time quitting smoking.

"Finally, I did quit for four years, and at the end of that period I went on vacation with my brother. We went fishing one afternoon. We caught our limit of brook trout, sat down on the bank, and my brother lit a cigarette—the brand I used to smoke. It looked so good, I said, 'Well, I'll have just one.' To make a long story short, at the end of my one-week vacation I was smoking over a pack a day. I gradually built up to three packs a day, plus pipes and cigars. It got to the point that I used to roll my own cigarettes with pipe tobacco because nothing seemed strong enough.

"As I watched my dad deteriorate, I kept telling myself, 'I've got to quit smoking.' And I tried several times over the next two years, but nothing seemed to work. I decided that if I couldn't kick the habit, I could at least strengthen my lungs. So I started to run. At first I just ran around the block, then I gradually started running farther and farther.

"I continued to smoke during the time I started running, and after two years I ran my first marathon. At that point, I got more hooked on running than on smoking. Strangely enough, the running became so important to me that the smoking just kind of went away. I just said, 'Who needs it?' and quit."

That was 10 years ago. Hussey was 37 at the time. Since then, he's run in eight marathons and his picture appears on a Big League bubble gum card along with his international marathon running statistics. His job keeps him on the road a good deal, but it doesn't keep him from running. He trains by running around airport parking lots between flights, and up and down stairs in hotels and office buildings.

"That's the way the principle works," says W. Clement Stone. "It's hard work to replace bad habits with good ones, and it takes time. Cosmic Habit Force is not a miracle worker, nor is it some sort of psychological magic. It won't make something of nothing; it won't even tell you in which direction you should go. What it will do—if you continually repeat and reinforce the message—is force you to develop the habits you choose for yourself. Through the use of this principle you can transform your goals into a burning desire so intense that nothing on earth could stop you from achieving them.

"It can help you develop and habitually practice all the success principles outlined in this book until they become second nature to you. The Cosmic Habit Force principle can make you healthier mentally and physically; it can make you wealthy beyond anything you can imagine today. But most of all, it can make you happier with yourself, your co-workers, your family, and friends.

"This principle provides you with the final tool you need to make this philosophy of success work for you. Take it and make it a habit."

Chapter 19

The Formula

The enduring effectiveness of the Seventeen Principles of Success has been evident throughout this book. It is amply demonstrated by the many business leaders who have shared their experiences with us. These principles are, unquestionably, the building blocks of achievement.

The question that remains for each of us, however, is "How do I apply these principles in my own life?"

W. Clement Stone spent much of the last 20 years of his life seeking the answer to that question. His solutions are sprinkled throughout the foregoing text. This final chapter summarizes the three main points of W. Clement Stone's New Formula for Success.

"In my formula," Stone says, "the whole is equal to the sum of all its parts." This is not a cliché to be brushed aside lightly; it contains elements as profound as those in Einstein's $E = MC^2$. This formula is similar to Einstein's theory of relativity in another way, as well. The formula becomes simple and understandable only after you master all its elements. No one principle can assure success in any endeavor; it's the application of the entire formula that makes it work.

The people who successfully apply the Seventeen Principles do so, Stone says, because they have developed the habit of Recognizing, Relating, Assimilating and Applying information from all sources that will help them in achieving their goals. He calls this his R2A2 Formula.

Stone points to Norman Monath's book, *Know What You Want and Get It!*, as an excellent explanation of how to adapt various success principles from one discipline to another: "Monath's explanation is what I have always referred to as R2 (Recognize and Relate) A2 (Assimilate and Apply)," Stone says. "In order to attain any goal in life, you must first learn to recognize, relate, assimilate, and apply principles from what you see, hear, read, think, or experience.

"When you read an inspirational, self-help book, for example, you will not receive any benefit from the words unless you study, understand, comprehend, and *apply* the principles it sets forth.

"There is an art to reading such a book. The first thing you must do is concentrate. Read as if the author were a close personal friend and was writing to you—and you alone.

"Also, it is wise to *know what you are looking for*. If you really want to relate and assimilate into your own life the ideas that are contained between the covers of an inspirational book . . . *work at it*. A self-help book is not to be skimmed through the same way you might read a detective novel.

"Dr. Billy B. Sharp, a widely-respected educator and author of *Choose Success*, wrote; 'In a novel, the author usually controls the conclusion. *In a self-help book*, the reader writes the conclusion. This means action on your part.'

"'Since ideas come from unexpected places, it is important to read with a note pad at hand. Anything of interest (a flash of inspiration or an answer to a problem) should be jotted down immediately.

"'The reader should read, asking the question: *What does this mean to me*?

"'The reader will want to be alert for the *How tos*. A good self-help book will have *How to* information, as well as *What to*. Be alert for both, and the relationship between the two.'

"Here are some other suggestions that I have always found helpful when reading an inspirational, self-help book:

"Read the dedication, the index, and each page in sequence. Read the entire book. If you own the book, *underscore that which you feel is important*, especially that which you would like to memorize. Put a question mark next to a statement you question or don't understand. You can even write short notes in the margins of a page. Write on your note pad any inspiring ideas or potential solutions to any problem that flashes into your mind. Complete a chapter before you stop reading.

"After you have completed your first reading, read the book again for the purpose of *studying*, so that you understand and comprehend the information in each paragraph. Identify and *memorize* self motivators in the text. Again underscore additional words and phrases that are important to you.

"At some future date, read the book again. I remember that Napoleon Hill once had a problem and seemed unable to come up with an answer. How did he finally find the answer? By rereading his own book, *Think and Grow Rich*."

Another key element in Stone's Success Formula is allocating a regular time every day for creative thinking. This is the time when you just sit alone and think. It may be as little as a half hour a day, or as much as two full hours—the important thing is to *do it with regularity*.

"Choose the time of day when you do your best thinking," Stone says. "If you are a morning person, get up early, if you are a night person, stay up late. Go to a quiet place that is conducive to creative thinking, and keep a note pad handy to jot down ideas. Let your mind wander if you want, try to look at things from a different perspective, or in a different way than you have looked at them before.

"If you are trying to solve a particular problem or come up with a new idea, apply the R2A2 Formula. Consider information from other or unrelated fields; see if any of that information might be adaptable to your present problem.

"Evaluate your ideas objectively. Make a list of the positive aspects, and any negatives or problems that must be overcome to implement the idea. If the positives outweigh the negatives and the problems can reasonably be expected to be overcome, you have a good idea. The key here is to be *reasonable and objective*. Don't fool yourself into thinking the impossible. People that overcome impossible odds do so by thinking ideas through and minimizing the risks, solving problems one at a time as they come up."

The third element of Stone's Success Formula is learning

to tap the powers of your subconscious. If you don't fully understand this, go back and reread Chapter 14, "Creative Vision." If you are to truly achieve great success in any endeavor, you must master this technique.

"Don't expect miracles at first," Stone cautions, "it takes time for the process of activating your subconscious to become effective. Like anything else, however, the more you practice, the better you will become at it. Once the habit is established, you don't have to do anything but let the process work."

Begin by defining the problem or the objective; make sure you know exactly what you are trying to accomplish. Whether you are trying to develop a better sales presentation or invent a new product, you must first know exactly what you want to achieve before you can ever have any hope of doing so.

Next, read all the information available about the subject. Check trade journals, read self-help books, or any other literature that might be appropriate to the subject. Read and study everything ever written about your topic, however unrelated the information might appear at the time.

Once again, use the R2A2 Formula. Remember Edison's experience with charcoal and the light bulb. The fact that burning wood doesn't consume itself without oxygen doesn't seem to have any relevance to electric lights unless you consider that when the famous scientist made this association his problem was that filaments kept burning up. Once he removed the oxygen from the bulb, his problem was solved.

Allow time for the idea to incubate. You may get a solution to your problem right away, or it may take a few days, weeks, even months or years. You may be able to relax and let your mind drift until your subconscious mulls over the idea and transmits the solution to your conscious mind, or you may wake up in the middle of the night with the perfect solution. It may come while you are shaving, driving to work, or having your hair done. But it will come. When the ideas start flowing, you will very likely have several in a row, any one of which may be workable, or maybe only one is *the* right answer. Write down all your ideas as they occur.

After the excitement of creation has passed, it's time to evaluate the ideas objectively. When you are convinced that you have chosen the one that will work best, get busy and act on it while it is new and exciting.

Generating ideas is fun, but the real test is the implementation. It may require a lot of hard work and perseverance, but there is nothing more exciting than making your idea work at creating wealth or jobs, or helping others in ways that would not have existed without the power of your mind.

You now have the principles that have helped so many others achieve success beyond their wildest dreams. You now have the formula for applying those principles in your own life.

So go to it. As W. Clement Stone says: "Do it now!"

Notes

Chapter 1

1. Laurie M. Sachtleben, "The Man who Fashioned a New Spiegel," *PMA Adviser* (August 1983), p. 3.
2. Sydney J. Harris, "Winners Learn To Handle Themselves Intelligently," *Chicago Sun-Times* (October 11, 1984), p. 57.

Chapter 2

1. Robert Rosenthal, "The Psychology of the Psychologist," *Psychology and Life* Ed. Floyd L. Ruch (Glenview, Ill.: Scott, Foresman and Company, 1963, 1967), p. 651.
2. "Napoleon Hill Revisited: On A Positive Mental Attitude," *PMA Adviser* (March 1985), p.6.
3. "W. Clement Stone: On Your Potential," *PMA Adviser* (January 1984), pp. 3,6.

Chapter 3

1. Denis Waitley, "Goal Setting: The Wheel of Fortune," *PMA Adviser* (April 1984), pp. 2,5. Adapted from *Seeds of Greatness: The Ten Best-Kept Secrets of Total Success.*
2. Ron Willingham, *The Best Seller!* (Englewood Cliffs, N.J.: Prentice-Hall, Inc., 1984) pp. 11-12.
3. Tom Monaghan with Robert Anderson, *Pizza Tiger* (New York: Random House, 1986) pp. 222-23.
4. "A Sense of Achievement," *The Royal Bank Letter* (The Royal Bank of Canada), Vol. 65, No. 6 (November/December 1984), p. 2.

Chapter 4

1. Jerry G. Bowles, "The Quality Imperative," a special advertising section, *Fortune* (September 29, 1986).
2. "Napoleon Hill Revisited: On Going The Extra Mile," *PMA Adviser* (February 1983), p. 6.

Chapter 5

1. William Hoffer, "The King of Conversation," *Success!* magazine (July 1983), p. 25.
2. Robert Levering, Milton Moskowitz, and Michael Katz, *The 100 Best Companies to Work for in America* (Reading, Mass.: Addison-Wesley, 1984), pp. 221-22.
3. Phoebe Hawkins, "Noteworthy Success from Bad Glue," *Insight* magazine (July 21, 1986), p. 43.
4. Merle Haggard with Peggy Russell, *Sing Me Back Home: My Story* (New York: Pocket Books division of Simon & Schuster, 1981), pp. 154, 169-70.

Chapter 6

1. "Business Leaders Who Helped Build America Remain Largely Unknown," *Commerce Today*, published by the U.S. Department of Commerce (July 7. 1975), pp. 3-4.
2. *Stories Behind Everyday Things* (Pleasantville, N.Y.: The Reader's Digest Association, Inc., 1980), p. 133.
3. Tom Peters and Nancy Austin, *A Passion For Excellence* (New York: Random House, 1985), pp. 325-27.
4. Stevenson Swanson, "Leading Question: What Kind of People Do Others Follow?" *Chicago Tribune* (November 29, 1984), pp. 1, 3.

Chapter 7

1. Lee Iacocca with William Novak, *Iacocca: An Autobiography* (New York: Bantam Books, 1984), pp. 269-70.
2. "Napoleon Hill Revisited: On Enthusiasm," *PMA Adviser* (August 1983), p. 6.
3. Grant G. Gard, *Championship Selling* (Englewood Cliffs, N.J.: Prentice-Hall, Inc., 1984), p. 26.

Chapter 8

1. Philip M. Albert, "Something New in Selling," a review of *Modern Persuasion Strategies: The Hidden Advantage in Selling*, by Donald J. Moine and John H. Herd, *PMA Adviser* (January 1986), p. 3.
2. Hank Trisler, *No Bull Selling* (New York: Bantam Books, 1985. Frederick Fell edition published in 1983), pp. 10-11.

3. Lloyd Purves, *Secrets of Personal Command Power* (West Nyack, N.Y.: Parker Publishing, Inc., 1981), pp. 83-84.
4. "The Winning Ways of Carlos Karas Recruit Ranks of Loyal Fans." *Texaco Marketer* (February 1986), p. 4.

Chapter 9

1. Maxwell Newton, Your Business, "Peter Grace at 72: Amazing Career Continues," *New York Post* (May 15, 1986), p. 58.
2. Robert G. Allen, *Creating Wealth* (New York: Simon and Schuster, 1983), p. 51.
3. Albert E.N. Gray, "The Common Denominator of Success," an address delivered at the National Association of Life Underwriters Convention in 1940. Reprinted and distributed in pamphlet form by the NALU.
4. Wally Armbruster, *Where Have All the Salesmen Gone?* (St. Louis: Piraeus Press, 1982), pp. 68-70.
5. From *George Washington Carver* by Anne Terry White (New York: Random House, 1953).
6. "Napoleon Hill Revisited: On Self-Discipline," *PMA Adviser* (July 1985), p. 6.

Chapter 10

1. "Making the Most of Time," *The Royal Bank Letter* (The Royal Bank of Canada), Vol. 67, No. 1 (January/February 1986), p. 1.
2. Peter A. Turla and Kathleen L. Hawkins, M.A., *Time Management Made Easy* (New York: E.P. Dutton, Inc., 1983), pp. 15-16.
3. Alan Lakein, *How to Get Control of Your Time and Your Life* (New York: New American Library, 1973), pp. 26-27.

4. W. Clement Stone, *The Success System That Never Fails* (New York: Pocket Books division of Simon & Schuster, Inc., 1962), pp. 18-19.
5. Allan D. Willey, *Making the Most of What You've Got* (Eugene, Oregon: Harvest House Publishers, 1982), p. 55.
6. Venita Van Caspel, *Money Dynamics for the New Economy* (New York: Simon and Schuster, 1986), pp. 27-30.

Chapter 11

1. "Napoleon Hill Revisited: On Maintaining Sound Physical and Mental Health," *PMA Adviser* (October 1984), p. 6.
2. Dr. Irving Dardik and Denis Waitley, Ph.D., *Quantum Fitness: Breakthrough to Excellence* (New York: Pocket Books, 1984), from "Building Blocks to True Fitness." *PMA Adviser* (October 1984), p. 4.
3. William D. Brown, Ph.D., *Welcome Stress! It Can Help You Be Your Best* (Minneapolis: CompCare Publications, 1983), p. 6.
4. Ibid., pp. 163-64.
5. Carol Kleiman, "It's Not Being On Top That's Unhealthy—It's Being In the Middle," *Chicago Tribune* (May 7, 1984), Section 3, p. 3.
6. Herbert Benson, M.D., with William Proctor, *Beyond the Relaxation Response* (New York: Times Books, 1984), p. 8.
7. Ibid., pp. 106-17.
8. Stuart M. Berger, M.D., "Nutrition's The Key to Mental Health," *New York Post* (August 26, 1986), p. 18.
9. Peter M. Miller, Ph.D., *The Hilton Head Executive Stamina Program* (New York: Rawson Associates, 1986), pp. 45-56.
10. Matt Clark with Karen Springen, "Running for Your Life: a

Harvard Study Likens Exercise with Longevity," *Newsweek* (March 17, 1986), p. 70.

Chapter 12

1. Napoleon Hill, "Master-Mind Alliance," *Law of Success* (Chicago: Success Unlimited, Inc., 1979), p. 98.
2. J.P. Donlon, "Technology Venturer Bobby Inman Nears the First Hurdle," *Chief Executive* (Spring 1986), pp. 30, 32-33.
3. George Russell, "The Big Three Get in Gear," *Time* (November 24, 1986), p. 64.
4. "Ore-Ida's Crop of Homegrown Entrepreneurs," *Business Week* (June 11, 1984), p. 154 H, 154 J.
5. Daniel Goleman, "Influencing Others: Skills Are Identified," *New York Times*, (February 18, 1986). pp. Cl, C15.
6. "How To Lead A Group,' *PMA Adviser* (March 1983), pp. 2, 5.

Chapter 13

1. "World Champion Mets," *Good Morning America* (New York: America Broadcasting Company, October 28, 1986).
2. Don Oldenburg, "Teamwork on the Job Can Be Good Business," *Chicago Sun Times* (February 28, 1985), p. 59.
3. "Making Quality Circles Ring True for You," PMA Adviser (January 1985), p. 5-6.
4. Alvin Toffler, *The Adaptive Corporation* (New York: McGraw-Hill, 1985), reviewed by Philip Albert in *PMA Adviser* (January 1985), p. 4.
5. Stephen L. Pistner, "Savvy, Management Utilizes Every Employee's Best Traits," *Crain's Chicago Business* (June 18, 1984), p. 11.

Chapter 14

1. James W. Botkin, Mahdi Elmandjra, and Mircea Malitza, *No Limits to Learning*: *Bridging the Human Gap, a Report to the Club of Rome* (Oxford: Pergamon Press, 1979).
2. "Spotting Trends," *PMA Adviser* (May 1984), p. 5.
3. Betty Edwards, *Drawing on the Right Side of the Brain* (Los Angeles: J.P. Tarcher, Inc., 1979; distributed by St. Martin's Press, New York), pp. 37, 57.
4. Garrison Keillor, *Lake Wobegone Days* (New York: Viking, 1985), p. ix.
5. Rance Crain, "Can't Sleep? It's Genius Calling," *Crain's Chicago Business* (June 25, 1984), p. 10.
6. Willis Harman, Ph.D., and Howard Rheingold, *Higher Creativity: Liberating the Unconscious for Breakthrough Insights* (Los Angeles, Jeremy P. Tarcher, Inc., 1984, distributed by Houghton Mifflin Co., Boston).

Chapter 15

1. Irving Stone, *The Agony and the Ecstasy* (Garden City, N.Y.: Doubleday & Company, Inc., 1958) pp. 679-82.
2. Daniel Goleman, "Concentration Is Likened to Euphoric States of Mind," *The New York Times* (March 4, 1984), pp. C1, C3.
3. Sydney J. Harris, "Winners Learn to Handle Themselves Intelligently," *Chicago Sun-Times* (October 11, 1984), p. 57.
4. Irving Stone, *The Passions of the Mind* (Garden City, N.Y.: Doubleday & Company, Inc., 1971), pp. 493-94.
5. Banesh Hoffmann with the collaboration of Helen Dukas, *Albert Einstein, Creator & Rebel* (New York: New American

Library, 1972), pp. 19-20.
6. Greg Daugherty, "The Manager With the 'Most' Tells How He Got It," a review of *Managing*, by Harold Geneen (Garden City, N.Y.: Doubleday & Company, 1984), *PMA Adviser* (September 1984), p. 4.
7. R. Buckminster Fuller, *Critical Path* (New York: St. Martin's Press, 1981) p. 109.

Chapter 16

1. Roger von Oech, *A Kick in the Seat of the Pants* (New York: Harper & Row, 1986), pp. 95-96.
2. Kevin Shyne, "A Good Habit: Accurate Thinking," *PMA Adviser* (June 1983), p. 2.
3. *PMA Science of Success* (Columbia, S.C.: The Napoleon Hill Foundation, 1961, 1983), Lesson 13, pp. 3-4.
4. Chris Andersen, "Meet the Presidents, Milo Jones," *Good Housekeeping* (September 1986), pp. 148-50.

Chapter 17

1. Tom Monaghan with Robert Anderson, *Pizza Tiger* (New York: Random House, 1986), pp. 5-6.
2. Will and Ariel Durant, *The Lessons of History* (New York: Simon and Schuster, 1968), pp. 43, 50-51.
3. Paul Zuromski, "Metal Bending: A New Twist in Demonstrating the Possible You," *Psychic Guide* (December 1986), pp. xiii-xiv (January & February, 1987), p. 88.
4. *Aristotle on Man in the Universe*, ed. Louise Ropes Loomis (Roslyn, N.Y.: Walter J. Black, Inc., 1943), pp. xiii-xiv.
5. W. Clement Stone, *The Success System That Never Fails*

(New York: Pocket Books division of Simon and Schuster, 1962), pp. 82-83.
6. Monaghan, *Pizza Tiger,* p.6.
7. *The Royal Bank Letter,* The Royal Bank of Canada, Vol. 65, No. 1 (January/February 1984), p. 4.

Chapter 18

1. Floyd L. Ruch, *Psychology and Life*, 7th Edition (Glenview, Ill.: Scott, Foresman and Company, 1967), pp. 215-216.
2. Harold W. Berkman and Christopher C. Gilson, *Consumer Behavior* (Encino, Calif.: Dickenson Publishing Company, Inc., 1978), p. 228.
3. "Napoleon Hill Revisited: On Cosmic Habit Force," *PMA Adviser* (April 1986:), p. 6.
4. "Napoleon Hill Revisited," p. 6.
5. John C. Maxwell, *Your Attitude, Key to Success* (San Bernardino, Calif.: Here's Life Publishers, Inc., 1984), p. 131.

INDEX

INDEX